Critiquing Free Speech

First Amendment Theory and the Challenge of Interdisciplinarity

LEA'S COMMUNICATION SERIES

Jennings Bryant/Dolf Zillmann, General Editors

For a complete list of other titles in LEA's Communication Series, please contact Lawrence Erlbaum Associates, Publishers

Critiquing Free Speech

First Amendment Theory and the Challenge of Interdisciplinarity

Matthew D. Bunker

University of Alabama

LAWRENCE ERLBAUM ASSOCIATES, PUBLISHERS
2001 Mahwah, New Jersey London

Lawrence Erlbaum Associates, Inc., Publishers
10 Industrial Avenue
Mahwah, NJ 07430

Cover design by Kathryn Houghtaling Lacey

Library of Congress Cataloging-in-Publication Data
Bunker, Matthew D.
Critiquing free speech: First Amendment theory and the challenge of interdisciplinarity
/ Matthew D. Bunker
    p.   cm.
Includes bibliographical references and index.
ISBN 0-8058-3751-5 (cloth: alk. paper)
    1. Freedom of speech—United States. 2. United States. Constitution. 1st Amendment. 3.
Interdisciplinary approach to knowledge. I. Title.

KF4772.B86 2001
342.73'0853—dc21   00-057683
                                                         CIP

Books published by Lawrence Erlbaum Associates are printed on acid-free paper, and their bindings
are chosen for strength and durability.

Printed in the United States of America
10 9 8 7 6 5 4 3 2 1

For Lois

Contents

Preface

This book is the culmination of several years of thinking about interdisciplinary legal studies and the First Amendment. Although I'm quite sure some of the answers I propose will be found wanting by some, I hope that at least the questions raised will prove worthwhile. This last statement I make with some trepidation, aware as I am of the dictum of that quintessential postmodern professor, Morris Zapp, a character in the academic novels of author David Lodge. As Professor Zapp once mused: "Any damn fool, he maintained, could think of questions; it was *answers* that separated the men from the boys."[1] Be that as it may (and passing over the sexist wording), sometimes the act of questioning an existing theoretical structure can prove at least as valuable as any answers to which the questioning may lead. Definitive answers are few and far between in this business. At times, interdisciplinary legal scholars present their work as if their own assumptions and theoretical commitments were beyond question. As I hope to show in these pages, this is simply not the case.

---

[1]David Lodge, Changing Places 45 (1975).

I would like to thank the University of Alabama for support in writing the book. I was fortunate enough to receive two separate summer research grants and a sabbatical that allowed me to work on portions of the manuscript. In particular, thanks to my department chair, Ed Mullins, and my dean, Cully Clark, for their most generous support. Many thanks also to Jennings Bryant, the series editor, for his kindness and his enthusiasm for the project. I'm most grateful to a large number of thoughtful colleagues, including anonymous reviewers, who read and commented on earlier versions of portions of this work. Some earlier versions of chapters herein appeared as articles in the journal *Communication Law and Policy*, and I appreciate the insights gained from those who read those pieces. In particular, many thanks to Sandra Braman, Bill Chamberlin, Carrie Crenshaw, Paul Gates, Don Gillmor, Tim Gleason, Steve Helle, Susan Dente Ross, Tom Schwartz, and Bob Trager. Despite all of their invaluable suggestions and valiant attempts to enlighten me, I, of course, remain responsible for all errors and faulty interpretations. I would also like to thank Linda Bathgate, communications editor at Lawrence Erlbaum Associates, for her marvelous support for the project and her gracious help through the publication process. The greatest debt of all is owed to my wife, Lois Graham, without whose encouragement and support the book would not have been possible.

Introduction

Mainstream First Amendment theory is under assault. Free speech should be protected, liberal theorists[1] have proposed, for a number of important reasons, including democratic self-governance, self-realization, respect for individual autonomy, the search for truth, and a variety of other reasons.[2] While these classical free speech justifications still have significant influence, free speech theory is nonetheless in a state of great ferment. The notion that government should extend to individuals the greatest possible rights of free expression (long nearly a truism among scholars in law, communication, and related disciplines) has become subject to significant challenges. The old consensus of expanding free expression rights has been challenged in a series of critiques by feminist legal scholars, critical legal theorists, communitarian theorists, critical race theorists, literary

---

[1]*Liberalism* here and throughout this book refers broadly to the political tradition that advocates protection of individual rights, equality before the law, and similar values. It should be noted that liberalism in this sense—with roots in the thought of Locke, J. S. Mill, and many others—is embraced by many on both the political left and right in the United States.

[2]Rodney Smolla, Free Speech in an Open Society 3–17 (1992).

theorists, and others.[3] Some of these critics argue that the theoretical assumptions that underlie free speech theory, assumptions that extend back to Milton, Locke, Kant, and others, are no longer tenable.[4] Traditional liberal theory's picture of "atomistic" individualism is unconvincing, the critics contend, in light of the socially constituted nature of human beings. Moreover, the critics suggest that certain forms of speech that are largely immune from regulation under current First Amendment doctrine, including hate speech and pornography, should not be protected because of their detrimental social impact.[5]

These critiques arise out of a shift that has occurred globally within legal theory; that is, the increasing use of vocabularies and paradigms from other disciplines to study law. Interdisciplinarity has become a transforming force within legal studies. Not only do legal scholars borrow from other disciplines, but scholars in other disciplines—including political science, communication, philosophy, economics, history, psychology, sociology, literary studies, and critical and cultural studies—not infrequently study law. In recent decades, the pace of interdisciplinary legal study has accelerated considerably. In the heyday of legal formalism in the late 19th and early 20th centuries, legal scholars assumed the autonomy of law from all other disciplines. Now, however, that autonomy is in serious doubt.[6]

There are obvious advantages to legal interdisciplinarity. Legal scholars can develop important insights about law by delving into social scientific and humanistic disciplines that intersect with legal studies. Historical scholarship can help illuminate the intentions of those who drafted consti-

---

[3]*See* Kathleen M. Sullivan, Free Speech Wars, 48 S.M.U. L. Rev. 203 (1994).

[4]*E.g.*, Linda C. McClain, "Atomistic" Man Revisited: Liberalism, Connection, and Feminist Jurisprudence, 65 S. Cal. L. Rev. 1171 (1992).

[5]*E.g.*, Catharine A. MacKinnon, Only Words (1993); Mari J. Matsuda et al., Words that Wound: Critical Race Theory, Assaultive Speech, and the First Amendment (1993).

[6]On the relationship of law and other disciplines generally, *see* Laura Kalman, The Strange Career Of Legal Liberalism (1996); Charles W. Collier, Interdisciplinary Legal Scholarship in Search of a Paradigm, 42 Duke L.J. 840 (1993); Charles W. Collier, The Use and Abuse of Humanistic Theory in Law: Reexamining the Assumptions of Interdisciplinary Legal Scholarship, 1991 Duke L.J. 191 (1991); Harry T. Edwards, The Growing Disjunction Between Legal Education and the Legal Profession, 91 Mich. L. Rev. 34 (1992); Lawrence M. Friedman, Popular Legal Culture: Law, Lawyers, and Popular Culture, 98 Yale L.J. 1579 (1989); Edward Rubin, Law and Society & Law and Economics: Common Ground, Irreconcilable Differences, New Directions: Law and the Methodology of Law, 1997 Wis. L. Rev. 521 (1997); Edward L Rubin, The Practice and Discourse of Legal Scholarship, 86 Mich. L. Rev. 1835 (1988); Brian Z. Tamanaha, The Internal/External Distinction and the Notion of a "Practice" in Legal Theory and Sociolegal Studies, 30 Law & Soc Rev. 163 (1996); Ernest J. Weinrib, Legal Formalism: On the Imminent Rationality of Law, 97 Yale L.J. 949 (1988).

tutional provisions. Literary studies can yield insights about the interpretation of legal texts. Economic analyses can help identify the consequences (both intended and unintended) of various legal rules. Psychological studies can answer important empirical questions about the prejudicial effects of pretrial publicity on jurors or the competence of individuals to stand trial. Various critical and cultural approaches can, among other things, critique the biases and blind spots of existing legal rules. Many other fields of scholarship have the potential to enrich the study of law.

Nevertheless, interdisciplinarity is not an unalloyed good. Much of the recent wave of interdisciplinarity seems to have been deployed to argue for greater limits on free speech rights. Stanford legal scholar Kathleen Sullivan has dubbed these new interdisciplinary challenges to First Amendment verities "free speech wars."[7]

It goes without saying, of course, that First Amendment theory—that body of philosophical and (less frequently) empirical reflection on the nature, purposes, and value of free speech—was always, and already, interdisciplinary. Legal scholars, political and moral philosophers, historians, and many others have, over the years and particularly in the 20th century, contributed to First Amendment theory. This book's focus on interdisciplinarity is directed toward more recent interdisciplinary incursions into the field from communitarians, feminist legal scholars, critical legal scholars, lawyer/economists, literary theorists, and others. It cannot be stressed enough that the critiques of these thinkers presented here are, in nearly all cases, not aimed at the substantive *ends* the theorists seek (such highly desirable goals as gender equity, an end to racism, stronger bonds of community, and the like) but only at the theoretical *means* they wish to employ to reach these goals. Sometimes, as the saying goes, the cure is worse than the disease.

Summary of Chapters

This book does not aspire to be an exhaustive treatment of First Amendment theory and interdisciplinary scholarship. Rather, it is a series of related, but distinct, essays that explore various aspects of that relationship—sometimes through the close examination of a particular theorist, in other cases by focusing on a group of thinkers whose ideas are closely connected.

---

[7]Kathleen M. Sullivan, Free Speech Wars, 48 S.M.U. L. Rev. 203 (1994).

Chapter 1 of the book will provide a general overview of mainstream First Amendment theory. The chapter will suggest that while classical First Amendment theory is not without its flaws, it is an important repository of values that we neglect at our peril.

Chapter 2 will examine how interdisciplinary thinkers may, by the very nature of their projects, engage in an unsatisfactory reductionism that ignores values implicit in the First Amendment. This chapter will focus on two scholars: economic theorist and federal judge Richard Posner and feminist theorist Susan H. Williams. The chapter will analyze each scholar's work and then proceed to use that work to make some fundamental points about the problems of free speech reductionism. This reductionism takes the form of a wholesale disciplinary "takeover" that omits irreducible constitutional values from its theoretical framework.

Chapter 3 will analyze and critique the work of First Amendment and literary theorist Stanley Fish. Fish has asserted, in the title of a famous essay, that "There's No Such Thing as Free Speech." The chapter will suggest that Fish's deconstructive approach to the First Amendment has important failings.

Chapter 4 will explore the work of a number of important theorists, predominantly communitarian thinkers, who problematize the conception of the "self" that engages in free expression or partakes of other individual rights. A number of communitarian theorists have suggested that liberal "rights" regimes place too much emphasis on the individual and not enough on the community from which the individual is "socially constituted." The chapter will analyze these critiques, noting that they may provide valuable additions to our understanding of free expression. Nonetheless, the chapter will suggest that the "liberal" picture of a relatively autonomous self still has many attractive features, normatively if not descriptively.

Chapter 5 will explore the work of a group of legal scholars I call "new realists." New realists, drawing on interdisciplinary critiques developed by an earlier group of scholars, the Legal Realists of the 1920s and 1930s, seek to modify current First Amendment law through their scholarship. They claim that private action, no less than action by government, can give rise to First Amendment violations. This approach would fundamentally alter free speech jurisprudence by converting the First Amendment from a "shield" against government censorship to a "sword" that requires active government intervention in the marketplace of ideas. The chapter will point out key analytical difficulties with this approach and suggest that, while new realist claims have some merit, it may not be wise to extend them as far as their proponents might wish.

Chapter 6 will focus on the current intense debate over whether the techniques of moral philosophy should be imported into constitutional and First Amendment jurisprudence. The proponents, led by noted theorist Ronald Dworkin, contend that recourse to moral philosophy is not only desirable, but unavoidable as we contemplate the meaning of our Constitution. A number of critics disagree, concerned that importing philosophical methods into judging leaves judges with too much discretion and is fundamentally at odds with the rule of law. The chapter will examine this debate and suggest that it may be impossible to avoid some variety of normative thinking about constitutional issues. Nonetheless, constitutional thinkers should apply these techniques carefully and remain thoroughly grounded in more traditional styles of legal reasoning.

Chapter 7 will summarize the findings of the book and, based upon the earlier chapters, offer some thoughts on the extent to which First Amendment theory should avail itself of the wisdom of other disciplines. The chapter will sketch the outlines of a theoretical approach that can benefit from interdisciplinary insights while remaining grounded in constitutional reality.

CHAPTER

1

Classical First Amendment Theory

The legal scholar now confronts a dizzying array of competing disciplines and approaches. Law has become a sort of meeting ground for academic ideas and trends. And because it has become an interdisciplinary crossroads—affected and infected by so many different influences—law has become, as perhaps never before in American history, one of the most absorbing intellectual subjects.

—J. M. Balkin[1]

The United States Supreme Court has not singled out one overriding theoretical justification for free speech, although it has its favorites among the theories discussed in this chapter. Still, the Court has been quite eclectic in its use of these theories, leading theorist Thomas Emerson to make an observation some thirty years ago that is no less true today: "The outstanding fact about the First Amendment today is that the Supreme Court has never developed any comprehensive theory of what that constitutional guarantee means and how it should be applied in concrete cases."[2] Some commentators have been vexed by the Court's theoretical eclecticism, while others have viewed it as a strength of First Amendment jurisprudence.

---

[1]J. M. Balkin, Interdisciplinarity as Colonization, 53 Wash. & Lee L. Rev. 949, 970 (1996).
[2]Thomas I. Emerson, The System of Freedom of Expression 15 (1970).

Before critiquing some of the contributions of the new interdisciplinarians, it may be helpful to sketch briefly what this book refers to as "classical" First Amendment theory, which I am defining as those works that emerged out of a shared Anglo-American, liberal (as that word is used in political philosophy) perspective. Strictly speaking, of course, the First Amendment is a purely American invention, and its text encompasses rights other than free speech. Moreover, much discussion of freedom of speech is philosophical in nature rather than merely descriptive of existing constitutional rights. Nonetheless, because the term *First Amendment theory* is widely adopted in the disciplines of law and communication, it will be used here. *Classical* may strike some readers as slightly pretentious, but because *traditional* has a whiff of the pejorative, *classical* it shall be.

This chapter will review a number of important contributions to First Amendment theory. This review is necessary both to establish a baseline for the chapters that follow—to encapsulate, in brief, the tradition against which the interdisciplinarians are reacting—and to underscore the importance of freedom of speech in the estimation of a number of outstanding thinkers. Although its detractors sometimes seem to outnumber its supporters these days, it is hoped that this brief overview will suggest that classical First Amendment theory, while imperfect, is still a vital and important resource.

Marketplace Theory

The marketplace of ideas theory, so named because of Justice Oliver Wendell Holmes's famous passage in *Abrams v. United States*,[3] represents one of the most powerful images of free speech, both for legal thinkers and for laypersons. Marketplace theory is often traced to English poet (and censor) John Milton's powerful 17th-century defense of unlicensed printing in the *Areopagitica*:

> Though all the winds of doctrine were let loose to play upon the earth, so Truth be in the field, we do injuriously by licensing and prohibiting to misdoubt her strength. Let her and Falsehood grapple; whoever knew Truth put to the worse, in a free and open encounter?[4]

---

[3]50 U.S. 616 (1919).
[4]John Milton, Areopagitica and Of Education 50 (George H. Sabine ed., Harlan Davidson 1987) (1644).

Milton's optimism about truth routinely overcoming falsehood seems misplaced after the horrors of the 20th century, and the scope of his tolerance famously did not extend beyond his fellow Protestants, but his is an important beginning nonetheless.[5] The notion of a transcendent, nonrelative "truth" has, of course, itself been contested of late, as will be discussed in more detail later.

Marketplace theory grew in sophistication as a result of British philosopher John Stuart Mill's 1859 defense of free speech in "On Liberty."[6] Mill noted that when government (even when aligned with the popular will) sought to silence an unpopular opinion, three possible conditions obtained. First, the unpopular opinion could conceivably be true. Even though those who seek to silence the opinion could, in good faith, believe it to be false, they are not infallible. Mill reminds us that many of our greatest certainties are liable to overturned at some point:

> Yet it is as evident in itself, as any amount of argument can make it, that ages are no more infallible than individuals; every age having held many opinions which subsequent ages have deemed not only false but absurd; and it is as certain that many opinions, now general, will be rejected by future ages, as it is that many, once general, are rejected by the present.[7]

One of the chief merits of human beings, Mill argues, is that they are able to listen to criticisms of their opinions and modify those views where necessary.

If the unpopular opinion thus turns out to be correct, suppressing it would have been a terrible mistake. It would have been more terrible, Mill maintains, because Milton was wrong:

> But, indeed, the dictum that truth always triumphs over persecution, is one of those pleasant falsehoods which men repeat after one another till they pass into commonplaces, but which all experience refutes. History teems with instances of truth put down by persecution. If not suppressed for ever, it may be thrown back for centuries.[8]

---

[5]For an account of the argument that Milton does not truly deserve his modern role as "herald" of free speech, see Francis Canavan, Freedom of Expression: Purpose as Limit 42–45 (1984).
[6]John Stuart Mill, On Liberty (Crofts Classics 1947) (1859).
[7]*Id.* at 18.
[8]*Id.* at 27–28.

Second, Mill suggests, the unpopular opinion might, in fact, be false, and the received opinion in the society, true. Even in that case, the unpopular opinion should not be suppressed, Mill argues. He suggests instead that doing battle with incorrect opinions is the only way an educated person can be quite sure of her premises. Without deep knowledge of competing opinions and the cultivation of the ability to defend one's own views, the received opinion is held as dead dogma only. An educated person must, Mill maintains, hear opposing arguments, not from those who would refute them, presumably by setting up straw persons or otherwise diluting the force of the arguments, but from their most ardent and articulate defenders. The educated person

> must know them in their most plausible and persuasive form; he must feel the whole
> difficulty which the true view of the subject has to encounter and dispose of; else he
> will never really possess himself of the portion of the truth which meets and
> removes that difficulty. Ninety-nine in a hundred of what are called educated men
> are in this condition; even of those who can argue fluently for their opinions. Their
> conclusion may be true, but it might be false for anything they know. . . ."[9]

In fact, Mill suggests, if fluent opponents should prove unavailable, it would be necessary to invent them. The devil's advocate is a critical component in the search for knowledge.

Mill acknowledges the argument that not all people need to engage in such mental labors. If a knowledgeable elite can marshal the intellectual firepower necessary to support the received opinion, perhaps the masses need not be bothered. They can simply accept the received wisdom, secure in the knowledge that someone, somewhere, can defend it against all comers. In the course of a discussion that reveals Mill's rather nasty anti-Catholic bias, he argues that without uninhibited free discussion, broadly practiced within the society, the received opinion itself is diminished. Without the almost structural relationship between an idea and its competitors, the idea itself loses some key portion of its significance: "Instead of a vivid conception and a living belief, there remain only a few phrases retained by rote; or, if any part, the shell and husk only of the meaning is retained, the finer essence being lost."[10] Mill gives the example of religious doctrines, which gain meaning in their struggle against rival theological conceptions, but gradually fade and die when they

---

[9]*Id.* at 36.
[10]*Id.* at 39.

achieve victory. Mill suggests that 19th-century Christianity is in exactly this sort of senescence—received as true by professing Christians, but rarely practiced with any rigor when its tenets conflict with the customs of a believer's country or class. The early Christian Church, on the other hand, had a much more vigorous grasp of doctrine because of its struggle against real enemies.

Mill admits that genuine human progress necessarily involves the overcoming of disagreements and the acceptance of an increasing number of truths that have no extant rivals. Still, he argues that some means of challenging received views, even if contrived, is necessary for true learning. Mill cites the dialogues of Plato as an early and skillful example of this genre.

Finally, Mill considers the possibility that the unpopular opinion that is sought to be suppressed is neither entirely true nor entirely false, but some mixture of the two, and that it shares this condition with the received opinion it challenges. Popular opinion, he points out, is often only partially true, or a limited or distorted version of the truth. Unpopular opinions—Mill calls them "heretical" opinions—often contain parts of the truth suppressed by the received opinion. In a more contemporary vernacular, unpopular opinions point to "marginalized" truths or portions of truth. Mill cites Rousseau's challenge to the Enlightenment *philosophes'* worship of civilization and progress: "The superior worth of simplicity of life, the enervating and demoralizing effect of the trammels and hypocrisies of artificial society, are ideas which have never been entirely absent from cultivated minds since Rousseau wrote; and they will in time produce their due effect. . . ."[11] Mill's point, of course, is not that the Noble Savage is to be preferred to doctrines of progress and civilization, but simply that the Enlightenment view was somewhat one-sided and found a useful corrective in Rousseau's thought.

Mill thus urges that the third condition—the partial truth of the received opinion and its rival—points toward the necessity of free discussion. Only by competition between the two can the truth in each be discovered. He admits that true partisans are unlikely to be moved by the free airing of alternative views, and in fact may become even more dogmatically entrenched in their views when confronted with the opinions of their ideological enemies. Nonetheless, Mill argues, the grain (or more) of truth contained in the unpopular opinion can be grasped by

---

[11]*Id.* at 47.

more judicious listeners only in the open combat between it and the received view.

Mill purported to show that whether an unpopular view is true, partially true, or entirely false, it should not be suppressed. While many thinkers continue to acknowledge the power of Mill's insights, suitably amended, numerous other commentators have questioned his entire enterprise. Some critiques have focused on the hyperrational character of Mill's hypothetical public. The assumption that rationality will characterize many, or even most, hearers in the debate between unpopular opinions and received views seems wildly optimistic to some. Again, the intervening century—along with work in such fields as psychology and communication theory—has cast some doubt on the rationality of the average citizen. If the average listener is either irrational or a slave to some socially constructed worldview that inhibits free and rational mental processes, Mill may be in error. Moreover, postmodernism and related movements have problematized the claims of reason *itself* to be anything more than a local, parochial, and historically situated faculty, often fatally infected by existing power relations.

Defenders of marketplace theory generally assert that reason, while imperfect, is the best tool humanity has, and that while people may accept false ideas over true ones in the short run, truth will emerge over the long run. One problem, of course, is that the long run can be quite long (as Keynes put it, in the long run we are all dead) and that false ideas can do great harm in the here and now. Another problem, as theorist Frederick Shauer pointed out, is that even if a populace is not likely to accept some false idea, great harm can nevertheless be produced by the false idea's side effects: "By side effects I mean those consequences that are not directly attributable to the *falsity* of the views expressed. People may be offended, violence or disorder may ensue, or reputations may be damaged. It is foolish to suppose that the expression of opinions never causes harm."[12] Marketplace theorists have generally assumed, with little empirical evidence, that the benefits of an unregulated marketplace of ideas far outweigh such side effects.

Millean marketplace theory probably first became instantiated in American law through the unlikely person of Justice Oliver Wendell Holmes. Holmes, in good pragmatist fashion, was highly skeptical about the existence of objective truth. Nonetheless, Holmes believed that such

---

[12]Frederick Schauer, Free Speech: A Philosophical Enquiry 28 (1982).

provisional truth as human beings could achieve was attained through the open competition of ideas. In a memorable formulation, Holmes expressed this view in his powerful 1919 dissent in *Abrams v. United States*, which is worthy of quoting at length:

> Persecution for the expression of opinions seems to me perfectly logical. If you have no doubt of your premises or your power and want a certain result with all your heart you naturally express your wishes in law and sweep away all opposition. To allow opposition by speech seems to indicate that you think the speech impotent, as when a man says that he has squared the circle, or that you do not care wholeheartedly for the result, or that you doubt either your power or your premises. But when men have realized that time has upset many fighting faiths, they may come to believe even more than they believe the very foundations of their own conduct that the ultimate good desired is better reached by free trade in ideas—that the best test of truth is the power of thought to get itself accepted in the competition of the market, and that truth is the only ground upon which their wishes safely can be carried out. That at any rate is the theory of our Constitution. It is an experiment, as all life is an experiment. Every year if not every day we have to wager our salvation upon some prophecy based upon imperfect knowledge. While that experiment is part of our system I think that we should be eternally vigilant against attempts to check the expression of opinions that we loathe and believe to be fraught with death, unless they so imminently threaten immediate interference with the lawful and pressing purposes of the law that an immediate check is required to save the country.[13]

Holmes' view was that whatever emerged from the marketplace simply was "truth," provisional though that truth might be. Truth was not some preexisting property that inhered in certain statements; on the contrary, truth, in a Jamesian, pragmatist sense, was *produced* by the marketplace. This skeptical and relativistic view of truth is one that we will meet again in these pages.

Other critiques of marketplace theory have focused on the analogy between it and laissez-faire economics, which, of course, gives the theory part of its intuitive appeal (at least to some). Much as Adam Smith's invisible hand was claimed to produce the optimal production of competitively priced goods and services, marketplace speech theory seems, to some, to assume a similar mechanism that produces truth. Some theorists have suggested a kind of "market failure" analysis by noting that, in the real world,

---

[13] Abrams v. United States, 250 U.S. 616, 630 (Holmes, J., dissenting) (1919).

certain dominant groups control the mass media and tend to exclude view-points that challenge the status quo.[14] Legal scholar Jerome Barron was an early advocate of the view that the marketplace is skewed away from non-mainstream ideas and that there should be a right of access to the mass media for individuals and groups advocating such ideas.[15] Much as antitrust law operates to break up anticompetitive practices in the economic markets, perhaps courts should abandon the myth of the perfect marketplace of ideas and enforce reforms to ensure that nonmainstream groups and ideas have a sufficient voice to allow the marketplace to function properly. Of course, recent developments toward the demassification of communication, such as the rise of the Internet, may at least partially undercut the thesis that the communication channels are monopolized by a powerful elite bent on silencing "different" voices.

Marketplace theory can also be criticized because of its tendency to elevate communal values over individual ones. If the only value of unimpeded communication is its contribution to overall social welfare, it becomes quite easy to justify restrictions on speech in a sort of cost-benefit analysis that overlooks the value of the speech as pure self-expression. This exclusive focus on collective welfare can result in a speech regime that privileges the perspective of the hearer over that of the speaker.

Marketplace theory, while flawed, has great value as one justification for the protection of free speech. The core insight of marketplace theory—fallibilism—leads us to exercise great caution before silencing viewpoints with which we disagree. Because the urge to censor such viewpoints seems a powerful, and perhaps universal, human drive, marketplace theory can act as a stabilizing force against it.

Self-Government Theory

Alexander Meiklejohn, perhaps the leading proponent of the self-government theory, argued that the freedom of speech guaranteed by the First Amendment was the means by which democracy functioned. For unless self-governing citizens had access to information and opinions relevant to issues about which they must ultimately make decisions, the democratic experiment could not succeed. The speech protected by the

---

[14]For a good discussion, *see* C. Edwin Baker, Human Liberty and Freedom of Speech 37–46 (1989). Baker ultimately rejects the adoption of market failure theories as First Amendment doctrine.

[15]*See* Jerome Barron, Access to the Press—A New First Amendment Right, 80 Harv. L. Rev. 1641 (1967).

First Amendment, Meiklejohn argued, was speech aimed at enhancing citizen participation in political issues. "We the people who govern, must try to understand the issues which, incident by incident, face the nation," he wrote. "We must pass judgment upon the decisions which our agents make upon those issues. And, further, we must share in devising methods by which those decisions can be made wise and effective, or, if need be, supplanted by others which promise greater wisdom and effectiveness."[16].

Meiklejohn, however, had a relatively narrow view of freedom of speech. It was not, he contended, a right of each citizen to express her views on whatever matters she pleased. Instead, it was a collective right that applied only to information germane to democratic decision making. Thus, in Meiklejohn's scheme, it is only speech for public purposes that deserves absolute protection under the First Amendment. Purely private speech is subject to regulation under a much weaker standard.

Meiklejohn used the metaphor of a New England town meeting to illustrate his theory. At the town meeting, participants must speak under rules that guarantee the relevance of their comments. The town meeting is not Hyde Park Corner, Meiklejohn noted, but is instead an institution devoted to advancing the public's business through the moderated discussion of public policy. So it is with free speech under the First Amendment. As Meiklejohn famously put it:

> The First Amendment, then, is not the guardian of unregulated talkativeness. It does not require that, on every occasion, every citizen shall take part in public debate. Nor can it give assurance that everyone shall have opportunity to do so. . . . What is essential is not that everyone shall speak, but that everything worth saying shall be said.[17]

Meiklejohn distinguished his self-governance theory from the marketplace of ideas theory by noting that the latter was a means to identify truth, while the former was "a device for the sharing of whatever truth has been won."[18] This distinction can hardly be considered as hard edged as the quoted statement suggests, however. Many commentators have noted that there is at the least some overlap between the two approaches, although,

---

[16]Alexander Meiklejohn, The First Amendment Is an Absolute, 1961 Sup. Ct. Rev. 245, 255 (1961)

[17]Alexander Meiklejohn, Free Speech and Its Relation to Self-Government 25 (1948).

[18]Alexander Meiklejohn, Political Freedom: The Constitutional Powers of the People 75 (1965).

of course, the marketplace metaphor has significantly broader application across a range of human enterprises.

Meiklejohn and his epigones[19] have been subject to significant criticism because of the relative narrowness of the theory's protection of speech. One early critic, famed First Amendment theorist Zechariah Chafee, Jr., in referring to the Framers, argued that "these politicians, lawyers, scholars, churchgoers and philosophes, scientists, agriculturalists, and wide readers used the phrase [the freedom of speech or of the press] to embrace the whole realm of thought."[20] Meiklejohn himself eventually broadened his notion of political speech to include the expression of artistic, scientific, and cultural ideas as well as political ones, although the former were always in the service of the latter. He came to argue that the First Amendment protects "[f]orms of thought and expression within the range of human communications from which the voter derives the knowledge, intelligence, sensitivity to human values: the capacity for sane and objective judgment which, so far as possible, a ballot should express."[21] Still, for many critics, this concession was inadequate, since it seemed to condition protection for great works of art or science solely on their usefulness to voters.[22] It seemed a bizarre rationale to protect William Shakespeare or James Joyce primarily because their writings might assist someone in choosing a Democrat over a Republican in some obscure congressional race. Moreover, Meiklejohn's maneuver highlights the unrestrained proliferation of protected speech, which tends to undermine the plausibility of a rationale based exclusively on democracy. As Rodney Smolla pointed out: "If laws get passed on all aspects of culture, then it is vital that freedom of speech extend to all aspects of law."[23] Thus, the ultimate, and almost inevitable, extensions of the theory tend, in the end, to undermine its explanatory power.

Self-government theory has also been criticized because it casts free speech in a democracy into a purely instrumental role. For thinkers of a less consequentialist bent, free speech has intrinsic value for human beings that cannot be ignored.

---

[19]*See, e.g.,* Robert Bork, *Neutral Principles and Some First Amendment Problems,* 47 Ind. L.J. 1 (1971).

[20]Zechariah Chafee, Jr., Book Review of Meiklejohn's "Free Speech," 62 Harv. L. Rev. 891, 896 (1949).

[21]Meiklejohn, *supra* note 16, at 255.

[22]Steven H. Shiffrin, The First Amendment, Democracy, and Romance 48 (1990).

[23]Rodney S. Smolla, Free Speech in an Open Society 15 (1992).

Checking Value Theory

A theoretical perspective closely related to Meiklejohn's approach is Vincent Blasi's "checking value" theory of the First Amendment. Blasi's approach, while recognizing the importance of numerous other rationales for free speech, emphasizes the role of free speech in checking the abuse of official power. "The central premise of the checking value," Blasi wrote, "is that the abuse of official power is an especially serious evil—more serious than the abuse of private power, even by institutions such as large corporations which can affect the lives of millions of people."[24] Official power is particularly a concern given government's monopoly on the sanctioned use of violence. This monopoly on violence suggests that only the force of public opinion and outrage can act as an effective check on the abuse of official power.

The checking value posits that government officials will carry out their duties more fairly and effectively if their activities are closely watched and reported upon. Blasi's theory takes an essentially pessimistic view of how human beings react when given the reins of governmental power. The corrupting effect of power is assumed to be a constant. The theory thus regards free speech as both an *ex post* constraint on corrupt government functionaries and as an *ex ante* disincentive to corruption. The tangle of illegal activities known collectively as "Watergate," which was subsequently exposed by some brilliant journalism, is often cited as a prime example of the checking value in action.

Checking value theory is a useful way to conceptualize free speech, but, as Blasi freely admitted, it is hardly exhaustive. As an exclusive theory, it has some of the same drawbacks as self-government theory—it focuses too much on political speech and, in doing so, elides many other important values of free expression.

Individual Autonomy Theory

Unlike the largely instrumental theories discussed earlier, the individual autonomy theory holds that free speech is an important component of individual liberty, regardless of its products. First Amendment theorist Vincent Blasi has noted that in individual autonomy theory, free expression is "valuable in and of itself because it figures prominently in our

---

[24]Vincent Blasi, The Checking Value in First Amendment Theory, 1977 Am. Bar Found. Res. J. 521 (1977).

vague notions of what it means to be human."[25] Autonomy supporters often argue that a democratic society requires freedom of speech—not simply for the Meiklejohnian goal of promoting self-governance, but because freedom of speech is a fundamental liberty that a democratic (and properly limited) government must not infringe. Freedom of speech contributes to individuals' opportunities to develop their rational faculties and to make critical decisions about the pursuit of a good life. As scholars Robert Trager and Donna L. Dickerson note:

> As humans, we need to be able to think about not only all of the possibilities of life available to us, to imagine the future and reflect on the past, but we also need to be able to express openly those possibilities through words, clothing, dance, decoration, architecture, music, art, literature.[26]

This need to both express oneself and to hear the expression of others can be said to contribute to ordinary happiness (although not all human beings in fact experience the link between expression and happiness, and indeed some people might prefer the comfort of simply following plans laid down by others) or to a more complex, Aristotelian notion of happiness as realizing one's potential through growth and development, even should ordinary happiness escape one.[27]

Numerous political theorists from John Locke to John Rawls have recognized the importance of some dimension of individual autonomy, whether expressed in terms of natural rights, contractarianism, or some other theoretical framework. As Kent Greenawalt points out, autonomy theory in the realm of free speech has both consequentialist and nonconsequentialist variants. Consequentialist autonomy theory stresses the development of individual judgment and personality through the free discussion of ideas. Human beings cannot develop their humanity or, in a slightly different formulation, achieve self-realization[28] under a regime that restricts freedom of thought and expression. Nonconsequentialist autonomy theory often emphasizes, as Greenawalt put it, the claim "that the government should always treat people as if they were rational and autonomous by allowing them all the information and advocacy that might be helpful to a rational, autonomous person making a

---

[25]*Id.* at 544.
[26]Robert Trager and Donna L. Dickerson, Freedom of Expression in the 21st Century 101 (1999).
[27]*See* Schauer, *supra* note 12, at 49.
[28]*See, e.g.*, Martin Redish, Freedom of Expression: A Critical Analysis (1984).

choice."[29] Under the latter theory, even if freedom of speech does not, in fact, further human development, attempts to limit communication are illegitimate. This normative position would undermine, for example, attempts by social scientific theories about human social and cognitive processes to weaken the theoretical justification for free speech by calling into question the empirical accuracy of the "self-realization" approach.

One of the most thoughtful autonomy theorists is C. Edwin Baker, who has advocated what he calls a "liberty theory" of free speech. As Baker describes the theory: "The liberty model holds that the free speech clause protects not a marketplace, but rather an arena of individual liberty from certain types of governmental restrictions. Speech or self-expressive conduct is protected not as a means to achieve a collective good but because of its value to the individual."[30] Baker's liberty theory seeks to protect noncoercive expressive activities that are freely chosen by the speaker and that operate only through free acceptance by some listener.

Autonomy theory is often justified with hypothetical social contract arguments, in which free and autonomous agents planning government structures would not be willing to cede control over either their own expression or that of others to government. This argument, often based on something akin to John Rawls's imagined "original position," has undeniable intuitive appeal but nonetheless has been subject to strong criticism. For example, Kent Greenawalt argues that

> at this preliminary stage autonomous people might well agree to foreclose some inputs for themselves which they would ideally like to have in some situations. That sacrifice might be an acceptable price for preventing some inputs from other people who are not rational and autonomous when they receive the communications or who, though autonomous, may commit antisocial acts.[31]

Thus, while one might enjoy such violent Hollywood spectacles as *Good Fellas* or *The Matrix*, the awareness that others would view such fare and thereby be influenced to commit acts of violence might result in a willingness to enter into a social contract that limits freedom of expression to some (perhaps significant) degree.

---

[29]Kent Greenawalt, Free Speech Justifications, 89 Colum. L. Rev. 119, 150 (1989).
[30]Baker, *supra* note 14, at 5.
[31]Kent Greenawalt, Speech, Crime, and the Uses of Language 115 (1989).

Autonomy theory is related to, but at least partially distinguishable from, what might be called "equality theory." Under this variant, which often has a Kantian flavor, the individual's freedom of expression is critical, but based less upon the priority of liberty *qua* liberty or upon the goals of self-realization and more upon the moral imperative of recognizing citizens' equality, dignity, and moral agency. As Ronald Dworkin expresses this imperative:

> Government insults its citizens, and denies their moral responsibility, when it decrees that they cannot be trusted to hear opinions that might persuade them to dangerous or offensive convictions. We retain our dignity, as individuals, only by insisting that no one—no official and no majority—has the right to withhold an opinion from us on the ground that we are not fit to hear and consider it.[32]

Dworkin points out that this moral imperative is applicable, not only to the citizen as listener, seeking to form her own opinions, but to the citizen as speaker, seeking to communicate her view of justice, truth, or the good life, no matter how offensive that view might be to some.

Dissent Theory

Law professor Steven Shiffrin has argued that the other dominant theories of the First Amendment fail to capture its true essence, which lies in the protection of dissent for its own sake. In his book *The First Amendment, Democracy and Romance*,[33] Shiffrin invokes the tradition of such nonconformists as Ralph Waldo Emerson and Walt Whitman to argue for a "romantic" conception of free speech, which emphasizes the continual need to shatter established forms and orthodoxies. The First Amendment thus serves as an ongoing antidote against conformity and closure in the realms of politics and culture. As Shiffrin eloquently expresses his thesis:

> If an organizing symbol makes sense in first amendment jurisprudence, it is not the image of a content-neutral government; it is not a town hall meeting or even a robust marketplace of ideas; still less is it liberty, equality, self-realization, respect, dignity, autonomy, or even tolerance. If the first amendment is to have an organizing symbol . . . let it be the image of the dissenter. A major purpose of the first amendment . . . is to protect the romantics—those who would break out of classical forms:

---

[32]Ronald Dworkin, Freedom's Law: The Moral Reading of the Constitution 200 (1996).
[33]Shiffrin, *supra* note 22.

the dissenters, the unorthodox, the outcasts. The first amendment's purpose and function in the American polity is not merely to protect negative liberty, but also affirmatively to sponsor the individualism, the rebelliousness, the antiauthoritarianism, the spirit of nonconformity within us all.[34]

Shiffrin argues that other free speech theories, such as the marketplace of ideas or the self-government model, fail to achieve the necessary comprehensiveness—they always leave out part of the picture or wind up favoring one type of speech over another. The dissent theory, on the other hand, is capacious enough to include those other visions, and can thus serve as a "repository" of free speech values. Moreover, he points out, during the periods of greatest repression of speech—such as the recurrent "red scares" of the 20th century—it is always dissent from political orthodoxy that is the first casualty of those who would destroy freedom of speech. If dissent were the organizing symbol of free speech, such outcomes might be less likely. Attention to the dissent theory would also, Shiffrin argues, help promote progressive change in countless hierarchies of power: "Dissent does not invariably seek change, let along desirable change, nor does it invariably combat power, let along illegitimate power. My claim, however, is that the sponsoring and protection of dissent generally have progressive implications."[35]

Other theorists have urged the protection of dissent, often not for its own sake but in order to maintain social stability. Thomas Emerson, for instance, noted that one of the key justifications for freedom of expression is "achieving a more adaptable and hence a more stable community, of maintaining the precarious balance between healthy cleavage and necessary consensus."[36] In some formulations, the protection of dissent serves as a safety valve that allows the disaffected to express their frustrations with the status quo through either speaking or listening to "subversive" ideas, in the hopes that they will refrain from more violent expressions of discontent. Free speech is thus presumed to perform a cathartic function. One potential difficulty with this view is that empirical studies—at least in the area of violent material—have tended to dispute the cathartic benefit.[37]

---

[34]*Id.* at 5.

[35]*Id.* at 96.

[36]Emerson, *supra* note 2, at 7.

[37]*See* David K. Perry, Theory and Research in Mass Communication: Contexts and Consequences 158–71 (1996).

Tolerance Theory

Lee Bollinger has suggested that the value of the First Amendment goes beyond merely protecting speech. Instead, the First Amendment is a cultural ideal that creates the conditions for the development of a certain kind of citizen. In *The Tolerant Society*,[38] Bollinger argued that freedom of speech "involves a special act of carving out one area of social interaction for extraordinary self-restraint, the purpose of which is to develop and demonstrate a social capacity to control feelings evoked by a host of social encounters."[39] Intolerance is a powerful force in social life, and protecting free speech through the First Amendment helps to teach tolerance by exposing citizens to diverse views they might not otherwise be inclined to endure. Bollinger thus portrays the First Amendment as a pedagogical tool. Although he acknowledges that other First Amendment theories may have some utility, Bollinger claims that his position suggests a major shift in free speech thought.

Bollinger's view, for all its obvious appeal, may claim too much. As one critique cogently pointed out, tolerance theory has rather limited explanatory or predictive power:

> It is by no means clear that previous perspectives can be dismissed as passé, or that his new perspective can be usefully applied to the full range of first amendment problems. Is public access to criminal trials or pretrial proceedings a way of increasing our tolerance—and if so, our tolerance of whom: the police, the press, or criminals? And what of commercial speech—should we give it constitutional protection to increase our tolerance for hucksterism? In these and other areas of litigation, such as the expanding public forum area or campaign finance, Bollinger's tolerance theory seems to have very little to say.[40]

In addition, even if Bollinger is right that freedom of expression encourages tolerance, this may be a desirable side effect of free speech rather than a defensible normative basis.[41] The fact that toleration may follow from free speech does not necessarily suggest that it should be the normative focus of First Amendment theory.

---

[38]Lee Bollinger, The Tolerant Society (1986).
[39]*Id*. at 10.
[40]Daniel A. Farber and Philip P. Frickey, Practical Reason and the First Amendment, 34 UCLA L. Rev. 1615, 1625 (1987).
[41]Greenawalt, *supra* note 31, at 29.

Eclectic Theories

Some First Amendment theorists eschew "unified" theories of free speech. These theorists look with suspicion on foundationalist approaches to free speech and instead advocate approaches that recognize diverse values that support, but do not necessarily "undergird," freedom of expression. Harry Kalven, Jr., for example, expressed skepticism about academic attempts at grand theorizing. Kalven, like a good common lawyer, preferred the case-by-case development of legal doctrine that remained thoroughly contextual to the airy abstractions of some theorists. Kalven's approach suggested that the development of First Amendment doctrine, particularly in the Supreme Court, is representative of a broader cultural tradition of free speech.[42]

Likewise, some philosophical pragmatists have suggested that monistic theories of free speech are both incomplete and unconvincing and that, as well, they tend to require Ptolemaic contortions in analyzing actual cases in order to make the theory fit with actual or preferred results. As pragmatists Daniel A. Farber and Philip P. Frickey argued:

> [W]e don't have a tower of values with free speech somewhere in the middle, and more basic values underneath. Instead, we have a web of values, collectively comprising our understanding of how people should live. Foundationalism errs in seeking to reduce the complex relationships among our values to a linear arrangement in which a few values have privileged status as fundamental.[43]

Conclusion

The classical First Amendment theories presented in this chapter are certainly not without their problems, as I have tried to indicate. Nonetheless, they represent an important resource in our constitutional tradition—a resource we ignore at our peril. As mentioned earlier, recent interdisciplinary work in First Amendment theory has called the classical models into question. It is to the approaches of two of these interdisciplinary theorists that we now turn.

---

[42]Harry Kalven, Jr., A Worthy Tradition (Jamie Kalven ed., 1988).
[43]Farber and Frickey, *supra* note 40, 1641 (1987).

CHAPTER

2

Imperial Paradigms and Reductionism

In the past two decades, fancy law review scholarship has replicated the intellectual history of the past three centuries. Against an unholy combination of Locke, Bentham, and Hobbes that was well ensconced in the scholarship of the fifties, the right-and-principles people pulled out Kant. Of course, if Kant can be put to good use, it takes no great leap of mind to recognize that Marx and the Frankfurt school can be pressed into service as well. From there things began to accelerate rapidly. Someone retaliates with Wittgenstein. Others respond with French structuralists. From there it is a small step to Derrida. Too far for some: They answer back with Dilthey and Gadamer. But for every Gadamer, there is a Habermas. And every Habermas has his Foucault. Foucault is dead. We are running out of Europeans.

—Pierre Schlag[1]

Interdisciplinary approaches to law have many virtues. Interdisciplinary thinkers can deploy new models and vocabularies that allow us to look at legal phenomena in new and intellectually fruitful ways. These new approaches can strip away some of the blind spots of the received tradition and can open up a new space for debating the merits of established approaches.

Despite these advantages, however, there may be serious drawbacks to interdisciplinary approaches as well. In particular, claims that law or legal theory can be "reduced" to the language and concepts of other disciplines pose serious difficulties. Reductionists sometimes claim that legal

---

[1]Pierre Schlag, Comment: The Brilliant, the Curious, and the Wrong, 39 Stan. L. Rev. 917, 918 n. 1 (1987).

theory is not only *not* an autonomous domain of knowledge, but that law would be better accounted for by using the explanatory tools or vocabulary of another discipline. As Kathleen Lennon and David Charles explained, "[R]eductionist accounts aim to show that where we thought we had two sets of concepts, entities, laws, explanations, or properties, we in fact have only one, which is most perspicuously characterized in terms of the reducing vocabulary."[2]

Reductive claims are common in a number of disciplines. For example, the argument is made that psychology can be reduced to neurophysiology, or that biology is reducible to chemistry, which in turn is reducible to physics. As philosopher John Searle explained, at least some types of reductionism are eliminative. "We get rid of the reduced phenomenon by showing it is really something else," Searle writes. "Sunsets are a good example. The sun does not really set over Mount Tamalpais; rather the appearance of the setting sun is an illusion entirely explained by the rotation of the earth on its axis relative to the sun.[3]

In the study of law, claims of the desirability—or unavoidability—of reduction have become commonplace. For example, proponents of critical legal studies (CLS) sometimes argue that legal decisions are simply politics under the deceptive guise of the rule of law. CLS scholars argue that legal rules do not determine judicial decisions. Instead, such rules are indeterminate and can support virtually any result in a given case. As a result, law is best explained in terms of the political preferences and class biases of the judge.[4] As one commentator put it, for CLS, "the dependence of law on politics is masked by a formal apparatus designed to create the impression that law is autonomous and neutral.[5] The upshot of this approach is that the study of legal rules and legal theory as an independent realm of knowledge collapses, and the law must now be accounted for using the reducing vocabulary of CLS. Like a sunset, law is simply an illusion.

At the other end of the political spectrum, scholars identified with the "law and economics" movement often argue for a reduction of legal concepts and rules to the language of economic efficiency. Some "law and

---

[2]Kathleen Lennon and David Charles, Introduction 2, in Reduction, Explanation, and Realism (1992).
[3]John R. Searle, The Mystery of Consciousness, New York Review of Books, Nov. 2, 1995, at 63.
[4]This view is not original with critical legal studies. A significant academic movement in the 1920s and 1930s—the legal realists—made similar claims. *See e.g.*, Laura Kalman, Legal Realism at Yale, 1927–1960 (1986).
[5]Bernard Schwartz, Main Currents in American Legal Thought 606 (1993).

economics" scholars urge that economic rigor and quantitative analysis, based on the consequences of legal outcomes, should replace normative legal theory that draws upon controversial and sometimes ill-defined notions of individual rights, morality, and justice.[6]

This chapter will first briefly examine the recent history of American legal thought and the growing influence of other disciplines on law. Next, it will explore two interdisciplinary free speech analyses—one from a postmodern feminist perspective and the other from a law and economics framework. Although this critique does not assume that the works examined are necessarily *representative* of all interdisciplinary First Amendment scholarship, they do illustrate some of the difficulties inherent in attempts to fit free speech doctrine and theory into the methodology or vocabulary of other disciplines. Finally, the chapter will suggest some of the possible limits on interdisciplinary free speech scholarship in light of these reductionistic difficulties.

"Law and . . ."

A brief history of American legal thought may help set the stage for an examination of legal interdisciplinarity. This history is necessarily partial, but it captures at least some of the dominant views in American legal theory over the last century or so.

In the beginning, there was Langdellian formalism. Christopher Columbus Langdell, dean of Harvard Law School from 1870 to 1895, maintained that once true legal propositions had been identified, the results of individual cases could be derived deductively. Langdell's views had an enormous influence in the legal thought of the late 19th century, both in legal education and in legal scholarship. Langdell considered law to be a science that identified fundamental legal principles from the vast corpus of reported cases. As he wrote in his contracts book, published in 1871: "Law, considered as a science, consists of certain principles or doctrines. To have such a mastery of these as to be able to apply them with constant facility and certainty to the ever-tangled skein of human affairs, is what constitutes a true lawyer. . . ."[7] Legal formalism assumed that law—in particular, the common law—had generated universal truths that,

---

[6]On such reductions generally, *see* Stephen W. Ball, Facts, Values, and Normative Supervenience, 55 Phil. Stud. 143 (1989).

[7]Christopher Columbus Langdell, Law of Contracts vi (1871).

once identified, assured arriving at the proper results in cases through simple syllogistic logic.[8]

Formalism was not without its critics, even in the 19th century. Oliver Wendell Holmes challenged the premises of formalism with his famous claim that

> [t]he life of the law has not been logic: it has been experience. The felt necessities of the time, the prevalent moral and political theories, institutions of public policy, avowed or unconscious, even the prejudices which judges share with their fellow-man, have had a good deal more to do than the syllogism in determining the rules by which men should be governed.[9]

Holmes's attack on formalism proved influential in the "sociological jurisprudence" of Roscoe Pound, which sought to study the social impact of legal doctrine,[10] and in the jurisprudential critique of formalism launched by the legal realists in the 1920s and 1930s.[11] The realists, including such figures as Karl Llewellyn and Jerome Frank, attacked formalism aggressively and urged, among other things, recourse to the social sciences to understand the nature of law and judicial behavior and to chart the proper course for legal development.[12] As Stanley Fish put it, the realists went "from one essentialism, identified with natural law or conceptual logic, to another, identified with the strong empiricism of the social sciences."[13] Although the realists' actual application of social scientific research to law was infrequent and sometimes amateurish, the realist critique posed a strong challenge to formalism and brought into question the notion of law as an autonomous discipline.

In the decades after the realists faded from prominence, beginning in the 1940s, a new orthodoxy emerged among legal academics in the form

---

[8]*See* Kermit L. Hall, The Magic Mirror 221–22 (1989). *See also* Thomas C. Grey, Langdell's Orthodoxy, 45 U. Pitt. L. Rev. 1 (1983).

[9]Oliver Wendell Holmes, The Common Law 1 (1881).

[10]"Roscoe Pound and Benjamin Cardozo were the most important of the many jurists who followed Holmes in seeing law as an instrument for the conscious pursuit of social welfare, an instrument whose master term was policy rather than principle, whose master institution was the legislature rather than the courts, and whose servants should devote themselves to social engineering rather than doctrinal geometry." Thomas C. Grey, Modern American Legal Thought, 106 Yale. L.J. 493, 498 (1996) (book review).

[11]*See generally* Kalman, *supra* note 4.

[12]Realism was not a unified intellectual movement, but consisted of a number different strands. *See* Gary Minda, Postmodern Legal Movements 25–33 (1995).

[13]Stanley Fish, There's No Such Thing as Free Speech 210 (1994).

of the "legal process" school. The process school, whose most influential members were Henry Hart and Albert Sacks of the Harvard Law School, incorporated some of the insights of the realists but tried to cabin the latters' more radical claims of legal indeterminacy. As Gary Minda described the process view: "Process theorists defended the view that right answers could be developed from a conceptual understanding of the institutional functions and competency of different governmental agencies in the legal system." Moreover, process theorists "asserted the autonomy of the legal process" and "rejected the claims of those realists who advocated the development of nonlegal criteria for judicial decision making."[14] Legal process scholars also developed notions of consistency, reasoned elaboration, and "neutral principles" as the essentials of proper adjudication.[15]

Beginning in the 1960s and 1970s, however, a series of jurisprudential movements emerged that would challenge the hegemony of the process school and its intellectual progeny. In the last few decades, law and economics, critical legal studies, feminist theories of law, critical race theory, law and literature, law and society, and a variety of other interdisciplinary movements began to challenge the autonomy of law, with varying degrees of success. In legal journals, the application of neoclassical economic notions, along with disciplinary tools borrowed from anthropology, literary theory, philosophy, continental social theory, and numerous other perspectives, became increasingly common. Theorists applied principles and techniques drawn from microeconomics, public choice theory, deconstruction, hermeneutics, critical theory, poststructuralism, postmodernism, and a host of other "isms."

One critic noted that the changing nature of legal scholarship is dramatically demonstrated by articles from two issues of the *Yale Law Journal*, one from 1897 and the other from 1988.[16] The 19th-century articles are doctrinal and almost laughably prosaic, with titles such as "Injunction in the Federal Courts" and "The Law of Icy Sidewalks in New York State." Roughly one hundred years later, the journal contains "Critical Legal Studies and the Liberal Critic" and "Don' t Know Much bout the Middle Ages: Posner on Law and Literature." The comparison suggests that, at elite institutions at least, legal interdisciplinarity has transformed

---

[14]Minda, *supra* note 12, at 34.

[15]*See, e.g.*, Herbert Wechsler, Toward Neutral Principles of Constitutional Law, 73 Harv. L. Rev. 1 (1959).

[16]Charles W. Collier, The Use and Abuse of Humanistic Theory in Law: Reexamining the Assumptions of Interdisciplinary Legal Scholarship, 1991 Duke L.J. 191 (1991).

the landscape of academic legal scholarship. Of course, much doctrinal scholarship is still written and published, but clearly interdisciplinary scholarship has made significant inroads.

Legal interdisciplinarity has undoubtedly done much to enrich legal scholarship and to deepen the understanding of law and legal theory. The following sections examine two interdisciplinary attempts to come to terms with free speech theory and doctrine. While the analysis of these efforts is at times critical, readers should infer no hostility toward such scholarship in general, and certainly none toward the excellent scholars whose works are examined. It is hoped, however, that by examining these exemplars with close attention to their reductive strategies, some useful observations about legal interdisciplinarity may be generated.

Free Speech and Postmodern Feminism

Feminist jurisprudence has had a significant impact on free speech theory. For example, feminist scholars such as Catharine MacKinnon have called for new legal restrictions on pornographic material that eroticizes rape and sexual violence and that presents women as sexual objects.[17] Feminist scholars have not written from a single theoretical perspective, of course. Some feminist theorists emphasize the different voice that arises from women's moral reasoning, while others emphasize the subordination of women inherent in male-dominated legal structures.[18] Still others explore the intersection of gender and race. Although feminist concerns traverse the full range of legal doctrine, an increasing number of feminist theorists are turning their attention to questions of free speech theory and doctrine.

Susan H. Williams addressed free speech theory with great sophistication in a 1994 article, "Feminist Jurisprudence and Free Speech Theory."[19] While Williams's thoughtful work has much to recommend it, it also illustrates the reductive tendencies of interdisciplinary free speech scholarship that draws on certain strands of feminist theory, as well as closely aligned postmodern approaches.

Williams's thesis is that free speech issues are often epistemological issues. That is, the search for truth is the central free speech justification,

---

[17]*See, e.g.*, Catharine A. MacKinnon, Only Words (1993).
[18]*See generally* Feminist Legal Theories (Karen J. Maschke ed., 1997).
[19]68 Tul. L. Rev. 1563 (1994). Some of Williams's points are discussed at greater length in Susan H. Williams, Feminist Legal Epistemology, 8 Berkeley Women's L J. 63 (1993).

and thus the nature of truth and knowledge is critical to free speech theory. As articulated by Milton, Mill, Holmes, and many others, free speech is the means to arrive at truth, however defined; moreover, this claim is one that the U.S. Supreme Court has, both explicitly and implicitly, embraced in its First Amendment jurisprudence.

Williams links the truth theory of free speech with what she refers to as "Cartesianism" (an eponymous reference to French philosopher René Descartes). Cartesianism is defined much more broadly than simply as Descartes's rationalism:

> Cartesianism is a collection of assumptions that together form a vision of the nature of truth and human knowledge. In the Cartesian view, there exists an external and objective reality that is accessible to individual knowers through the use of their reason, perhaps combined with their sense perception. Knowledge attained through this process is universally true, true for all people, rather than merely true for a particular person in a particular time and place. This traditional epistemology is so widely accepted and so much a part of our social institutions that it becomes extremely difficult to even imagine an alternative view.[20]

This suspect Cartesian view underlies free speech theory, Williams contends, and to the extent that Cartesianism is seriously flawed, free speech theory reflects those flaws. As Pierre Schlag memorably expressed the relationship: "Thus, it might be said of the liberal enlightenment thinker and the First Amendment exactly the inverse of what is said about New York: If you cannot make it here, you cannot make it anywhere."[21] Williams identifies a number of key feminist critiques of Cartesianism. While Cartesianism assumes the existence of an objective reality that one can know, the feminist critique emphasizes the social construction of knowledge and truth. This social construction takes place because, among other things: (1) "problems" to be studied must first be recognized as problems; (2) "facts" or "data" about the problems are identified based on preexisting cultural categories rather than obtained in some "brute," prepackaged form and are themselves theory laden; and, (3) once the data have been assembled, multiple theories can account for them. At each level—problem identification, data gathering, and theory construction—cultural presuppositions, emotions, and values intrude.

---

[20]Williams, Feminist Jurisprudence, *supra* note 19, at 1564–65.

[21]Pierre Schlag, How to Do Things with the First Amendment, 64 U. Colo. L. Rev. 1095, 1097 (1993).

The result of this recognition that knowledge and truth are inextricably intertwined with values and emotions leads, Williams contends, to the realization that knowledge and truth are not universal entities, but rather are dependent upon one's perspective. "Once we recognize the impact of culture, values, and emotions on knowledge, it becomes plain that knowledge may be situated rather than universal," Williams writes. "We could be faced, then, with not one but many equally valid interpretations of reality."[22] Truth is not absolute; it is both socially constructed and fundamentally perspectival.

Williams acknowledges that this perspectival account of truth is not uniquely feminist—it is common to a host of viewpoints influenced by neopragmatism, postmodernism, poststructuralism, and related movements. "Perspectivism" is often traced to the philosophy of Nietzsche, of whom at least some readings of his work claim that "there is no sensible conception of a world independent of human interpretation and to which interpretations would correspond if they were to constitute knowledge."[23] The roots of perspectivism lie much further back in the history of philosophy, however, as the next section will discuss. In any event, Williams suggests that perspectivism is, in some sense, a uniquely feminist concern, possibly because women may have special access to the insights of perspectivism, and more definitely because Cartesian epistemology has led to the subjugation of women. The latter claim is based on the notion that Cartesian dichotomies such as reason/emotion and objective/subjective have contributed to the construction of sexual roles, with the men claiming the preferred (first) half of the dichotomy for themselves while ascribing the inferior (second) part to women.

With truth transformed from universal to perspectival, Williams turns to the implications for free speech theory. Here her account becomes somewhat less than clear. She acknowledges that the demotion of truth claims to matters of perspective might lead some to conclude that free speech could serve no valid purpose—if there is no such thing as objective truth, a search seems futile. However, Williams contends that localized truth serves important purposes, including social cohesion:

> In this alternative epistemology, truth and knowledge grow out of and form the basis for a shared social life. As such, they are the foundation for a whole range of human

---

[22]Williams, Feminist Jurisprudence, *supra* note 19, at 1570.
[23]Alexander Nehamas, Nietzche, Friedrich, in A Companion to Epistemology 304–305 (Jonathan Daney and Ernest Sosa eds., 1992).

goods, none of which is possible without that shared life—goods like friendship, community, and love, but also goods like self-respect, comfort, and safety. One goal of this new epistemology is to ensure the widest possible participation in this shared life. The ability to participate in the process of knowledge formation is one guarantee of being a part of this shared social life, and exclusion from it is a kind of internal exile. A second goal of this epistemology is to provide the conditions under which such a shared life is possible. . . . That is why, under this new epistemology, truth is still desirable both for individuals and for societies and is still important enough to justify a fundamental constitutional right.[24]

In Williams's epistemology, speech is an important method of constructing localized truth in an open dialogue that respects diverse perspectives. Thus, speech is still important, although not for the Cartesian goal of attaining universal truth. Speech is one means by which cultures are constructed, maintained, criticized, and reconstructed—ideally, with broad participation from persons with a variety of perspectives. Speech is a way of attaining the "truth" that can only arise through dialogue, mutual understanding, and the integration of a multitude of individual perspectives, none of which can stand alone. Williams suggests that this dialogic model is at least implicit in current free speech theory but has been overshadowed by the objectivist assumptions of Cartesianism.

What implications does this new epistemology have for free speech theory and doctrine? Williams claims that, among other things, commercial speech—speech that tries to persuade consumers to purchase goods and services—may receive less protection. Because commercial speech is designed merely to sell a product or service and, in the process, to impose a perspective upon the consumer, it is not part of the dialogic construction of truth, and thus may not be worthy of First Amendment protection. On the other hand, her model might offer firmer protection for speech that is less rational and more emotive, such as the symbolic desecration of the American flag.[25]

Moreover, when the diverse perspectives needed to create Williams's conception of truth are inhibited—for example, by monolithic media con-

---

[24]Williams, Feminist Jurisprudence, *supra* note 19, at 1572.

[25]Although a majority of the Court ruled that flag burning was protected speech in Texas v. Johnson, 491 U.S. 397 (1989), a strong dissent by Chief Justice Rehnquist questioned the First Amendment status of such "inarticulate" speech. One wonders how seriously the Court would take such a position upon full reflection, however, especially given the fact that art, music, and other cultural products that unquestionably receive full First Amendment protection often speak to an audience at a level that is less than fully "rational."

glomerates—regulation to create access may be necessary. In order to warrant extensive protection, speech must contribute to the formation of truth. When it fails to do so, government regulation designed to enhance less frequently heard voices may be required.

Williams reserves her most extensive consideration of the implications of her epistemology for a discussion of hate speech. Hate speech, in Williams's view, does have some value:

> It shocks us into a reconsideration of our own assumptions, about ourselves and about the community in which we live. The fact that it represents a perspective which must be rejected on substantive moral and political grounds does not alter its effectiveness as speech that produces the position of truth and plays a role in the community's construction of social reality.[26]

The mere fact that hate speech has some value, however, does not guarantee its full protection, Williams maintains. Certain contexts—college campuses, for example—might dictate speech regulations to protect young, vulnerable students. Such regulations might not be constitutionally appropriate in other contexts, such as parks and street corners. Williams implicitly suggests that such contextualism both is absent from current free speech jurisprudence and necessarily follows from her epistemology:

> Regardless of one's ultimate stance on the particular balance at issue here, the point is that a feminist epistemology would lead us to examine the issue of hate speech in a highly contextual fashion, not to expect some blanket answer to whether such regulations are constitutional that would apply in all times and places.[27]

Contextuality is vital, Williams argues, because the production of truth in her feminist epistemology depends upon conditions that encourage dialogue and that do not result in silencing competing perspectives. Hate speech on campuses may cause such silencing,[28] and thus inhibit the search for a mutually supportive and inclusive social reality. Interestingly, Williams notes that this inhibition claim helps account, not only for an increased governmental interest in regulating (the focus of much First Amendment doctrine), but also for a reduction in the value of the speech

---

[26]Williams, Feminist Jurisprudence, *supra* note 19, at 1576.
[27]*Id.* at 1577.
[28]*See, e.g.*, Mari J. Matsuda et al., Words that Wound: Critical Race Theory, Assaultive Speech, and the First Amendment (1993).

itself. That is, silencing inhibits the search for Williams's version of truth, and thus diminishes the intrinsic value of the speech, value that derives in Williams's view from its dialogic, communal character.

Williams concludes by noting that speech is an important value, but only one among many others, including equality. Thus, a court's decision to favor speech in a hate speech or pornography case cannot be either easy or algorithmic—there are serious costs either way. Both hate speech and pornography cause significant harm. Thus, tragic choices are inevitable.

The Truth About Truth?

Professor Williams's free speech views are eloquently stated and thought-provoking. However, they raise a number of difficulties. Williams first implies that the marketplace of ideas theory—presented as a search for objective truth—is the fundamental justification for free speech. Next, she proceeds to call into question the very existence of objective truth (henceforth referred to as "T1"), including any claim of correspondence of true statements with a mind-independent reality. She claims, not only that there is no such correspondence, but also that no such reality exists at all. Finally, she argues that misconceptions about the nature of truth have serious implications for free speech jurisprudence.

Williams's account of the injection of values into inquiry is a valid one, but its implications may be less far-reaching than she suggests. The notions, for example, that human interests have some influence on the "facts" a researcher identifies or that theories are underdetermined by the world they describe have some validity, as even the most hard-bitten positivists now generally recognize. It is simply a non sequitur, however, to move from this interest-laden picture of empirical investigation to the claim that *there is no objective reality* independent of human interests and values. Of course, one's view of the world is influenced by one's values and interests.[29] This rather uncontroversial point about the unavailability of absolute objectivity generates no particular support for the philosophical idealist notion that no reality exists independently of our representa-

---

[29]As a proscientific critique of one strand of feminist epistemology put it: "No serious thinker about science, least of all scientists themselves, doubts that personal and social factors influence problem choice and the acceptance of results by the scientific community." Paul R. Gross and Norman Levitt, Higher Superstition: The Academic Left and Its Quarrels With Science 139 (1994).

tions of it.[30] Such a claim confuses epistemology with ontology.[31] Philosopher John Searle pointed out that

> the whole idea of a "view" is already epistemic and [the existence of an external reality] is not epistemic. It would be consistent with realism to suppose that any kind of "view" of reality is quite impossible. Indeed, on one interpretation, Kant's doctrine of things in themselves is a conception of a reality that is inaccessible to any "view." . . . [R]ealism . . . is not as it stands an epistemic thesis at all.[32]

By conflating a theory of knowledge with "what is," Williams apparently sought to add force to her argument. However, this reductive account simply does not advance her thesis that there is no T1 toward which the marketplace of ideas could, even in theory, lead.[33]

Perhaps the most serious objection to Williams's account is the relativism inherent in her version of truth and knowledge. This relativism is reductive in that it removes the entire notion of "truth," as generally conceived in free speech theory, and redefines it as *nothing but* what some group or culture happens to agree upon. Philosopher Donald Davidson noted that "relativism is a heady and exotic doctrine, or would be if we could make good sense of it."[34] Relativism in various forms is, of course, not new. In

---

[30]Perspectivism need not mean that there is no such thing as truth, but simply that one only gets closer to the truth by incorporating many diverse perspectives. Such a view is, of course, not far from some traditional views of free speech, and it avoids the relativism of Williams's account.

[31]*See, e.g.*, Sergio Sismondo, Science Without Myth: On Constructions, Reality, and Social Knowledge (1996) (noting that constructivisms "don't cohere with our understanding of the distinction between epistemology and ontology, since they deny that the order of being is distinct from the order of knowing." *Id.* at 11).

[32]John R. Searle, The Construction of Social Reality 154 (1995). Searle goes on to note: "It is somehow satisfying to our will to power to think that 'we' make the world, that reality itself is but a social construct, alterable at will and subject to future changes as 'we' see fit. Equally, it seems offensive that there should be an independent reality of brute facts—blind, uncomprehending, indifferent, and utterly unaffected by our concerns. And all of this is part of the general intellectual atmosphere that makes antirealist versions of 'poststructuralism' such as deconstruction seem intellectually acceptable, even exciting." *Id.* at 158.

[33]Philosopher Kai Nielsen notes that, despite the claims of postmodernists, "there is no doubt at all that fire burns, that water is wet, that snow is normally white, that cats are different than dogs, that people grow old and die, that people are sometimes selfish, that pain is bad, that pleasure is good, that there is some order in nature, and a host of other things. These truths are vague and in most circumstances their assertion is banal, but they are truths and we are more certain of them than we are of any theory which would deny them or try to provide a foundation for them." Kai Nielsen, Naturalism Without Foundations 319 (1996).

[34]Donald Davidson, On the Very Idea of a Conceptual Scheme, in Relativism: Cognitive and Moral 66 (Jack W. Meiland and Michael Krausz eds., 1982).

Plato's *Theaetetus*, Socrates offers several refutations of Protagorus' view that "man is the measure of all things."[35] Relativism in general—and Williams's view of truth in particular—is subject to the objection that it appears to be a general truth-claim that general truth-claims do not exist. That is, all truth is relative, except for the claim "all truth is relative," which itself states an absolute truth about how things "really are." Philosopher Thomas Nagel summarized the implications of this objection nicely:

> To put it schematically, the claim "Everything is subjective" must be nonsense, for it would itself have to be either subjective or objective. But it can't be objective, since in that case it would be false if true. And it can't be subjective, because then it would not rule out any objective claim, including the claim that it is objectively false. There may be some subjectivists, perhaps styling themselves pragmatists, who present subjectivism as applying even to itself. But then it does not call for a reply, since it is just a report of what the subjectivist finds it agreeable to say. If he also invites us to join him, we need not offer any reason for declining, since he has offered us no reason to accept.[36]

Of course, Williams's version of truth—call it "T2"—is not, strictly speaking, a subjectivist one. It is an intersubjective conception that defines truth as a socially constructed product. In this conception—common to a variety of postmodernist, poststructuralist, and neopragmatist thinkers— truth is relative, not to individual knowers, but to some paradigm, culture, interpretive community, episteme, form of life, dominant discourse, or conceptual framework.[37] This "framework" relativism asserts that truth is always produced by internal relationships within some conceptual frame- work, not by relationships of correspondence between true statements and an objective reality that exists independently of the framework.

Philosopher Harvey Siegel has offered a contemporary restatement of Plato's views on relativism as expressed in the *Theaetetus*.[38] The restate-

---

[35]Plato, Theaetetus, in Complete Works 157 (John M. Cooper ed., 1997).

[36]Thomas Nagel, The Last Word 15 (1997).

[37]See generally Relativism: Cognitive and Moral (Jack W. Meiland and Michael Krausz eds., 1982). The literature on these issues is enormous. Some particularly helpful works include: Steven Best & Douglas Kellner, Postmodern Theory (1991); Catherine Z. Elgin, Between the Absolute and the Arbi- trary (1997); Thomas Kuhn, The Structure of Scientific Revolutions (2d ed. 1970); Christopher Nor- ris, Reclaiming Truth (1996); Karl R. Popper, The Myth of the Framework (1994); Richard Rorty, Consequences of Pragmatism (1982); Peter C. Schanck, Understanding Postmodern Thought and its Implications for Statutory Interpretation, 65 S. Cal. L. Rev. 2505 (1992).

[38]Harvey Siegel, Relativism Refuted (1987).

Contents

About the Author

Lee Prescott was born in Liverpool, England, at the height of Beatlemania. Much to his disappointment, being unrelated to any of the Fab Four (DNA test pending), he found himself having to be educated and gain employment status, achieving the former at the Universities of Leeds and Strathclyde and the latter through a quarter of a century working in information technology. While not aimlessly wandering around the world's mountainous regions, Lee lives in Glasgow, Scotland, with his family. *Slowly Slowly* is his first book.

Acknowledgements

A very special thanks to my family for putting up with me through the process of writing *Slowly Slowly*. My thanks to Sasha and Vanessa for the feedback on the initial draft. Spasibo to Baba for setting up the writing desk in La Chapelle-sur-Erdre. I am deeply indebted to Martin Mammatt for all the hours of proofreading, extensive enhancements to the text and repeatedly correcting my systemic grammatical shortcomings; hopefully, the free beer night in Otley will act as some recompense. Many thanks to Allan Denovan for his efforts proofreading, the scientific corrections, cultural observations and his encouragement along the way. Merci beaucoup pour tout à M. Piu Piu for the proofreading, correcting my French, such as it is, and the suggestion for a stronger ending. Thanks to Ewan Cameron for all his help with the artwork. Lastly, my gratitude to all the wonderful Nepali folks who took care of me along the way; I couldn't have written this book without you.

ment, Siegel notes, applies equally to "framework" relativism and to the sort of subjective relativism apparently advocated by Protagorus. Siegel's most telling argument is that relativism is incoherent: it cannot be "right," because if relativism is correct, no theory is right as a description of how things really are. Siegel called this argument the "undermines the very notion of rightness" ("UVNR") argument. It is quite difficult to be a consistent relativist because of the difficulty of making arguments at all without at least implicitly appealing to nonrelativistic criteria. As Siegel applied the UVNR argument to cultural or framework relativism:

> To "defend" framework relativism relativistically (i.e. "according to my framework, framework relativism is true (correct, warranted, etc.)") is to fail to *defend* it, since the non-relativist is appropriately unimpressed with such framework-bound claims. But to defend framework relativism non-relativistically is to give it up, since to defend it in this way is to acknowledge the legitimacy of framework-neutral criteria of assessment of claims, which is precisely what the framework relativist must deny."[39]

This pitfall predictably haunts Williams's feminist epistemology: she wants simultaneously to claim that perspectivism is superior to "Cartesianism" (in fact, that "Cartesianism" is wrong) and to claim that there are many, equally valid interpretations of reality (in fact, that "reality" itself is socially constructed all the way down). One position or the other *could* be correct, but one cannot hold both simultaneously without some degree of incoherence.[40] Moreover, Williams makes no distinction between different domains of knowledge and truth to which her views might be more or less applicable. Perhaps, for example, scientific truth—or simple, everyday experience—differs in kind from truth in historical studies. For that matter, truth in the natural sciences may be

---

[39]*Id.* at 43–44. For another perspective on the self-refuting nature of relativism, *see* Hilary Putnam, Reason, Truth and History 113–24 (1981).

[40]One could, of course, accept Williams's perspectivism at face value and argue that the particular discourse or paradigm that 20th-century Americans occupy is simply one that speaks in terms of objectivity. Eric Blumenenson noted the argument that "we who have inherited the Enlightenment vocabulary should embrace the objectivist language of human rights, moral obligation, and equality as our own local practice, unimpeachable as the product of our history. The perspectivist thesis cannot hold that such language is untrue without invoking a kind of correspondence theory in reverse, by which our language should correspond to the nonmetaphysical-way-the-world-really-is. But since the thesis starts with a rejection of the correspondence theory of truth, there remain only ' language games' and 'forms of life' (in Wittgenstein's terms) which can be neither true nor false." Eric Blumenson, Mapping the Limits of Skepticism in Law and Morals, 74 Tex. L. Rev. 523, 537–38 (1996) (citations omitted).

a very different animal than its counterpart in the social sciences.[41] Or perhaps the truths of logic and mathematics are significantly different from truth in the realm of moral philosophy. Williams's relativism seems relentlessly absolutist in this regard; all truth of any kind is illusory, simply a product of one's paradigm.

As a matter of free speech theory, it is interesting to note that many theorists who challenge the marketplace of ideas theory of free speech reinscribe the logic of truth-seeking theory through their own writings. When one argues against the search for T1, one is already presupposing something like a marketplace of ideas in which only those ideas that can pass muster, based upon appropriate arguments and reasons, will be accepted. If one assumes that one must produce evidence or persuasive arguments for one's assertions that readers will accept or reject based on their adequacy or fit with how things are, one's strategy is already parasitic upon the existence of something quite like T1. The very act of making arguments performatively contradicts one's claims.[42]

Of course, the fact that Williams's T2 suffers from these relativistic difficulties does not prove that it is incorrect (whatever "correct" might mean in this context). Perhaps objectivism is simply embedded in everyday language and thought to such an extent that alternative epistemologies only seem incoherent. Or perhaps, as some have argued, the very objections raised against relativism beg the question by improperly smuggling in an objective or absolute conception of truth.[43] It may be that no knockdown argument is possible. Clearly, however, the seemingly incoherent nature of framework relativism must, at the least, raise a red flag concerning T2. In addition, it must put one on guard against other claims that seem to transgress the boundaries of Williams's epistemology.[44]

---

[41]*See, e.g.*, Alexander Rosenberg, Philosophy of Social Science (1988). On the crucial distinction between the social construction of *social* objects versus *material* objects, *see* Sismondo, *supra* note 31, at 84–85.

[42]Blumenson makes a related point when he suggests that many "postmodern and pragmatist writings provide a mixed message. . . . They are, after all, arguments, a medium which presumes that reasons and evidence can have objective weight and are not merely revelations about the people who proffer them. And they are arguments that invoke an extracultural standard to tell us that our culture's Enlightenment discourse has gone wrong." Blumenson, *supra* note 40, at 547. Of course, one might simply claim that one's arguments are deployed "rhetorically" to convince hearers, but without the intent to describe how things really are. *See* Schanck, *supra* note 37, at 2550–51 (discussing similar claims).

[43]*See generally* Siegel, *supra* note 38, at 23–25.

[44]*See, e.g.*, Sismondo, *supra* note 31, at 87. ("Neo-Kantian social constructivism . . . gives the political critic some tools with which to work: a debunking attitude toward traditional philosophies of science and some interpretive skills for recognizing interestedness. But it withholds a key tool: the concept of *mis*representation.")

Indeed, Williams's epistemic views often seem to clash with other positions she wishes to adopt. To take a trivial example, her statements about the harms of hate speech and pornography implicitly rely more upon positivist social science than they do upon perspectivism. On a more serious note, the UVNR argument would appear to apply, not only to Williams's grand theory (perspectivism), but to her moral claims as well. Williams seems to want to hold on both to her epistemology and to her absolute moral commitments.[45] The problem, of course, is that if one wishes to impute some sort of false consciousness to racists, sexists, and other unpleasant characters, there must be some implicit claim of moral truth that these people are either missing or blinded toward. Consider Williams's assertion about the value of hate speech: "The fact that it represents a perspective which must be rejected on substantive moral and political grounds does not alter its effectiveness as speech that produces the position of truth and plays a role in the community's construction of social reality."[46] Most reflective persons would certainly agree that hate speech "represents a perspective which must be rejected on substantive moral and political grounds," but it is not clear that Williams can get there from her epistemology.[47] Once one makes the perspectivist turn, one's epistemology appears to have a disabling effect on claims about the truth or correctness of moral and political positions. As legal scholar Eric Blumenson noted:

> Applied to ethics, perspectivism challenges the idea that ideals like justice and equality refer to anything at all, except as particular cultures come to define them.

---

[45]In fairness to Professor Williams, she has recognized something along these lines in a more extended discussion of her views. Williams, Feminist Legal Epistemology, *supra* note 19. In this article, Williams discusses other feminist theorists' attempts to find some independent standard on which to build a critique that overcomes the relativistic implications of social constructionism. Williams discusses, for example, Katherine Bartlett's attempt "to design an epistemological stance that will maintain the cultural contingency of the social constructionist argument while salvaging some basis for truth or objectivity that would allow for critique. In her approach, called 'positionality,' truth is always partial, incomplete, and founded on experience rather than unitary and transcendent. Nonetheless, it is possible to improve your knowledge by attempting to incorporate other perspectives by imaginatively understanding the viewpoints of others." *Id.* at 100. However, after discussing Bartlett and other theorists, including Drucilla Cornell and Martha Nussbaum, Williams concludes that the problem has not been resolved.

[46]Williams, Feminist Jurisprudence, *supra* note 19, at 1576.

[47]Feminist legal theorist Joan Williams noted that when "we as feminists reject Truth, and are left only with arguments in favor of our interpretations, we are brought face to face with the need to persuade others to see the world as we do." Joan Williams, Feminism and Post-Structuralism, 88 Mich. L. Rev. 1776, 1778 (1990).

The problem is not just that people have divergent ideals . . . but that they construct different descriptions of the world (is the fetus a person?): one can only make moral judgments with a picture of the world in mind, and what looks like discrimination in one picture will look natural and just in a different one."[48]

A number of feminist commentators have raised this problem and have expressed wariness about postmodern feminists' abandonment of truth in light of the need for criteria of justice.[49] At the very least, perspectivists must confront the difficulty head-on. Neopragmatist philosopher Richard Rorty, for example, unflinchingly observed the moral predicament his views create:

> Suppose that Socrates was wrong, that we have not once seen the Truth, and so will not, intuitively, recognize it when we see it again. This means that when the secret police come, when the torturers violate the innocent, there is nothing to be said to them of the form. "There is something within you which you are betraying. Though you embody the practices of a totalitarian society which will endure forever, there is something beyond those practices which condemns you."[50]

The point here, of course, is not that Rorty's observation points toward the existence of any "objective" moral truths, but that perspectivism tends to disable such claims.

Putting aside objections to T2 based on its incoherence, it may be worth exploring whether this reductive epistemology really has the unique

---

[48]Blumenson, *supra* note 40, at 529.

[49]*See, e.g.*, Jennifer Lynn Orff, Note and Comment: Demanding Justice without Truth: The Difficulty of Postmodern Feminist Legal Theory, 28 Loy. L. A. L. Rev. 1197 (1995); Lisa R. Pruitt, A Survey of Feminist Jurisprudence, 16 U. Ark. Little Rock. L.J. 183 (1994). *See also* Deborah L. Rhode, Feminist Critical Theories, 42 Stan. L. Rev. 617 (1990). Rhode notes that postmodern feminist theorists "are left in the awkward position of maintaining that gender oppression exists while challenging our capacity to document it. Such awkwardness is, for example, especially pronounced in works that assert as unproblematic certain 'facts' about the pervasiveness of sexual abuse while questioning the possibility of any objective measure." *Id.* at 620. Rhode, however, argues that the difficulty can be resolved by somehow moving beyond the "dualistic framework of truth and falsehood. . . . To disclaim objective standards of truth is not to disclaim all value judgments. We need not become positivists to believe that some accounts of experience are more consistent, coherent, inclusive, self-critical, and so forth." *Id.* at 626. While this suggestion has some intuitive appeal, it is not entirely clear, at least vis-à-vis Professor Williams's version of perspectivism, how criteria (such as consistency and coherence) are to be formulated that will survive the disabling consequences of perspectivism itself. For an argument that postmodern thought poses no danger to feminist theory, *see* Dennis Patterson, Postmodernism/Feminism/Law, 77 Cornell L. Rev. 254 (1992).

[50]Rorty, *supra* note 37, at xlii.

free speech implications Williams claims for it. Williams argues, for example, that a feminist epistemology would lead to increased contextuality in First Amendment doctrine—in particular, hate speech doctrine. Williams claims that the location of hate speech, for instance—whether on a street corner or a college campus—has much to do with the harm inflicted by the speech. She further asserts that a highly contextual analysis would be the norm if judges adopted her epistemology.

Williams here appears to have conflated two different levels of inquiry, on the one hand, metaphysical claims ("there is no such thing as T1, only T2"), and on the other, jurisprudential claims ("contextual standards are superior to broadly stated rules"). Legal scholar Matthew H. Kramer has argued persuasively that one's position on metaphysical matters has no necessary implications for normative legal or political questions:

> Metaphysical queries ask how things hang together, not how people ought to be treated. Thus, for instance, the metaphysical state of people does not concern the ways in which human beings *ought* to conduct themselves or organize themselves, but pertains instead to what human subjectivity is and how it works. A metaphysical probing into consciousness, be it psychological or epistemological, will look at how conscious beings hang together (in themselves or in connection with other things), rather than at how conscious beings should interact.[51]

Kramer's point is that notions of truth, knowledge, and subject formation have no particular implications for politics and law; throughout history, various epistemological positions have been aligned with conservatism, liberalism, and other political positions. The same is true for jurisprudential issues. Not only can one not derive a jurisprudential "ought" from an epistemological "is," but jurisprudence seems quite underdetermined by epistemology. Williams seems to assume that Cartesianism necessarily results in a regime of inflexible rules rather than contextual standards. However, one need only look at the fragmented state of current First Amendment doctrine to realize the questionable nature of this view. Not only is current First Amendment law highly contextual—with tremendous variation, depending upon the speaker, the category of

---

[51]Matthew H. Kramer, Critical Legal Theory and the Challenge of Feminism 6 (1995). *See also, e.g.,* Laurie Calhoun, Philosophy Unmasked: A Skeptic's Critique 25 (1997) (noting that perspectivism, which is a "meta-thesis," therefore "has no implications for action").

speech, the place or medium in which the speech takes place, and so on—but numerous scholars have argued that it is *too* contextual. Strictly as an empirical description of current constitutional law, a belief in T1 apparently need not lead to broad, inflexible legal rules. Quite the contrary has occurred in free speech law. Nor is it necessarily true that adopting T2 would lead to highly contextual decisions in free speech cases. One can easily imagine a judge operating from a perspectivist view of truth and knowledge and still concluding that broad rules, as opposed to flexible standards, made for better constitutional law. The perspectivist insight has no necessary consequences "on the ground."

Williams's claim about context is not really about contextuality in general, but about a specific issue of context that she implies has been ignored in hate speech cases. In her example, it is the need of young, vulnerable college students to have some protection against hate speech at a crucial stage in the formation of their identities. In fact, current First Amendment doctrine could, at least in theory, accommodate this interest—the Supreme Court has, on several occasions, held that the need to protect children from harm is a significant state interest that justifies overriding speech interests in certain situations.[52] Similarly, actions based upon the infliction of emotional distress are limited, but by no means completely foreclosed, by the First Amendment.[53] Thus, the jurisprudential resources are at least potentially available to extend some sort of protection from hate speech to young adults. Of course, the Supreme Court has also expressed some antipathy toward hate speech regulations,[54] but the point is that, at least conceptually, "Cartesian" First Amendment jurisprudence is fully equipped to provide contextual free speech adjudication, and it does so regularly. Would the Court sanction limitations on campus speech based on the psychological vulnerability of college students? Perhaps it would not, but the issue would almost certainly not be decided based on the justices' epistemic positions. Certainly the Supreme Court has not been unwilling in recent years to recognize new "compelling" interests that justify overriding free speech rights. In fact, some scholars contend that such interests are

---

[52]*See, e.g.,* New York v. Ferber, 458 U.S. 747 (1982) (upholding regulation of child pornography); FCC v. Pacifica Foundation, 438 U.S. 726 (1978) (upholding regulation of "indecent" speech by broadcasters).

[53]*See, e.g.,* Hustler Magazine, Inc. v. Falwell, 485 U.S. 46 (1988).

[54]R.A.V. v. City of St. Paul, 505 U.S. 377 (1992).

proliferating at an alarming rate.[55] The point, however, is that the change in doctrine Williams advocates is, at bottom, not a matter of epistemology at all. Styles of judging and the weighting of conflicting interests may have some attenuated connection to epistemological issues, but there is no *necessary* correspondence between them.

A similar point could be made regarding Williams's "silencing" argument. That is, she claims that her epistemology, which requires a dialogic creation of T2 with full participation from all citizens, would result in altered First Amendment doctrine because of the need for regulation to prevent the silencing of subjugated groups. It is not entirely clear that this doctrinal conclusion is primarily a matter of epistemology, either. One could just as easily suggest that the search for T1 also requires full participation by all citizens and that speech that silences some individuals and that has no real cognitive content (for example, face-to-face racial epithets) ought to be regulated in order to advance knowledge. The decision that "more speech" rather than more regulation is the proper course seems less a consequence of Cartesianism than of the traditional liberal distrust of government drawing such lines.

Indeed, Williams's approach is largely silent on this point. Williams seems sanguine about the notion of significant government regulation of speech, which is particularly odd for a scholar who appears to be quite attuned to issues of power and subordination. Government can, in her view, limit commercial speech, enforce access rights against mass media, and police hate speech, doing so consistently for good ends. One envisions, perhaps, a group of like-minded epistemologists appointed to the Supreme Court of the United States, judiciously upholding sound and sensitive social-constructivist legislation. Classic free speech theory recognized the dangers in such rosy scenarios, and this recognition is less a matter of epistemology than of unpleasant historical experience. Given the at least arguable dangers of abandoning the concept of T1 (assuming that is possible), increased governmental regulation of speech coupled with a slippery conception of truth seems a dangerous mix. There is certainly no particularly good reason to think that jettisoning T1 will result in the widespread adoption of an ethic of care. As philosopher André Comte-Sponville noted, there are genuine moral dangers in giving up a robust

---

[55]*E.g.*, Russell Galloway, Means-End Scrutiny in American Constitutional Law, 21 Loy. L. A. L. Rev. 449 (1988).

conception of truth. Speaking against Nietzchean perspectivism, Comte-Sponville asked:

> If there is no truth, how are you going to resist lies? . . . If there is no knowledge, how will you fight obscurantism and ignorance? If there are no facts but only interpretations, what objections will you make to the revisionists who maintain that the gas chambers are not, precisely, *a fact*, only a point of view, a mere hypothesis, a mere *interpretation* by certain historians connected to the Jewish lobby?[56]

Williams's work simply does not address this issue in any depth. Instead, her point seems to be that T1 is dogmatic and somehow operates to maintain hierarchy and inequality. Again, the problem appears to be one of conflating epistemology and concrete political positions that do not necessarily follow from any particular epistemology. Moreover, Williams seems to assume that the epistemic choice is stark—one must select either a fluid, postmodern perspectivism or a dogmatic, Cartesian absolutism.[57] This dichotomy is a false one, however. Rejecting relativism and embracing some form of T1 need not result in a dogmatic absolutism that assumes that its own conceptual framework has unique access to truth. As Siegel has pointed out, such "vulgar absolutism" is not compelled by a rejection of relativism. Yet Williams's argument gains apparent (and unearned) support by at least implying that vulgar absolutism is the only alternative to her feminist epistemology. Siegel suggested, on the contrary, a fallibilist absolutism that "requires not certainty, or 'ultimate' truth, but simply that knowledge-claims be evaluated nonarbitrarily, and that they be more or less warranted on the basis of reasons which serve to (fallibly) justify their acceptance."[58] Moreover, such a position does not forbid critical scrutiny of the criteria by which truth is produced. Fallibilism "requires not the identification of a uniquely privileged framework or evidential system, but . . . simply the possibility of objective, non-question-begging evaluation of putative knowledge claims, in terms of criteria which are taken as absolute but which nonetheless admit of criticism and

---

[56]Andre Comte-Sponville, The Brute, the Sophist, and the Aesthete: "Art in the Service of Illusion," in Why We are not Nietzcheans (Luc Ferry and Alain Renaut eds., Robert de Loaiza trans., 1997).
[57]For an interesting development of the argument that there is simply no such thing as a Western, metaphysical mode of thought (whether attributed to Descartes, Plato, or anyone else) that is the limiting matrix of all Western thought and rationality, *see* Matthew Stewart, The Truth About Everything (1997). *See also* Suzanna Sherry, The Sleep of Reason, 84 Geo. L.J. 453 (1996) (critiquing the view that "Enlightenment reason" is simply one possible way of knowing).
[58]Siegel, *supra* note 38, at 162.

improvement."[59] The fallibilist position, which of course has strong connections to traditional free speech theory, obviates the need for a false dichotomy between vulgar absolutism and Williams's abandonment of T1. The desire to avoid vulgar absolutism need not lead to relativism, but instead can lead to a fallibilist and pluralist view that admits of many useful frameworks for knowledge, all of which are admittedly limited and partial to some degree. Unlike Williams's epistemology, fallibilism does not commit one to self-refutation and paradox.

Finally, it must be noted that the suggestion that a belief in objective truth may somehow be connected with a history of inequality or unjust subordination does not undermine its claim to correctness. This is another claim that seems at least implicit in Williams's project. Even assuming that some adherents of "Cartesianism" might benefit from it by reaping the illicit rewards of the injustice it (supposedly) perpetuates, that fact alone is not dispositive. Even assuming, for the sake of argument, that Cartesianism, in some vague way, supported, or continues to support, unjust hierarchies does not refute its epistemology. One might just as easily claim, as philosopher Alvin I. Goldman has suggested, that those who oppose objective truth-claims do so simply for their own personal advantage. Proponents of such views "have an interest in purveying such stories, to sell their books and accumulate citations."[60] Goldman's point is not that this interest-based perspective actually describes the motivations of those who propound such views, but that interest-based analyses in general do not have any implications for the correctness of epistemic positions. This point seems obvious, but it is sometimes lost in the vague association of certain ways of thinking with unjust social practices. One can both oppose injustice and accept T1.

The Economics of Free Speech

> *[T]he black-letter man may be the man of the present, but the man of the future is the man of statistics and the master of economics.*
>
> —Oliver Wendell Holmes[61]

---

[59]*Id.* As John Searle pointed out: "The view that the world exists independently of our representations of it does not imply that there is a privileged vocabulary for describing it." Searle, *supra* note 32, at 155. *See also* Popper, *supra* note 37.

[60]Alvin I. Goldman, Social Epistemology, Interests, and Truth, 23 Phil. Topics 171, 185 (1995).

[61]Oliver Wendell Holmes, The Path of the Law, in Collected Legal Papers 167, 187 (1920).

The economic analysis of law, also known as "law and economics," has become an influential, indeed powerful, branch of legal scholarship. Law and economics has gained a strong foothold in the legal academy and has even seen some of its adherents elevated to the federal bench. Much law and economics scholarship has focused on the efficiency of legal rules in fields such as antitrust, torts, and contracts, with an eye toward overall wealth maximization.[62] Moreover, law and economics has both positive and normative aspects. As Gary Lawson explained the distinction:

> In its positive guise, law and economics purports to predict legal events, such as the general trend of outcomes of common law adjudications, or to describe the consequences of legal rules. . . . In its normative guise, law and economics, as does any other normative legal theory, purports to guide the decisionmaking of judges, legislators, and other legal actors. One can embrace some or all of the positive project(s) of law and economics while rejecting its normative component, and vice versa.[63]

One influential study of First Amendment law from a law and economics perspective is that of one of the new discipline's preeminent scholars, Judge Richard A. Posner. Posner's book, *Economic Analysis of Law*,[64] is one of the most widely used texts on the subject. Judge Posner has also been an extraordinarily prolific legal commentator in law review articles and scholarly books, and he recently gained notoriety as the court-appointed mediator in the Microsoft antitrust case.[65] One of Posner's most intriguing contributions to First Amendment theory came in a 1986 article, "Free Speech in an Economic Perspective."[66] Posner's article explores the First Amendment formula created by famed federal appellate judge Learned Hand in *United States v. Dennis*.[67] The facts in *Dennis* involved a Smith Act prosecution of Communist Party leaders for advocating the violent overthrow of the government. The formula Hand developed to determine if government could regulate such advocacy, a version

---

[62]*See generally*, Brian Bix, Jurisprudence: Theory and Context 159–80 (1996). For an early, and influential, critique of law and economics scholarship, *see* Arthur A. Leff, Economic Analysis of Law: Some Realism about Nominalism, 60 Va. L. Rev. 451 (1974).

[63]Gary Lawson, Efficiency and Individualism, 42 Duke L.J. 53, 56 (1992).

[64]Richard Posner, Economic Analysis of Law (3d ed. 1986).

[65]It should be noted that some of Posner's most recent writings suggest a reconsideration of some of his stronger claims about the economic analysis of law. *See, e.g.*, Richard A. Posner, The Problems of Jurisprudence (1990).

[66]20 Suffolk L. Rev. 1 (1986).

[67]183 F.2d 201, 206 (2d Cir. 1950), aff'd 341 U.S. 494 (1951).

of the "clear and present danger" test, required a high probability of harm for a governmental restriction on speech to be constitutional. As Posner explained Hand's formula, a court must

> ask whether the gravity of the 'evil' [i.e., if the instigation sought to be prevented or punished succeeds], discounted by its improbability, justifies such invasion of free speech as is necessary to avoid the danger. In symbols, regulate if but only if B < PL, where B is the cost of the regulation (including any loss from suppression of valuable information), P is the probability that speech sought to be suppressed will do harm, and L is the magnitude (social cost) of the harm.[68]

From that initial formulation, Posner proceeds to develop a more precise formula that divides B into two parts: V ("value"), which denotes social value of speech that may be suppressed, and E ("error"), which denotes "the legal-error costs incurred in trying to distinguish the information that society desires to suppress from valuable information."[69] Posner also "discounts" L (social cost) to its present value by accounting for the fact that the harm of dangerous speech may not be realized immediately. Thus, the ultimate Posnerian version of Hand's formula states that government can only regulate if "$V + E < P \times L / (1 + i)^n$" where n is the number of periods between the utterance of the speech and the resulting harm and i is an interest or discount rate which translates a future dollar of social cost into a present dollar."[70]

Posner's intention appears to be to provide a quantifiable analysis of free speech jurisprudence. Economic rigor is to replace fuzzy-headed First Amendment theory. For example, Posner measures the V variable (value of the speech) by an inquiry into the nature of the speech being suppressed (political, economic, artistic, etc.), the method of regulation, and the market robustness of the speech. He concludes that political speech has greater value than other types of speech because it is necessary to prevent the development of monopolies of political power in a democracy. In addition, Posner reasons that political speech would be less robust than, for example, pornography. Regulations on speech have the same basic effect as a tax on goods, Posner contends, because both limit the supply of an item by decreasing benefits to the supplier for providing it—be it a luxury yacht or

---

[68]Posner, *supra* note 66, at 8 (quoting *Dennis*, 183 F.2d at 212). Posner suggests that Hand meant "probability," not "improbability."
[69]Posner, *supra* note 66, at 8.
[70]*Id.*

political information. Posner uses the economic notion of elasticity to evaluate how much the marketplace of ideas will be affected by changes in the price of information. Posner eventually derives a demand curve that illustrates why the regulation of political speech may result in less than the socially optimal output of such speech. He concludes his analysis of V by noting that

> the upshot of this analysis is to restore political speech to its status as principal beneficiary of the first amendment's speech and press clause, and put commercial speech and pornography on a lower rung—without, however, having to make judgments about the relative social value of political and other ideas.[71]

Posner's article proceeds to provide tentative suggestions for placing values on the other parts of his version of the Hand formula, which he then applies briefly to a number of communication law topics, including commercial speech, defamation, the right of privacy, and obscenity. (The application, however, does not involve an actual quantification of the terms of the formula.) He concludes that much First Amendment law is largely consistent with the results that would be suggested using an economic approach, although with some exceptions.

The Dismal Science Meets the First Freedom

Judge Posner's analysis represents an intriguing first pass at applying economic analysis to free speech theory and doctrine. Posner has taken seriously—indeed, literally—Justice Holmes's "market" metaphor.[72] The insights he develops (in much greater detail than can be discussed in the present work) place familiar First Amendment truisms in a new and interesting light. Although his analysis leaves existing First Amendment law largely unaltered, his interdisciplinary approach has rather significant implications for how we think about free speech. Despite its illuminating novelty, however, Posner's analysis is troubling because of its reductive features. At times, it brings to mind the old saw about econo-

---

[71]*Id.* at 24.

[72]Abrams v. United States, 250 U.S. 616 (1919) ("the best test of truth is the power of thought to get itself accepted in the competition of the market . . ." *Id.* at 630 (Holmes, J., dissenting)). *See* Kathleen A. Sullivan, Free Speech and Unfree Markets, 42 UCLA L. Rev. 949 (1995) (arguing that the marketplace of ideas metaphor is inapt).

mists being "people who know the price of everything and the value of nothing."[73]

The most troubling aspects of Posner's analysis are the (largely undiscussed) presuppositions he uses to formulate his model.[74] Posner's economic approach to law is a direct descendant of utilitarianism, and it shares many of that theory's weaknesses in dealing with questions of individual rights. There are at least three serious difficulties with Posner's model. First, Posner's approach is exclusively consequentialist. That is, the value of speech is measured only in terms of results, outcomes, or states of affairs. Posner's concept of V (value) measures only the social loss from the suppression of information. Although Posner leaves this term relatively undefined, his subsequent explorations of free speech doctrine make clear that he assumes V to be based upon some sort of aggregative informational utility.[75] Such an approach leaves no room for a consideration of the intrinsic value of rights separate from the states of affairs that result from their adoption. Second, Posner's analysis is limited to macro, or social, outcomes, which means that individual perspectives are not considered in any significant way. Instead, individual *informational* utility is simply summed to determine the best collective result.[76] Among other things, this means that the value of speech is measured solely from the perspective of the listener rather than the speaker. Third, the decision to focus on the positive value of speech, however defined, precludes a serious consideration of the notion that one should look not primarily at the positive contribution of particular speech, but at the dangers of allowing governmental action in the

---

[73]For a development of the argument that there are definite limits to what economic analysis can contribute to scholarship on individual rights, *see* Thomas S. Ulen, Essay on the Bill of Rights: An Economic Appreciation of the Bill of Rights: The Limits and Potential of Law and Economics in Discussing Constitutional Issues, 1992 U. Ill. L. Rev. 189 (1992).

[74]For a thoughtful critique of Posner's approach, *see* Peter J. Hammer, Note: Free Speech and the "Acid Bath": An Evaluation and Critique of Judge Richard Posner's Economic Interpretation of the First Amendment, 87 Mich. L. Rev. 499 (1988).

[75]The assumptions underlying Posner's "V" are explored in Ronald A. Cass, Commercial Speech and the First Amendment: Commercial Speech, Constitutionalism, Collective Choice, 56 U. Cin. L. Rev. 1317, 1330–32 (1988). Other commentators have noted that Posner's approach is murky on the issue of how "V" is to be measured. *See, e.g.*, Kenneth Dau-Schmidt, Commercial Speech and the First Amendment: Comments on Commercial Speech, Constitutionalism, Collective Choice, 56 U. Cin. L. Rev. 1383, 1388–89 (1988) ("From Posner's article on the first amendment, it is unclear to me exactly what values he believes we should attempt to maximize in interpreting the Constitution." *Id.* at 1388).

[76]In a later work, Judge Posner acknowledges the validity of a similar criticism against wealth maximization as a normative legal standard. *See* Posner, *supra* note 65, at 376–77. I am unaware, however, of any later reconsideration of his "informational utility" model in the work under discussion.

expressive realm.[77] This approach—free speech's *via negativa*—is simply not an option in Posner's scheme, despite his inclusion of an "error" factor. These three presuppositions combine to create a free speech model that is reductive in the extreme.

It may be useful, by way of contrast, to consider briefly the range of traditional positive free speech theories and thus examine explicitly what considerations are simply elided by Posner's approach. Legal scholar Kent Greenawalt recently surveyed traditional free speech justifications, and his typology provides a helpful comparison.[78] Greenawalt noted that speech theories can be categorized in a number of ways, including consequentialist versus nonconsequentialist theories, individual versus social theories, and a variety of other schemes. Greenawalt chose the former, noting that any choice is less than perfect. In his typology, consequentialist theories of free speech include the following: (1) Truth Discovery, which holds that freedom of speech leads to, or assists in, the search for truth; (2) Interest Accommodation and Social Stability, in which free speech provides a means of ascertaining preferences, reaching some reasonable accommodation, and pacifying those whose preferences are not adopted; (3) Exposure and Deterrence of Abuses of Authority, which is perhaps more familiarly known as the "checking value" of free speech;[79] (4) Autonomy and Personality Development, cited here as consequentialist because of its role in individual growth; (5) Liberal Democracy, the self-governance theory often attributed to Alexander Meiklejohn; and (6) Promoting Tolerance, a theory developed most fully by Lee Bolinger.[80]

Free speech theory also recognizes a number of nonconsequentialist justifications, including: (1) Social Contract Theory, which holds that individuals consent to the authority of government and preserve certain rights against governmental power; (2) Recognition of Autonomy and Rationality, a Kantian respect for autonomy that is separate from any consequences of such respect; (3) Dignity and Equality, which accords freedom of speech on the basis of the basic respect with which human

---

[77]*See, e.g.,* Ruth Walden, A Government Action Approach to First Amendment Analysis, 69 Journ. Q. 65 (1992); Ronald A. Cass, The Perils of Positive Thinking: Constitutional Interpretation and Negative First Amendment Theory, 34 UCLA L. Rev. 1405 (1987).

[78]Kent Greenawalt, Free Speech Justifications, 89 Colum. L. Rev. 119 (1989).

[79]*See* Vincent Blasi, The Checking Value in First Amendment Theory, 1977 Am. B. Found. Res. J. 521.

[80]Lee Bollinger, The Tolerant Society (1986).

beings must treat each other; and (4) the Marketplace of Ideas, conceived, not as a device to produce truth, but, in a Holmesian, pragmatist sense, as the only *test* of truth. The first three nonconsequentialist justifications are, of course, also theories that rest on individual, rather than social, considerations. In other words, they are centered on speakers rather than hearers.

All of these justifications (which are not exhaustive) are powerful additions to free speech theory, and most have at least some doctrinal recognition.[81] The typology is useful because it makes clear what Posner's model ignores. Not only are the nonconsequentialist justifications elided in Posner's economic model, also elided are the consequentialist justifications in their individual, rather than collective, dimensions. It would be one thing if these values were dismissed on the basis of argument, but that is not the case. In Posner's reducing scheme, they simply never appear.[82] They fly beneath the radar of his methodology. The economic reduction of free speech theory necessarily impoverishes the reduced theory by omitting crucial elements simply by virtue of its presuppositions. The lack of attention to the fundamental claims of individual speakers is quite remarkable. It is at least arguable that such claims are the very bedrock of the free speech tradition. As legal scholar Burt Neuborne argued:

> It is fair to assert that throughout the formative period of our free speech heritage—from Milton's plea for unlicensed printing to Locke's plea for religious toleration; from the Holmes-Brandeis dissents to Justice Jackson's majestic articulation of the toleration principle in West Virginia State Bd. of Educ. v. Barnette . . . the paradigm beneficiary of the free speech principle has been a vulnerable speaker of conscience, impelled to speak out by the demands of humanity. . . . While the long-term interests of hearers are cited to justify protecting the speaker, the primary source of judicial

---

[81]Steven Schiffrin notes that "the Court has been generous about the range of values relevant in first amendment theory, and unreceptive to those who ask it to confine first amendment values to a particular favorite." Steven Schiffrin, The First Amendment and Economic Regulation: Away from a General Theory of the First Amendment, 78 Nw. U. L. Rev. 1212, 1252 (1983).

[82]Although generally supportive of the potential for economic analysis to contribute to free speech law, Daniel A. Farber recognized this limitation: "The inherent value of self-expression should not be dismissed as an important basis for freedom of speech. For example, it is questionable whether a satisfactory economic explanation can be given for protecting nonrepresentational art or instrumental music, which have no clear informational content." Daniel A. Farber, Free Speech without Romance: Public Choice and the First Amendment, 105 Harv. L. Rev. 554, 557 (1991). What Farber's example does not acknowledge, of course, is that even those forms of communication that *do* have informational content may also be protected on the basis of the inherent value of expression.

concern in the early free speech cases was the establishment and defense of breathing space—toleration—for the speaker's capacity for self-expression."[83]

Of course, Posner is not alone in concluding, for example, that free speech theory and doctrine should be based on social consequences rather than intrinsic individual rights. Charles Fried noted that this view infects Owen Fiss's recent claims that individual free speech can be limited in order to promote democratic values. Fried's analysis of Fiss applies equally to Posner's model: "The error Fiss commits right at the outset is to mistake an effect of the principle for the principle itself. The First Amendment protects liberty—liberty of expression—and it is an effect of this liberty that there is a wide and uninhibited discussion of political matters."[84] Similarly, Posner's model mistakes an effect (the social value of information) for a foundational principle. This may, in fact, be a widespread difficulty in the economic analysis of law: "efficiency" may be one effect of, say, tort or contract law, but it is not necessarily the single guiding normative principle of those areas of the law.

The reductive effects of Posner's methodology can be seen in the case analyses it generates. Posner questions the result in *Cohen v. California*,[85] in which the Supreme Court held that wearing a "Fuck the Draft" jacket in a courthouse was protected speech. Because *Cohen* is classified as an "obscenity" case in Posner's scheme,[86] he substitutes H (harm) for the PL $/ (1 + i)^n$ (or consequences) term. The substitution is appropriate, he suggests, because little is certain about the actual effects of pornography, but it is clear that "obscenity" is harmful, if only because "in some parts of the

---

[83]Burt Neuborne, The Third Abraham L. Pomerantz Lecture: The First Amendment and Government Regulation of Economic Markets, 55 Brooklyn L. Rev. 5, 14 (1989) (citations omitted). See also, Laurence H. Tribe, American Constitutional Law (1988) ("No adequate conception of so basic an element of our fundamental law . . . can be developed in purely instrumental or 'purposive' terms." *Id.* at 785); C. Edwin Baker, The Scope of the First Amendment Freedom of Speech, 25 UCLA L. Rev. 964 (1978) ("The liberty model holds that the free speech clause protects not a market-place, but rather an arena of individual liberty from certain types of governmental restrictions. Speech is protected not as a means to a collective good but because of the value of speech conduct to the individual." Id. at 966).

[84]Charles Fried, Speech in the Welfare State: The New First Amendment Jurisprudence: A Threat to Liberty, 59 U. Chi. L. Rev. 225, 226–27 (1992). *See also* Martin Redish, The Value of Free Speech, 130 U. Pa. L. Rev. 591 (1982) ("[P]olitical democracy is merely a means to—or, in another sense, a logical outgrowth of—the much broader value of individual self-realization." *Id.* at 604).

[85]403 U.S. 15 (1971).

[86]This is an odd classification for the *Cohen* case. In the Court's First Amendment jurisprudence, the mere use of vulgar slang would be insufficient to warrant the label "obscene," which is generally reserved for "hard core" sexual depictions and places the expression outside the protection of the First Amendment. *See* Miller v. California, 413 U.S. 15 (1973).

country there is intense dislike of it."[87] This is an interesting admission in at least two respects. First, one might question whether there is any more certain knowledge about the actual consequences of nonobscene utterances than those of "obscene" ones. There is certainly social scientific evidence about the effects of pornography,[88] and one might argue that this evidence, which notes considerable variation in individual responses, provides roughly the same degree of certainty (or uncertainty) as predictions about the consequences of any other speech—either categorically or in individual instances. Posner's becoming modesty about the consequentialist mode in the "obscene" domain actually casts doubt on his entire enterprise. Second, the equation of H with "intense dislike" by third persons highlights the dramatic discontinuity between Posner's model and conventional ways of conceiving of free speech under the First Amendment: it is generally assumed that mere dislike of speech, regardless of intensity, has little bearing on the protection of expression.

In any event, Posner's analysis of *Cohen* is that the value (V) of the speech lost by substituting some less scatological term was slight compared to the harm (H) suffered by unwilling viewers of the offending slogan. The same anti-draft message could have been communicated without profanity, resulting in less vehemence, perhaps, but only a slightly diminished V. This odd analysis brings into stark relief the distorting effect of Posner's reductionism. The justices in the majority viewed *Cohen*, not as a case about the value of the information to others, but as a case involving the exercise of a fundamental individual right, albeit a right that was defeasible under certain circumstances. As Justice Harlan memorably put it:

> For, while the particular four-letter word being litigated here is perhaps more distasteful than most others of its genre, it is nevertheless often true that one man's vulgarity is another's lyric. Indeed, we think it is largely because governmental officials cannot make principled distinctions in this area that the Constitution leaves matters of taste and style so largely to the individual.[89]

---

[87]Posner, *supra* note 66, at 44.

[88]*See, e.g.*, Jennings Bryant & Dolf Zillmann, Violence and Sex in the Media, in An Integrated Approach to Communication Theory and Research 195 (Michael B. Salwen and Don W. Stacks eds., 1996); Richard Jackson Harris, The Impact of Sexually Explicit Media, in Media Effects: Advances in Theory and Research 247 (Jennings Bryant and Dolf Zillmann eds., 1994); John S. Lyons, Rachel L. Anderson, and David B. Larson, A Systematic Review of the Effects of Aggressive and Nonaggressive Pornography, in Media, Children, and the Family: Social Scientific, Psychodynamic, and Clinical Perspectives 271 (Dolf Zillmann et al. eds., 1994).

[89]403 U.S. at 25.

Only under the reductive gaze of Posner's method is the result at all puzzling. Of course, Posner as theorist is not bound by the reasoning of the majority; he is applying his own distinctive analysis to the facts. But it is only by artificially excluding crucial premises of free speech theory that the result becomes problematic. The very counterintuitiveness of the reasoning suggests that important considerations are being elided: the reducing vocabulary simply omits the values of the reduced discourse, impoverishing it without comment in the process. Freedom of speech is conceptualized simply as a means to end—and a rather narrow end at that.[90] Indeed, the very notion that free speech must "pay its way" is a troubling one for a free society.[91]

Even ignoring the important free speech interests that Posner's model fails to account for, other reductive problems remain. However one calculates the value of free speech in Posner's equation, a troubling assumption is that all the relevant values can be compared on a single, quantitative scale, or, as Cass Sunstein put it, on a single metric.[92] That is, Posner assumes that one can simply balance consequences or harm against the value of speech, however defined or measured. This is apparently entirely unproblematic—both value and harm are simply numbers in the equation. Martha Nussbaum notes that those who subscribe to this "commensurability" thesis necessarily believe either that "all the valuable things are valuable because they contain some one thing that itself varies only in quantity . . . or despite the plurality of values, there is an argument that shows that a single metric adequately captures what is valuable in them all."[93] As Sunstein argues, such an approach flattens the way we think about important goods such as legal rights, and thus falsifies shared societal values.

---

[90]Compare, for example, Justice Brandeis's claim in *Whitney v. California*: "Those who won our independence believed that the final end of the State was to make men free to develop their faculties. . . . They valued liberty both as an end and as a means." 274 U.S. 357, 375 (1927) (Brandeis, J., joined by Holmes, J., concurring). Or compare the powerful statement of Justice Jackson in the 1943 flag salute case, *West Virginia Board of Education v. Barnette*: "If there is any fixed star in our constitutional constellation, it is that no official, high or petty, can prescribe what shall be orthodox in politics, nationalism, religion, or other matters of opinion. . . ." 319 U.S. 624, 642 (1943).

[91]*See* Neuborne, *supra* note 83, at 15 n. 46.

[92]Cass Sunstein, Free Markets and Social Justice (1997).

[93]Martha Nussbaum, Poetic Justice 14 (1995). *See also* Laurence H. Tribe, Constitutional Calculus: Equal Justice or Economic Efficiency? 98 Harv. L. Rev. 592, 596 (1985) ("The appeal of utilitarian policy analysis, as well as its power, lies in its ability to reduce the various dimensions of a problem to a common denominator. The inevitable result is not only that 'soft' variables—such as the value of vindicating a fundamental right or preserving human dignity—tend to be ignored or understated, but also that entire problems are reduced to terms that misstate their structure and that ignore the nuances that give these problems their full character." *Id.*).

Sunstein points out that legal rights are regarded as different in kind—qualitatively different—from other social interests. Rights are not simply of greater quantitative value on some monistic utility scale. This is an important distinction, which is captured, as Sunstein notes, in the "rights as trumps" approach of Ronald Dworkin and in political theorist John Rawls's claim that certain basic liberties retain priority even if abridgment of those rights would increase economic welfare. As Sunstein puts it:

> If we treat rights as "trumps," we may be taken to be saying not that they are infinitely or even extraordinarily valuable when viewed solely in terms of aggregate levels, but that they are valued in a distinctive way—a way quite different from, and qualitatively higher than, the way we value the competing interests. Because of the distinctive way that rights are valued, it is necessary that the competing interests be (a) of a certain sort and (b) extraordinary in amount or level, in order to count as reasons for abridgement.[94]

This incommensurability of values and competing harms is precisely what Posner wishes to—in fact, must—dispense with in order for his model to get off the ground. As the saying goes, when one is armed with a hammer, everything suddenly begins to resemble a nail. Everything must be measurable according to social utility or disutility, and all values must be instrumental—none are intrinsic. It is this monism that leads, for example, to Posner's *Cohen* analysis, in which the "slight" marginal value of using the expletive is more than offset by the "harm" to bystanders. Such a methodology leads to a free speech jurisprudence that is distorted almost beyond recognition. As Laurence Tribe argued:

> Being "assigned" a right on efficiency grounds, after an appraisal of the relevant cost curves, hardly satisfies the particular human need that can be met only by a shared social and legal understanding that the right belongs to the individual because the capacity and opportunity it embodies are organically and historically a part of the person that she is, and not for any purely contingent and essentially managerial reason.[95]

As Tribe's comment suggests, economic analysis is much more adept at identifying efficient means than it is at articulating appropriate ends.

---

[94]Sunstein, *supra* note 92, at 96.
[95]Tribe, *supra* note 93, at 596.

One objection to this critique is that Posner simply made more precise what already happens in First Amendment cases—whether for purely descriptive or predictive purposes. After all, his model simply elaborates Hand's formula. Although Hand's version of the clear and present danger test (known as the "grave and probable danger" test) is no longer used, current free speech doctrine involves the balancing of speech and conflicting interests via the strict scrutiny test and a number of similar devices. Such an objection would be misguided. Even though there may be flaws in strict scrutiny and related standards—either in theory or in application—the use of such doctrines exhibits a clear judicial respect for the value of fundamental rights which is lacking in Posner's approach. Under strict scrutiny, for example, fully protected speech is assumed to have significant value and can be regulated only in cases in which the competing interest is one of extraordinary magnitude—a "compelling" state interest. Although certainly manipulable, strict scrutiny in theory could never support the sort of "marginal" calculations of value that Posner's model proposes. Strict scrutiny recognizes that free speech is not an absolute value, but the test nonetheless requires an extraordinary showing before regulation is even possible. Posner, on the other hand, provides no protection for speech *at all* simply because it is speech: "Judge Posner treats first amendment speech as the equivalent of any other interest; it enjoys no special preference. It is subject to cost-benefit analysis under a balancing formula."[96] One might well argue that strict scrutiny has in recent years been weakened—it is no longer "strict in theory, but fatal in fact"[97]—and needs retooling, but it seems clear that it provides greater protection for speech, both quantitatively and qualitatively, than Posner's approach.[98]

Moreover, it seems abundantly clear that Posner wants to do more than simply describe and add precision to what judges already do in First

---

[96]C. Thomas Dienes, When the First Amendment Is Not Preferred: The Military and Other "Special Contexts," 56 U. Cin. L. Rev. 779, 834 n. 209 (1988). *See also* Frederick Schauer, *Harry Kalven and the Perils of Particularism*, 56 U. Chi. L. Rev. 397 (1989) ("It is not clear what role . . . speech plays in Posner's scheme. If in the evaluation of the cost of a particular speech, or the cost of a particular regulation, no special decision rules (presumptions, shifting of burden of proof, etc.) come into play because this is a speech rather than some other activity sought to be regulated, then it turns out that there is no principle of free speech, even though it may turn out that there is a great deal of freedom to speak." *Id.* at 413 n. 40).

[97]Gerald Gunther, Foreword: In Search of Evolving Doctrine on a Changing Court: A Model for a Newer Equal Protection, 86 Harv. L. Rev. 1, 8 (1972).

[98]The distinction made in the text between Supreme Court "balancing" in free speech cases and Posner's approach should not be seen as an endorsement of the former. The point is simply that Posner's analysis goes beyond positive explication and into the normative domain.

Amendment cases. He wishes to provide a prescriptive account of how much speech *should* be protected, not merely a case-deciding algorithm consonant with current free speech jurisprudence. Some confusion of positive and normative modes is evident throughout the work, and this confusion is a problem that has bedeviled law and economics scholarship generally.[99] Why, for example, if one wished to provide an ideal model for free speech, would one use Hand's *Dennis* formulation as the starting point of the analysis? Although Posner was enigmatic on this point, the assumption, apparently, is that Hand's test embodies some essential wisdom about free speech. In reality, however, it appears to have been a selection made on the basis of convenience—Hand's test is particularly congenial to elaboration in an economic mode. There is not even good reason to suppose that Hand himself believed his formulation was a worthy test for freedom of speech. A recent biography of Hand suggests, on the contrary, that his *Dennis* test was simply the work of a dutiful lower court judge bound by a Supreme Court precedent with which he did not particularly agree.[100] Hand, it appears, in fact favored a different and more speech-protective standard that he devised in 1917 in *Masses Publishing Co. v. Patten.*[101] Even without this wrinkle, there is no reason to suppose that Hand ever believed the *Dennis* test had any particular application beyond the facts of *Dennis*, which was a subversive advocacy case, much less that he put the test forward as the *sine qua non* of free speech doctrine. Of course, all subsequent use of Hand's creation is not necessarily foreclosed by the doubts of its creator. Nonetheless, Posner's adaptation needs some rather serious justification before it can simply be assumed to generate superior theory and doctrine.

Even more fundamentally, why is informational utility the central—indeed, the only—value that the First Amendment promotes in Posner's model? Posner argues that his model restores the primacy of political speech over commercial speech and pornography, in part on the basis of the market robustness of each type of speech and, thus, the vulnerability to suppression of each, "without, however, having to make judgments about

---

[99]Many commentators have made this point. *See, e.g.*, Henry Hansmann, The Current State of Law-and-Economics Scholarship, 33 J. Legal Educ. 217, 232–34 (1983) (noting that "strong claims that parts of the law-and-economics literature are strictly positive are suspect. Most of the work so advertised strikes me as having a distinctly normative edge–as having been written to prove a normative point rather than simply being a dispassionate exercise in objective social science." *Id.* at 233).

[100]Gerald Gunther, Learned Hand: The Man and the Judge 598–605 (1994).

[101]244 Fed. 535 (S.D.N.Y. 1917).

the relative social value of political and other ideas."[102] But, of course, a judgment about the central value of speech—that is, aggregate informational value—is built into the entire model *sub silentio*. Addressing similar claims, Laurence H. Tribe noted that

> rather than deal with the charge that their calculus inherently distorts the issues posed by the problems they address, the advocates of the technocratic mode continue to claim baldly that their methods offer a relatively noncontroversial, value-free approach to structuring policy choices. The persistent appeal of the technocratic mode may simply evidence an unfortunate if understandable human tendency to obscure complex choices by suppressing their controversial character.[103]

Even ignoring this central concern, Posner's analysis runs into difficulties. It is not clear, for example, that the market robustness argument is altogether sound. The market robustness of speech may often depend less on the *type* of speech and more on the resources of the speaker. Political speech by a wealthy ideologue running for president would be much hardier than commercial speech by a struggling start-up company.[104] Even if such objections are overlooked, however, the fundamental issue of why market robustness should have any connection whatsoever with free speech protection under the First Amendment remains unanswered. Not only is the entire approach questionable, it also has the potential to generate rather ominous limitations on speech that many would consider important.

Of course, greater protection for speech may not be normatively desirable. These are matters that can be rationally debated. The problem with Posner's approach is that it obscures the argument by simply announcing, but not defending, its method. It rigs the playing field before the game can even begin. The fundamental value of speech as some sort of overall informational utility is simply assumed, as is the notion that one can reduce the values of speech and other interests to some quantitative standard and thus compare them. Posner's article does not actually carry out such quantitative operations; it merely sets up the framework and discusses how these investigations might play out. But any actual attempt to carry out such analyses would be meaningless. As Sunstein pointed out:

---

[102]Posner, *supra* note 66, at 24.

[103]Tribe, *supra* note 93, at 595 n. 20.

[104]*See* Aleta G. Estreicher, Securities Regulation and the First Amendment, 24 Ga. L. Rev. 223, 249 (1990).

In disputes over free speech, large questions are whether speech ought to be valued in the same way as commodities to be traded on markets, and whether free speech values are unitary or plural. We might think that we ought not to treat free speech as an ordinary commodity and that we should recognize the diverse ends it embodies.[105]

Even assuming that speech can be valued like any other commodity, how could one possibly carry out the actual process of quantification in any but the most arbitrary way?[106] Unless precision is possible, the enterprise seems bankrupt.[107]

Not only is the reduction of values or harms to quantitative formulae impossible, it is pernicious as well. It gives an unwarranted aura of "science" to what can only be a rather inexact art. Assuming courts adopted such an approach, it could evoke the kind of pseudo-authority that often follows in the wake of quantification. Even though the reduction of genuine human values to numbers is spurious, the *image* thus created is one of scientific rigor. Robert C. Downs has noted this feature of law and economics scholarship generally: "Once a question is identified (excluding all others) and assumptions are taken as true, the answers are generated as though compelled by mathematical equations and thus take on the aura of objective truth."[108] This results in an illusion of increased certainty for the decision maker, and difficulty in challenging the analysis without adopting the reducing vocabulary or conceptual scheme.[109]

The Limits of First Amendment Interdisciplinarity

The two works explored here are not necessarily representative of interdisciplinary First Amendment scholarship. There are, of course, many important distinctions between the theorists explored here, as well as between their works and those of other interdisciplinary legal scholars. For one thing, Posner's model might be described as a pure "disciplinary"

---

[105]Sunstein, *supra* note 92, at 103–4.

[106]Posner himself concedes this point. "To try to measure the value of particular speeches (or writings) would often— though not always, as we shall see—involve intractable, subjective, and arbitrary inquiries, implying that E (error costs) would be very high." Posner, *supra* note 66, at 9.

[107]*See generally* Hammer, *supra* note 74.

[108]Robert C. Downs, Law and Economics: Nexus of Science and Belief, 27 Pac. L.J. 1, 21 (1995).

[109]For an exploration of this issue, as well as a thorough critique of judicial "balancing" methodologies in general, *see* T. Alexander Aleinikoff, Constitutional Law in an Age of Balancing, 96 Yale. L.J. 943 (1987).

reduction, while Williams's approach operates at a higher level of abstraction and might be better thought of as an "epistemic" reduction. Despite these and other differences, the works examined here do illustrate some of the problems—and the promise—of such efforts. This section will briefly discuss some attributes they share and suggest some of the possible limits of interdisciplinary free speech studies.

Both Williams and Posner are original thinkers who have made interesting and fruitful attempts to bring novel intellectual perspectives to bear upon the problem of free speech. Both of their efforts have certain features in common. First, each selects the marketplace of ideas theory as the primary free speech theory. Although each makes passing nods to other theories of free speech, the actual analyses proceed in the main as if the marketplace model were the only free speech justification: Posner by trying to put a value on the information thus adduced, and Williams by refurbishing "truth" in postmodern style. This analytic move immediately takes out of consideration other important free speech justifications, particularly those deriving from nonconsequentialist and individual perspectives. Moreover, both suggest that a critique and reconstruction of the marketplace of ideas theory is the key to an improved free speech jurisprudence. However, it seems clear that the marketplace theory is not necessarily the most defensible free speech justification—in fact, it may be for that reason that free speech critics often focus on it to the exclusion of other considerations. To avoid reductionistic analyses, however, it appears that those wishing to apply other disciplines to free speech must make some attempt to account for the full range of free speech theory, not merely the most convenient target. To the extent that interdisciplinary scholars attempt to force free speech theory into their conceptual frameworks, it is crucial that the reducing vocabulary make every effort to include as much of the richness of that theory as possible. Reductionism in its eliminative form is the claim that X is "nothing but" Y. Posner and Williams maintain that the value of free speech is nothing but the social utility of information, or the social constructivist possibilities of shared discourse. But by eliding so many other important considerations, interdisciplinary analysis may tend to falsify its object. Part of what constitutes a discipline is a series of agreed presuppositions that structure inquiry and screen out irrelevant considerations. Problems arise, however when the elements thus screened out are essential to the subject under consideration.

The second point of comparison is that both Williams and Posner approach free speech theory and doctrine from an external rather than an internal point of view. Although both scholars are, no doubt, accomplished doctrinalists, they choose, in varying degrees, to approach the free speech arena as foreign territory that their perspective must conquer. This is generally a matter of nuance and subtlety rather than bald assertion, but the suggestion here is that law is something like a culture, with its own familiar categories, modes of reasoning, and the like. Effective legal scholarship must proceed as a kind of "immanent critique" within that culture.[110] There is something ultimately unsatisfying in attempts at the wholesale importation of "alien" disciplinary frameworks and perspectives. It is as if someone had attempted to criticize the game of golf solely by reference to the principles of physics that apply to the sport. One cannot help but feel that somehow the analyst has missed something—which, of course, is a key reason why reductive approaches are often unconvincing. J. M. Balkin, himself an interdisciplinary legal scholar, theorized interdisciplinarity as, among other things, the attempt of one discipline to "colonize" another.[111] Balkin noted that for other disciplines to significantly influence law, they must at the least be translated into a rhetoric that is compatible with standard legal reasoning.[112]

But the objection goes deeper than matters of rhetoric and strategy. Although legal theory can be a helpful adjunct to construing constitutional provisions and other legal texts, theory must, in some sense, be derivable from law as a product of lawmaking institutions and from the values that inform those institutions.[113] Daniel A. Farber argued that "brilliant," counterintuitive legal theory is often unconvincing simply by virtue of its "brilliance":

> Most theories of constitutional law rest on some notion of the consent of the governed, either through tacit institutional acquiescence or some kind of social contract

---

[110]In a similar vein, feminist scholar Katharine T. Bartlett has noted that "feminist legal scholars are moving away from offering analyses that create distance between existing legal principles and women's interests toward approaches that attempt to articulate women's interests in light of these principles, as reformulated to accommodate those interests." Katharine T. Bartlett, Tradition, Change, and the Idea of Progress in Feminist Legal Thought, 1995 Wisc. L. Rev. 273, 341.

[111]J. M. Balkin, Symposium on Writing across the Margins: Interdisciplinarity as Colonization, 53 Wash. & Lee L. Rev. 949 (1996). On the cultural clash between lawyers' and economists' languages and worldviews, see Avery Wiener Katz. Positivism and the Separation of Law and Economics, 94 Mich. L. Rev. 2229 (1996).

[112]Balkin, *supra* note 111, at 968.

[113]This is, of course, not necessarily the case as to "pure" theory that has no discernible connection to the law of any particular jurisdiction or nation-state. Such theory might create ideal types that are not bound by the limitations of law in the real world. Both of the theorists discussed here, however, appear to desire their theoretical insights to have direct influence on actual First Amendment doctrine.

theory. A brilliant theory is by definition one that would not occur to most people. It is hard to see how the vast majority of the population can be presumed to have agreed to something that they could not conceive of.[114]

It is, of course, possible that a counterintuitive theory of legal behavior could account for people's actions in ways that do not require their conscious awareness of the underlying theory—many social scientific theories are of this type, and some even have predictive success. However, such theories can only be pure description, with no normative content. Genuine legal norms, whether constitutional or otherwise, of necessity must be adopted at some level by the relevant actors. And legal theory, to have any meaningful connection to law, must in some way spring from intentions, text, doctrinal developments, and other traditional sources of these norms.[115] As one commentator noted, even legal pragmatists frequently attend to such matters, despite their largely instrumentalist orientation: "Pragmatists nevertheless recognize that conforming to inherited legal doctrine and attending to history may be good for the community, so doctrinal integrity remains instrumentally important. Pursuing the good for this community requires us to know and respect its unique history."[116] This basic requirement of attention to, and respect for, the consensual nature of law further suggests, as Farber argued, that legal scholarship ought to, by and large, consist of Kuhnian "normal science" rather than paradigm-shattering theory construction. None of this is to claim that legal theory can never evolve, but rather that such evolution is likely to be gradual and incremental and to operate within existing normative frameworks, rather than proving sudden and revolutionary. As Posner himself recognized in more recent writings, stability and predictability are themselves important legal values: "A judicial holding normally will trump even a better-reasoned academic analysis because of the value that the law places on stability. . . ."[117]

Posner's project is more successful than Williams's at integrating its analysis within existing free speech theory and doctrine. He builds upon

---

[114]Daniel A. Farber, The Case Against Brilliance, 70 Minn. L. Rev. 917, 925 (1986). Farber admits his critique was somewhat tongue-in-cheek, but the point he makes is a valuable one. *See also* Daniel A. Farber, Brilliance Revisited, 72 Minn. L. Rev. 367 (1987).

[115]*Cf.* Hugh Baxter, Review Essay: Bringing Foucault into Law and Law into Foucault, 48 Stan. L. Rev. 449, 479 (1996) (suggesting that normative constitutional theory could not successfully apply Foucaultian theory without additional recourse to basic constitutional interpretation).

[116]David Luban, What's Pragmatic about Legal Pragmatism, 18 Cardozo L. Rev. 43, 43 (1996).

[117]Posner, *supra* note 66, at 95.

existing First Amendment categories, although reconceptualizing them in his own inimitable way. Much law and economics scholarship has operated in a similar way, often by assiduous attempts to show that existing legal doctrine already implicitly builds upon economic theory. But although Posner's work has a high degree of isomorphism with current doctrine, it omits from its analysis irreducible free speech values. William's work, although proposing relatively modest doctrinal revisions, is a more wrenching restructuring of existing theory because of its idealist epistemology. In both cases, the idea of law as necessarily linked, in at least some attenuated way, to text, intention, doctrine, and the like suggests that it is extremely odd simply to detach some area of law from its legal context, apply a completely alien conceptual scheme, and still expect something that one can recognize as "law" to emerge at the end of the process. Discussing "The Due Process Clause According to Wittgenstein" or "The Eighth Amendment According to Foucault" may be interesting intellectual exercises, but it is unlikely to succeed in producing legal theory that does not simply elide many of the values already either implicit or explicit in constitutional law.[118] These values include more than just the particular values associated with an individual constitutional provision; they also include both issues of overall constitutional structure and broader legal concerns such as *stare decisis* and its underlying rationales. As one commentator expressed the relationship of law to other disciplines: "Even when adjusted for the law's policy objectives . . . the learning of other disciplines needs further adjustment to meet such imperatives of the legal system as fairness, acceptability, stability, predictability, consistency of application, and reasonable administrability where truth is obscure."[119]

The crucial point is that legal theory in general, and free speech theory in particular, contain irreducible normative elements. An interdisciplinary scholar need not agree with those norms but must at least account for that disagreement in some fashion.[120] As philosopher Thomas Nagel noted,

---

[118]As Judge Posner himself noted, with some reservation, "[I]t can be argued that [judges] should not stray outside the bounds of conventional moral and political opinion in their society—and therefore that an American judge is not to decide cases on the basis of the ethics of Marx or Nietzsche. . . ." Posner, *supra* note 65, at 95.

[119]Phillip Areeda, Comment: Always a Borrower: Law and Other Disciplines, 1988 Duke L.J. 1029, 1040.

[120]On the need for theory to account for considered judgments in matters of morality and justice, *see* Nielsen, *supra* note 33, at 261–72.

many forms of failed reductionism share a common problem: "The perspective from inside the region of discourse or thought to be reduced shows us something that is not captured by the reducing discourse."[121] In free speech theory and doctrine, certain fundamental values, particularly individual self-realization and autonomy, are so central to the tradition that perspectives based upon the collective value of information or the social construction of reality can at best show only a small part of the picture.[122] Reductionism cannot convincingly displace existing questions of value by simply declaring an analytic framework that assumes its own values are fundamental. Posner's analysis simply assumes that the social value of information is fundamental, while Williams's account simply assumes that the undistorted construction of a communal reality is central to the value of speech. In each case, one would still have to ask why these assumptions are correct, which inevitably returns one to questions of value. Both Williams and Posner, it appears, are trying to claim some sort of automatic precedence for their projects without submitting to critical scrutiny the values that underlie them. Posner simply begins his analysis *in media res* by adopting, and then elaborating, the Hand formula, without questioning its subordination of individual and nonconsequentialist perspectives. Williams's view of the undistorted social construction of reality as the primary goal of speech has the same sort of subordination built in. Williams's analysis, moreover, seems to assume that her feminist epistemology somehow logically requires a dialogic construction project that legitimizes government suppression of some voices in order to encourage others. This confusion of "is" and "ought" impedes a serious consideration of whether such suppression is, in fact, normatively desirable. In fact, it seems far more likely that no particular normative principles necessarily follow from her constructivist philosophy.

This is not to say that perspectives from other disciplines cannot illuminate legal theory and doctrine, but simply to suggest that a wholesale disciplinary takeover is unlikely to yield "law" in any form consistent with the values that shape it—which is to say, in any recognizable form.

---

[121]Nagel, *supra* note 36, at 73.

[122]Burt Neuborne argues that "our traditional doctrinal protection of speech about religion, politics, science, and art is essentially noninstrumental, flowing from a toleration driven respect for the dignity of the self-affirming speaker and a prophylactic refusal to permit the government to pick and choose who should be tolerated. Such speaker-centered protection does not turn on the worth of the speech or the speech's value to the community." Neuborne, *supra* note 83, at 25. For an interesting argument against First Amendment monism, *see* Schiffrin, *supra* note 81.

This is particularly true when one is wielding controversial claims from social science or the humanities that bear little resemblance to the stock of cultural wisdom that currently informs legal practice. Moreover, in addition to its irreducibly normative aspect, law also has a practical orientation that repels totalizing theoretical constructs. Charles Collier nicely summarized this inevitable disjunction between "high theory" and law in practice:

> Our system of case law grants precedential authority to poorly reasoned and well reasoned opinions alike: indeed the system offers powerful rationales for leaving legal mistakes in place, instead of correcting them. . . . This is because the concerns of judges are not abstract or theoretical, but practical and prudential—disposing of a contentious case, for example, in circumstances where the court's authority is delicately balanced between grudging acceptance by the public and lukewarm support from the other branches of government. The better part of judicial valor may be to "muddle through" (as Alexander Bickle put it) with a patched-together pastiche of partial reasons, rather than to construct a sweeping intellectual synthesis that is, however, wholly out of touch with social and political reality. . . . [It] cannot be assumed that the body of judicial doctrine forms anything like a philosophical system. To base a legal theory on such an assumption is to build it on a house of cards.[123]

Although Collier's views may somewhat overstate the case against appropriately coherent theory in important constitutional domains such as free speech, his point is nonetheless well taken vis-à-vis attempts to "colonize" legal theory by other disciplinary frameworks.

One useful way to consider the relationship of interdisciplinarity to First Amendment law is provided by Philip Bobbitt's work on constitutional interpretation. Bobbitt's conceptualization is helpful because it demonstrates in a clear and fully articulated way the dangers of reductionism for constitutional interpretation in general, rather than for any particular subfield of constitutional law. Bobbitt argued that a diverse group of "modalities," or ways of arguing for constitutional propositions, provide the current structure of constitutional interpretation and guard against any sort of totalizing constitutional monism. Bobbitt suggested that there are six modalities of constitutional argument:

---

[123]Collier, The Use and Abuse, *supra* note 16, at 233.

Historical (relying on the intentions of the framers and ratifiers of the Constitution); Textual (looking to the meaning of the words of the Constitution alone, as they would be interpreted by the average contemporary "man [*sic*] on the street"); Structural (inferring rules from the relationships that the Constitution mandates among the structures it sets up); Doctrinal (applying rules generated by precedent); Ethical (deriving rules from those moral commitments of the American ethos that are reflected in the Constitution); and Prudential (seeking to balance the costs and benefits of a particular rule).[124]

These modalities, Bobbitt claimed, are the exclusive means of making legitimate constitutional arguments.[125] "Outside of these forms, a proposition about the U.S. constitution can be a fact, or be elegant, or be amusing or even poetic, and although such assessments exist as legal statements in some possible world, they are not actualized in our legal world."[126]

Examining the earlier discussion in light of Bobbitt's modal scheme, one thing becomes immediately apparent. Both Posner's and Williams's free speech theories, and much interdisciplinary free speech scholarship in general, operate exclusively in Bobbitt's "prudential" mode. These theorists look at First Amendment issues solely as a matter of costs and benefits—with Posner doing so quite literally. This is simply another way of saying that they are consequentialist theories, and for that reason reductive according to Bobbitt's scheme. The prudential modality is a seductive one, and those for whom it is a presupposition often have some difficulty seeing the limitations of their position.[127] Bobbitt argued against such unimodal approaches because of the important considerations they ignore. All of the modalities are important, Bobbitt suggested, because they provide various incommensurate ways of seeing the legal world and measuring theory against the demands of justice. Without a rich mix of

---

[124]Philip Bobbitt, Constitutional Fate: Theory of the Constitution 12–13 (1982).

[125]For a critique of Bobbitt's approach, *see* J. M. Balkin and Sanford Levinson, Constitutional Grammar, 72 Tex. L. Rev. 1771 (1994).

[126]Philip Bobbitt, Constitutional Interpretation 22 (1991).

[127]One commentator notes that a cost-benefit approach to constitutional law conceals "important questions of principle" and "also threatens the constitutive potential of constitutional law. American society addresses basic questions of social and political justice—such as the meaning of liberty, fairness, and equality—through the discussion of constitutional issues. Constitutional law directs our attention to the underlying premises of our governmental structure and forces us to consider whether we are, and wish to be, a society that permits or tolerates particular exercises of governmental power." Aleinikoff, *supra* note 109, at 993.

modalities, such reflection is diminished. There are other benefits to the modalities as well. Bobbitt argued, for example, that the fact that there is no meta-rule that requires one modality to trump all others allows for diverse groups to "claim the Constitution as their own in the face of reasoned but adverse interpretations."[128] Moreover, diverse modalities allow constitutional interpretation to change and evolve over time without the need to wholly repudiate the Constitution itself, thus providing some measure of political stability.

Posner and Williams both wish to provide their own prudential meta-rules, which ignore history, text, doctrine, and the other modalities—Posner through his cost-benefit calculations, and Williams through her exclusive focus on her epistemic reduction and the social constructivist project for speech that she contends it entails. Williams's prudential claims are more muted than Posner's, but her entire analysis suggests that the primary argument on behalf of free speech is its ability to produce the kind of "truth" that her epistemology values. Speech that imposes burdens on the production of such truth correspondingly loses its value. This is pure prudentialism. If prudential concerns were the only important values in constitutional law, interdisciplinarity as represented by Posner and Williams would be less problematic. But if, as Bobbitt suggests, a diverse mix of incommensurate modalities is necessary for constitutional interpretation to function properly, reductive schemes will inevitably fail to capture much that is important.[129] Reductive models ultimately distort by eliminating or transforming considerations that are central to the enterprise under study. As Bobbitt put it:

> If we import a model—economic, political, etc.—into law we invariably carve away those aspects of the legal situation to which the model is inapplicable. We forget that the model is merely a prototype, and so we resist the reality of the divergence of the actual from our model. In this way we do not enrich legal analysis by resort to coordinate disciplines; we impoverish it.[130]

What can interdisciplinarity offer to free speech theory and doctrine? It can serve as a useful heuristic; it can illuminate old problems with new

---

[128]Bobbitt, *supra* note 126, at 158.

[129]For a critique of law and economics on these grounds, *see* James Boyd White, Economics and Law: Two Cultures in Tension, 54 Tenn. L. Rev. 161 (1986).

[130]Bobbitt, *supra* note 126, at 173. For an interesting argument from a postmodern perspective that largely supports Bobbitt's modal view, *see* Dennis Patterson, Law and Truth 151–79 (1996).

perspectives. It can cast familiar doctrines in a new and unfamiliar light. It can add to the existing repertoire of free speech thought, but it is difficult to see how it can successfully replace that repertoire. It can never reduce free speech to a single, grand theory. It can enrich by its very strangeness, but it cannot create a monistic meta-rule for First Amendment interpretation. As Steven D. Smith noted: " In law as in life, we sometimes do better by reconciling ourselves to complexity than by insisting upon an artificial simplicity." [131] The dream of reductionism, of the perfect, all-encompassing system, is perhaps best left to the physicists.

---

[131] Steven D. Smith, Reductionism in Legal Thought, 91 Colum. L. Rev. 68 (1991).

3

Stanley Fish, Literary Theory, and Freedom of Expression

After a century as an autonomous discipline, academic law in America is busily ransacking the social sciences and the humanities for insights and approaches with which to enrich our understanding of the legal system.

—Richard Posner[1]

One of the most eloquent and disturbing critics of free speech theory, and of legal theory generally, is Stanley Fish. Fish, a Miltonist and literary theorist, has become an influential legal commentator by bringing his notions of poststructuralist literary theory to bear on law. Fish maintains that legal documents such as constitutional amendments or judicial opinions are "texts" in the same sense that a poem by Milton or a play by Shakespeare is a text. As a result, literary theory's assumption that there is no such thing as an "objective" text may properly be applied to law. Fish claims that the meaning of texts (literary or legal) lies, not in the text, nor in the individual reader, but in "interpretive communities" of which the reader is a member. Fish's approach thus undermines both the claim that law is

---

[1]Richard A. Posner, Law and Literature: A Relation Reargued, 72 Va. L. Rev. 1351, 1351 (1986).

inherently indeterminate (or subjective) and the claim that there is an objective meaning to legal materials that legal theory can assist one to discover.

In the realm of free speech theory, Fish has maintained that most arguments about the nature of free expression are incoherent, going so far as to claim in the title of a famous essay that "There's No Such Thing as Free Speech, and It's a Good Thing, Too."[2] Fish argues that all claims about free speech are fundamentally political and that no rational or objective grounds can be advanced to define which categories of speech should be protected and which should be unprotected. In a larger sense, his work also questions whether any approach to legal theory can guide or constrain judges in a way that would produce better legal decisions.

This chapter will review and critique Fish's contributions to legal theory, with particular attention to his recent claims about free speech. The chapter will first set forth Fish's views on interpretive communities, the relation of theory to practice, and the incoherencies of First Amendment thought. Next, it will analyze those views, focusing in particular upon the intersections between Fish's various claims and on the assumptions that underlie them. While the chapter focuses closely on Professor Fish's work, the claims he raises often resemble or share certain common assumptions with other recent critiques of the traditional understanding of free speech theory.[3] As a result, this work's analysis of Fish's claims has significance for the broader academic dialogue about free speech that is currently in progress.

Is There a Self in This Text?

To understand the implications of Fish's views for First Amendment theory, it is necessary to locate them in their intellectual context. As a distinguished literary critic, Fish spent his early career both interpreting literature and developing theories about how interpretation should be practiced. Fish's major contributions can be seen as coming in opposition to the dominant mode of literary criticism in the United States from roughly the 1930s to the 1960s—New Criticism.

---

[2]Stanley Fish, There's No Such Thing as Free Speech and It's A Good Thing, Too 102 (1994).

[3]*See, e.g.*, Freeing the First Amendment: Critical Perspectives on Freedom of Expression (David S. Allen and Robert Jensen eds., 1995); Tona Trollinger, Reconceptualizing the Free Speech Clause: From a Refuse of Dualism to the Reason of Holism, 3 Geo. Mason Indep. L. Rev. 137 (1994); Susan H. Williams, Feminist Jurisprudence and Free Speech Theory, 68 Tul. L. Rev. 1563 (1994).

New Criticism "concerned itself with treating works of literature 'objectively,' viewing them as self-contained, autonomous, and existing for their own sake."[4] Eschewing older critical traditions that relied upon authors' intentions and historical circumstances as clues to provide the "real meaning" of a work, New Critics instead adopted a self-consciously formalist and empirical approach that insisted on the unity and self-sufficiency of the text. A New Critic did not examine a poem by John Milton in order to gain some insight into Milton's time, Milton's peculiar psychology, or even Milton's true intention in writing the poem. Rather, the New Critic explicated the techniques of composition that stand outside and above such concerns as authorial intention. At the heart of the New Critics' approach was "the technique of 'close reading'—a mode of exegesis that pays scrupulous attention to the rich complexity of textual meaning rendered through the rhetorical devices of irony, ambiguity and paradox."[5] As numerous commentators have pointed out, part of the motive for the New Criticism's ruthless "objectivity" may have been the literary profession's desire to move its project out of the purely aesthetic realm in order to compete with the perceived rigor of the hard sciences.

Fish and other literary critics challenged the objectivist assumptions of the New Criticism with what came to be called "reader-response" criticism, which focused, not on the objective analysis of the literary work, but on the activities of readers as they "receive" texts.[6] Reader-response criticism undermined the notion of a literary work existing as a brute fact. Instead, "whether employing structuralist, psychoanalytic, phenomenological, or hermeneutic techniques, all reader-response criticism has shared in shifting critical attention from the inherent, objective characteristics of the text to the engagement of the reader with the text and the production of textual meaning by the reader."[7] Meaning did not exist as an essence contained in, say, *Hamlet*, but rather was produced experientially by the reader.

But while reader-response criticism escaped what some viewed as the arid formalism of the New Criticism, it had problems of its own. Moving the source of meaning from the textual features to the reader's experience

---

[4]Joseph Childers and Gary Hentzi, The Columbia Dictionary of Modern Literary and Cultural Criticism 205 (1995).

[5]Elizabeth Freund, The Return of the Reader 41 (1987).

[6]A related movement that also focuses on the role of the reader in constructing texts is "reception theory." *See* Arthur Asa Berger, Cultural Criticism: A Primer of Key Concepts 22–24 (1995).

[7]Childers & Hentzi, *supra* note 4, at 253.

resulted in an unavoidable slide toward radical subjectivism, to the point where the text as an objective entity was itself put into question. Once the text disappears as an objective source of meaning, each reader is capable of producing her own meaning, a meaning as "valid" as that of any literary critic.

Nor was the problem an exclusively literary one for Fish. By placing the objective truth of the text in question, one is not simply talking about alternate interpretations of Shakespeare. Rather, the availability of objective truth or determinate meaning in any domain of human life is called into question. It is at this point that the line between literary theory and philosophy begins to blur. Aligning himself with such thinkers as Richard Rorty, Jacques Derrida, and Thomas Kuhn, Fish suggests that no human activity, including the natural sciences, could ever offer access to an unmediated realm of truth. A brief examination of the thought of Rorty, Derrida, and Kuhn will prove helpful at this point.

Richard Rorty's neopragmatism, also known as antifoundationalism, argues against the traditional philosophic quest for absolutes, such as "Truth" or "Goodness," against which human beings can compare their time-bound and language-bound knowledge.[8] One commentator described the quest as the idea

> that ultimate reality,—God in some formulations, the physical universe in others, "the good" in others, the structure of human consciousness in still others—establishes an objective basis for our inquiries and thus enables us (in principle) to determine once and for all that the universe is billions rather than thousands of years old, that William Faulkner is a better writer than Margaret Mitchell, that peace usually is better than war, and that democracy is a better system of government than National Socialism.[9]

Rorty claims that this quest for absolutes, which began with Platonic philosophy, turned out to be an epistemological dead end. So did Cartesian epistemology, beginning with René Descartes's attempt to build all knowledge upon undoubted foundations.[10] Rorty advocates turning away from these impossible standards, and instead embracing a pragmatic and contingent view of truth in all human endeavors. As Rorty pointed out in his influential book, *Consequences of Pragmatism*, he is not offering a new approach to foundations of knowledge; rather, he is merely pointing out the misguided nature of the entire enterprise:

---

[8]Rorty is perhaps best known for Philosophy and the Mirror of Nature (1979).
[9]Richard A Posner, Overcoming Law 448 (1995).
[10]*See generally* Bertrand Russell, A History of Western Philosophy 563–68 (1972).

When [pragmatists] suggest that we not ask questions about the nature of Truth or Goodness, they do not invoke a theory about the nature of reality or knowledge or man which says that "there is no such thing" as Truth or Goodness. Nor do they have a "relativistic" or "subjectivist" theory of Truth or Goodness. They would simply like to change the subject. They are in a position analogous to that of secularists who urge that research concerning the Nature, or the Will, of God does not get us anywhere. Such secularists are not saying that God does not exist, exactly; they feel unclear about what it would mean to affirm His existence, and thus about the point of denying it. Nor do they have some special, funny, heretical view about God. They just doubt that the vocabulary of theology is one we ought to be using.[11]

French theorist Jacques Derrida's strategy of deconstruction approaches the problem of foundations from a slightly different direction. Derrida, one of the originators of the poststructuralist movement, contends that meaning—and thus the foundations of any knowledge—is always unstable.

In traditional theories of meaning, signifiers [words] come to rest in the signified [concepts] of a conscious mind. For poststructuralists, by contrast, the signified is only a moment in a never-ending process of signification where meaning is produced not in a stable, referential relation between subject and object, but only within the infinite, intertextual play of signifiers.[12]

Deconstruction often focuses on so-called binary oppositions contained in language; that is, deconstruction emphasizes the concept that words exist only in relationship to other words, for example, truth versus falsity, self versus other, mind versus body, and other such oppositions.[13] Deconstruction demonstrates how these oppositions collapse into themselves to undermine the whole system of meaning, in particular Western

---

[11]Richard Rorty, Consequences of Pragmatism xiv (1982). Rorty's work acknowledges a debt to American pragmatist philosophers of the late 19th and early 20th centuries, including Charles Pierce, William James, and John Dewey. For a brief overview of pragmatism, see Richard C. Solomon and Kathleen M. Higgins, A Short History of Philosophy 259–263 (1996).

[12]Steven Best & Douglas Kellner, Postmodern Theory 21(1991).

[13]Derrida's deconstructive strategy is not premised on a simple inversion of binary oppositions. As Alan D. Schrift pointed out, "Derrida is often read simply as privileging, for example, writing over speech, absence over presence, or the figurative over the literal. But such a reading is overly simplistic; like Heidegger before him, Derrida realizes that in overturning a metaphysical hierarchy, one must avoid reappropriating the hierarchical structure. It is the hierarchical oppositional structure itself that is metaphysical, and to remain within the binary logic of metaphysical thinking reestablishes and confirms the closed field of these oppositions." Alan D. Schrift, Nietzsche's French Legacy: A Genealogy of Poststructuralism 16 (1995).

philosophical attempts to build meaning "from the ground up" from firm foundational principles. Terry Eagleton illustrated this point nicely when he pointed out that often, "[f]irst principles . . . are defined by what they exclude."[14] Eagleton went on to explore the binary opposition between "man" and "woman" in male-dominated societies as a deconstructionist might:

> Woman is the opposite, the "other" of man: she is non-man, defective man, assigned a chiefly negative value in relation to the male first principle. But equally man is what he is only by virtue of ceaselessly shutting out this other or opposite, defining himself in antithesis to it, and his whole identity is therefore caught up and put at risk in the very gesture by which he seeks to assert his unique, autonomous existence. Woman is not just an other in the sense of something beyond his ken, but an other intimately related to him as the image of what he is not, and therefore as an essential reminder of what he is. Man therefore needs this other even as he spurns it, is constrained to give a positive identity to what he regards as no-thing.[15]

Deconstruction thus reverses the "privileged" terms in Western discourse and demonstrates that these "first principles" themselves have no essence and are simply parasitic upon other terms in language.[16] The link between Derrida's thought and Rorty's antifoundationalism becomes clear particularly in Derrida's notion of "logocentrism," which has been defined as "the illusion that the meaning of a word has its *origin* in the structure of reality itself and hence makes the *truth* about that structure seem directly present to the mind."[17] This "metaphysics of presence"[18] represents the Western obsession with knowing the truth about the world in a direct and unmediated way, something Derrida contended is not possible, given the representational character of all human knowledge. Thus Derrida, like

---

[14]Terry Eagleton, Literary Theory: A Introduction 132 (1983).

[15]*Id.* at 132–33.

[16]Derrida's writings are themselves notoriously difficult. This brief summary can only present a limited view of a very complex subject. For other treatments, *see, e.g.*, Robert Con Davis and Ronald Schleifer, Contemporary Literary Criticism (1989); J. M. Balkin, Deconstructive Practice and Legal Theory, 96 Yale L.J. 743 (1987); Joseph Margolis, Deconstruction; or, The Mystery of the Mystery of the Text, in Hermeneutics and Deconstruction 138 (Hugh J. Silverman and Don Ihde eds., 1985).

[17]John M. Ellis, Against Deconstruction 36–37 (1989). *Logocentrism* as used by Derrida seems to have a number of different, but related, meanings. According to Roger Scruton, it means both "the privileging of speech over the written word, and, more importantly, the belief that the world really is as our concepts describe it." Roger Scruton, Modern Philosophy 478 (1995).

[18]J. M. Balkin defines the metaphysics of presence as "the irrepressible desire for transcendental signified presence, the thing itself, or truth." Balkin, *supra* note 16, at 748 n. 13.

Rorty, is often read as claiming that human beings are bound up in languages that have no necessary connection to a "real" world existing somewhere "out there." Moreover, there are no firm foundations upon which knowledge can be built—only different vocabularies.

This view, of course, is consistent with some readings of historian of science Thomas Kuhn's influential book, *The Structure of Scientific Revolutions*.[19] Kuhn's work is often cited for the proposition that the history of science is not one of continuous progress toward some deeper understanding of the world. Instead, scientific history reveals periodic shifts in theoretical frameworks—"paradigms"—which do result in increased success in prediction and control, but are not "true" in any absolute sense of direct correspondence to reality. According to this view, "the reason that scientific theories do not build on their predecessors is very roughly that they constitute irreconcilably different conceptual schemes, and accurate translation between them is impossible."[20] Thus Kuhn's work, like Derrida's and Rorty's, emphasizes the nature of all human knowledge as "made" rather than "found."

Armed with the claims of Rorty, Derrida, and Kuhn, as well as his own unique insights, Fish thus faced the problem of determining where literary meaning lay. Reader-response criticism had already dethroned the text as a source of determinate meaning. Fish's innovation was to depose the individual reader (or "self") as well. He took this step in the enormously influential work, *Is There a Text in This Class?*[21] This work emphasized the role of "interpretive communities," rather than individuals, in deriving meaning from texts. Fish claimed that it was interpretive communities, groups such as literary critics who share certain interests and concerns, that determine the meaning of texts. More precisely, Fish defined an interpretive community as

> not so much a group of individuals who shared a point of view, but a point of view or way of organizing experience that shared individuals in the sense that its assumed distinctions, categories of understanding, and stipulations of relevance and irrelevance were the content of the consciousness of community members who were therefore no longer individuals, but insofar as they were embedded in the community's enterprise, community property.[22]

---

[19]Thomas S. Kuhn, The Structure of Scientific Revolutions (2d ed. 1970).
[20]Alexander Rosenberg, Philosophy of Social Science 13–14 (1988).
[21]Stanley Fish, Is There a Text in This Class? The Authority of Interpretive Communities (1980).
[22]Stanley Fish, Doing What Comes Naturally: Change, Rhetoric, and the Practice of Theory in Literary and Legal Studies 141 (1989).

Fish thus denied either the existence of an objective textual meaning or a radical subjectivism in which each person is free to form her own interpretation.

Individuals, Fish argued, are inescapably bound by the modes of thought made available by the interpretive communities to which they belong. Interpretive communities both constrain meaning and, to some extent, "constitute" the individual members. Fish wrote that "since the thoughts an individual can think and the mental operations he can perform have their source in some or other interpretive community, he is as much a product of that community (acting as an extension of it) as the meanings it enables him to produce."[23] The objective features that readers see in texts are created by the strategies and modes of thought made available to individuals by the interpretive community.

In the title essay of *Is There a Text in This Class?* Fish characteristically makes his point with a story in which he describes how a colleague at Johns Hopkins University faced a question from a student on the first day of class. The student asked Fish's colleague the seemingly simple question, "Is there a text in this class?" Fish's colleague naturally assumed the student wanted to hustle off to the bookstore to buy the assigned textbook, and replied with the name of the book. But that was not what the student wanted to know. "No, no," she said, "I mean in this class do we believe in poems and things, or is it just us?"[24] The colleague, Fish tells us, thereupon recognized that the student was inquiring into his views on the objective meaning of texts and said to himself, "Ah, there's one of Fish's victims!"[25]

The story makes the point that words (in this case, the student's question) are always ambiguous and that the way interpreters (here, the professor) give meaning to words is by participation or membership in a structure of beliefs and intentions that gives words meaning: an interpretive community. Interpretation is not a conscious act, but rather a condition of one's consciousness. As Fish put it:

> One does not say "Here I am in a situation: now I can begin to determine what these words mean." To be in a situation is to see the words, these or any other, as already meaningful. For my colleague to realize that he may be confronting one of my vic-

---

[23]Fish, *supra* note 21, at 14.
[24]*Id.* at 305.
[25]*Id.* at 313.

tims is *at the same time* to hear what she says as a question about his theoretical beliefs.[26]

Moreover, the way in which Fish's colleague creates meaning is not subjective or solipsistic. On the contrary, it is the interpretive community that makes the creation of meaning possible at all:

> [A]n individual's assumptions and opinions are not "his own" in any sense that would give body to the fear of solipsism. That is, *he* is not their origin (in fact it might be more accurate to say that they are his); rather, it is their prior availability which delimits in advance the paths that his consciousness can possibly take.[27]

In Fish's thought, individual consciousness is, in some sense, created by the interpretive community. Transposing the concept from literature to law, Fish pointed out that

> a professional reader of contracts (a lawyer or judge) does not choose to work within concepts such as offer, acceptance, consideration, or duress. Rather these concepts (which he certainly does not originate) are the content of his consciousness, and they are not applied to or "laid over" the contract; they are features of the contract as he sees it, not after a first, innocent reading, but immediately.[28]

Fish's interpretive communities seem to erase individuality, to propose a "self" that is entirely determined by forces beyond its control. Fish himself has noted that "individuality is the casualty of this process."[29]

Fish's interpretive community thesis has significant implications for First Amendment theory, which largely rests upon an assumption of free and autonomous selfhood. Recall that Fish's theory is not one that merely relates to reading Milton—it is a theory of how human beings interact with a language-bound world. As one critical primer put it: "Because for many existence and knowledge are only available within

---

[26]*Id.* at 313.

[27]*Id.*at 320.

[28]Stanley Fish, How Come You Do Me Like You Do? A Response to Dennis Patterson, 72 Tex. L. Rev. 57, 59–60 (1993).

[29]*Id.* at 58. *See also* Pierre Schlag, Fish v. Zapp: The Case of the Relatively Autonomous Self, 76 Geo. L.J. 37, 43 (1987).

systems of signification, it has become a commonplace to hear *the world itself referred to as a text.*"[30] In Derrida's well-known formulation, "There is nothing outside the text."[31] Although Fish himself does not explicitly say so, it is clear from his examples—"baseball, law school, classrooms in general, marriages, halfway houses"[32]—that the claimed reach of his theory is very wide indeed.

The implications of the theory of interpretive communities for First Amendment theory are momentous. Nearly all strands of First Amendment theory—whether of the democratic self-government, individual autonomy, or marketplace of ideas variety—assume at bottom an autonomous, freely choosing self. How can individuals make free and informed political choices, or choose among competing versions of the good life if their very modes of interpretation, the structures that create meaning, are not free but rather are determined by some shadowy aggregate? Fish's interpretive community construct is also closely connected with his claim that legal theory cannot affect the development of the law, which the next section will articulate.

The Uselessness of Theory

Professor Fish challenges traditional notions of First Amendment theory at a second level; he claims that "theory" cannot guide or constrain judicial practice. Of course, the notion that theory is useless is disturbing to many. It is, for example, part of the purpose of theoretical First Amendment scholarship to have at least some impact on how First Amendment doctrine is shaped. If theoretical scholarship has—and can have—no effect whatsoever on how judges decide concrete free speech cases, the enterprise seems bankrupt.

Fish illustrates his argument about the irrelevance of theory to practice with another story in an essay titled, "Dennis Martinez and the Uses of Theory."[33] In 1985, Fish relates, then–Baltimore Orioles pitcher Dennis Martinez spoke to a sports reporter about what Martinez's manager, Earl Weaver, had told him before a game. The reporter wanted to know "what words of wisdom had been imparted by the

---

[30]Childers and Hentzi, *supra* note 4, at 303 (emphasis added).
[31]Jacques Derrida, Of Grammatology 158 (Gayatri Chakravorty Spivak trans., 1976).
[32]Fish, *supra* note 28, at 58.
[33]Fish, *supra* note 22, at 372.

astute Weaver."[34] Martinez, recounting an exchange Fish claims is typical between "fully situated members of a community," told the reporter that Weaver said, "Throw strikes and keep 'em off the bases," to which Martinez replied, "O.K."[35] The reported conversation, Fish claimed, is a "rebuke" to an outsider who expects that there is some arcane wisdom or theory that the manager could share with his pitcher that could possibly affect the actual practice of baseball. If that were not enough, Fish writes, Martinez "drives the lesson home with a precision Wittgenstein might envy: 'What else could I say? What else could he say?' In other words, 'What did you expect?'"[36]

Fish's point is that fully socialized members of interpretive communities, by virtue of that socialization, are already so embedded in that particular "form of life" that no abstract formula or principle can guide their practice. For the sports reporter, a practitioner of "theory talk," the game may consist of such principles, but for those who actually play it such talk is beside the point. For both Weaver and Martinez, Fish contended,

> what they know is either inside of them or (at least on this day) beyond them; and if they know it, they did not come to know it by submitting to a formalization; neither can any formalization capture what they know in such a way as to make it available to those who haven't come to know it in the same way.[37]

Fish concedes that some baseball players do take a theoretical approach to the game but contends that this fact does not make them better players. Fish then proceeds to make the same point using an anecdote about industrial research. Theory, in short, is irrelevant.

Fish intends "theory" in a special and limited sense, however. He defines theory as

> an abstract or algorithmic formulation that guides or governs practice from a position outside any particular conception of practice. A theory, in short, is something a practitioner consults when he wishes to perform correctly, with the term "correctly" here understood as meaning independently of his preconceptions, biases, or personal preferences.[38]

---

[34]*Id.* at 372.
[35]*Id.*
[36]*Id.*
[37]*Id.* at 373.
[38]*Id.* at 378.

Using this definition, Fish writes that he wishes to exclude from the category of theory "high-order generalizations, or strong declarations of basic beliefs, or programmatic statements of political or economic agendas, or descriptions of underlying assumptions."[39] Whatever is left of theory after these wholesale exceptions, Fish tells us, is, he contends, without consequences.[40]

Preliminary anecdotes and caveats now out of the way, Fish moves on to his real target: law. Despite the confusions of legal academics, Fish writes, judges do not decide cases based on legal theory. On the contrary, they do not need, or use, theory, yet this state of affairs does not render judging arbitrary or ad hoc. Judges may "use" theory in the sense of justifying their decisions after the fact, but they do not employ it in the actual process of deciding cases. Like Dennis Martinez, judges are fully socialized members of their interpretive community and thus do not require theorizing to play the game they play—a game in which they render judicial decisions. "Judging, in short, cannot be understood as an activity in the course of which practitioners regularly repair for guidance to an underlying set of rules and principles," Fish writes.[41] Judges, in other words, "just do it."

Fish criticizes legal philosopher Ronald Dworkin for his claim that judges should strive for "'articulate consistency,' a way of deciding cases that ties the most recent decision to 'some comprehensive theory of general principles and policies that is consistent with other decisions also thought right.'"[42] Needless to say, this is the same point First Amendment theorists urge when they advance theories of democratic self-governance, individual autonomy, the checking value, and other free speech theories that prescribe how the speech and press clauses should be interpreted. Dworkin contended that good judges operate with "articulate consis-

---

[39]*Id.*

[40]It is possible that Professor Fish might contend that First Amendment theory is not "theory" as he defines it, and thus refute some claims of this chapter. However, Fish is on record as suggesting that other general methods of interpreting the Constitution are "theory" in his special sense—for example, originalism versus nonoriginalism, or textualism versus supplementalism. "I regard these two positions as theoretical," Fish writes, "because they amount to alternative sets of instructions for reaching correct or valid interpretive conclusions." *Id.* at 329. Advocating a reading of the First Amendment that focuses on the value of, say, self-government, seems little different from advocating a reading of the amendment based on the intentions of the Framers. It would seem that either both methods of interpretation are "theory" as Fish defines it, or neither is.

[41]*Id.* at 384.

[42]*Id.* at 385.

tency," but that less reflective judges are apt to produce ad hoc or arbitrary decisions.

Fish will have none of this. A judge is already a "repository of the purposes, values, understood goals, forms of reasoning, modes of justification, etc.," of the legal enterprise. "It would follow, then," Fish writes, "that an agent so embedded would not need anything external to what he already carried within him as a stimulus or guide to right—that is, responsible—action; in short, he would not need a theory."[43] A judge, in other words, is already a member of an interpretive community and needs no further guidance.[44]

However self-sufficient Fish's notion of practice, theory does have a role to play. When judges hand down written opinions, they may, in fact, invoke theory. This use of theory, Fish maintains, is simply a matter of "self-presentation—a mode in which a present decision is explained or justified by an assertion of its fit with the principles underlying past decisions."[45] In this mode, judges are not offering an account of how they reached the decision, but one intended to persuade others of the validity of the decision. Written opinions are judicial "rhetoric" (a term, Fish argues, that is unfairly maligned); they are not accurate accounts of the decision process. Fish's claim here seems to parallel those of some of the legal realists[46]—judges first decide cases and then "construct a certain kind of story in which [the] decision is more or less dictated by the inexorable laws of the judicial process."[47]

Aside from the fact that judges, baseball players, and other members of interpretive communities do not need theory to perform their tasks, theory is an "impossible project" for another reason as well, Fish argues.[48] Theory

---

[43]*Id.* at 386.

[44]As one commentator noted, Fish uses a variety of terms seemingly interchangeably to denote interpretive communities, including "context," "interpretive constructs," and "conventions." Daryl J. Levinson, The Consequences of Fish on the Consequences of Theory, 80 Va. L. Rev. 1653, 1656 n. 7 (1994).

[45]Fish, *supra* note 22, at 388.

[46]*See, e.g.,* K. N. Llewellyn, The Bramble Bush 39 (1975). On the Realists generally, *see* Laura Kalman, Legal Realism at Yale, 1927–1960 (1986). It is not only legal realists—and their more recent successors in critical legal studies—who share Fish's atheoretical account of how judges operate. For example, Lon Fuller, decidedly *not* a legal realist, subscribed to a similar view, although less sanguinely than Fish does. Fuller wrote in 1934 that judges often "decide the case first on the basis of 'non-technical' considerations. Then armed, not with rack and wheel, but with the intellectual equivalents of those instruments of torture—fictions, analogies, 'theories,'—he proceeds to wring from his code or other body of doctrine the legally acceptable basis for his decision." L. L. Fuller, American Legal Realism, 82 U. Penn. L. Rev. 429, 435 (1934).

[47]Fish, *supra* note 22, at 392.

[48]*Id.* at 320.

is always an attempt to step outside of a local, contingent, situated perspective and achieve some Archimedean point by which to identify some truth about the world, and so more effectively direct practice.[49] No such point is available to human beings, Fish contends, because we are always embedded in some context or other. Fish's antifoundationalism asserts that

> questions of fact, truth, correctness, validity, and clarity can neither be posed nor answered in reference to some extracontextual, ahistorical, nonsituational reality, or rule, or law, or value; rather . . . all of these matters are intelligible and debatable only within the precincts of the contexts or situations or paradigms or communities that give them their local and changeable shape.[50]

In Fish's view, the very fabric of human thought and language is always based on some limited perspective; moreover, thought and language are impossible without that (or some other) perspective. Objectivity, in short, is unavailable. "[Theory] will never succeed because the primary data and formal laws necessary to its success will always be spied or picked out from within the contextual circumstances of which they are supposedly independent," Fish writes. "The objective facts and rules of calculation that are to ground interpretation and render it principled are themselves interpretive products: they are, therefore always and already contaminated by the interested judgments they claim to transcend."[51] Because "theory," properly defined, is an impossibility, it is incapable of having consequences for practice.

But Fish the antifoundationalist is not intending merely to chastise Dworkin and other legal thinkers who would promote theory as a guide to better judicial decisions. Dworkin and fellow legal foundationalists (for example, First Amendment theorists) believe that proper first principles and theoretical structures will guide the course of the law better than unreflective practice. Without adequate theory, arbitrariness will reign. Another group of legal thinkers, however, believes that by recognizing the impossibility of foundational theory in law, the effect will be emancipatory. The recognition of law's plasticity and contingency will free the

---

[49]Descartes wrote that "Archimedes, in order that he might draw the terrestrial globe out of its place, and transport it elsewhere, demanded only that one point should be fixed and immoveable; in the same way I shall have the right to conceive high hopes if I am happy enough to discover one thing only which is certain and indubitable." 1 Philosophical Works of Descartes 149 (Elizabeth S. Haldane and G. R. T. Ross trans, 1969).

[50]Fish, *supra* note 22, at 344.

[51]*Id.* at 320.

oppressed from the stubborn illogic of "liberal legal thought." These thinkers, usually identified with the critical legal studies movement, contend that legal theory is a sham that helps certain social groups maintain domination over other groups.[52] CLS writers have argued that undermining the myth of legal foundations will loosen the grip that this myth has on how we think about law. As Fish put it, "the lesson that we are always and already interpretively situated . . . becomes a way of escaping its implications."[53] Thus, while Dworkin and other foundationalists are concerned that a breakdown of legal theory will lead to hopeless subjectivity and chaos, those sympathetic to CLS trust instead that such a breakdown will have liberating consequences.

Fish rejects both views as mistaken precisely because theory has no consequences. The foundationalists are overcome with "theory fear," while the CLS scholars are indulging in "theory hope." "Theory fear" is easily disposed of, Fish claims, because (as we have seen) judges are, always and already, embedded in the practice called judging and thus could not, consistent with that practice, simply impose their arbitrary whims. Their way of seeing the world is already shaped for them by their socialization into the interpretive community, and "insofar as practice is always practice of *something* (of law, literary criticism, baseball), its gestures are already informed by the sense of value and continuity that make that something a distinct activity."[54]

Antifoundationalist "theory hope" is unwarranted as well. Fish describes the CLS view as "the characteristically left error of assuming that an insight into our convictions (they come from culture, not from God) will render them less compelling."[55] The fact that law is not grounded in some acontextual objectivity does not loosen the grip of legal thinking on legal actors. Antifoundationalist theory hope is based on the fallacious notion of stepping outside of one's interpretive constructs by recognizing that they are human creations rather than preexisting and, somehow, necessary categories. As Fish repeatedly argues, however, such "stepping outside" is impossible because it is only through interpretive constructs that one can know the world at all. "To put the matter baldly," Fish wrote, "already-in-place interpretive constructs are a condition of

---

[52]On critical legal studies generally, *see* Andrew Altman, Critical Legal Studies: A Liberal Critique (1990); Gary Minda, Postmodern Legal Movements (1995).
[53]Fish, *supra* note 22, at 437.
[54]*Id.* at 369.
[55]*Id.* at 395.

consciousness."[56] Again, there is no Archimedean point from which to examine, consider, or perhaps revise one's interpretive constructs. In short, "law . . . will not fade away because a few guys in Cambridge and Palo Alto are now able to deconstruct it."[57]

The challenge of Fish's ideas regarding First Amendment theory is unspoken but clear. Theory cannot guide First Amendment law because neutral and objective principles are unavailable. Moreover, if such principles were available, judges do not need them and would not use them to decide cases.

Deconstructing Free Speech

Fish's work as examined thus far has not directly addressed free expression questions. Fish rectified that omission with the 1994 publication of a provocatively titled essay, "There's No Such Thing as Free Speech and It's a Good Thing Too," in a book of the same title.[58] In the essay, Fish argues that all claims about free speech are fundamentally political and that no rational or objective grounds can be advanced to differentiate protected speech from unprotected speech.

Fish argues that there is no such thing as "free speech" in at least two senses. First, free speech is not, and cannot be, an absolute or independent value, but is instead an empty and partial concept that is always filled with some political agenda or other. Fish cites Milton's *Areopagitica* as a prime example of this: Milton argued for unregulated publication but then proceeded to exclude Roman Catholics from such tolerance. Milton's view is not merely an anomaly, Fish claims. On the contrary, it is always the exception to an (apparently) absolute realm of free speech that defines that realm. "I want to say that all affirmations of freedom of expression are like Milton's, dependent for their force on an exception that literally carves out the space in which expression can emerge," Fish writes.

> I do not mean that expression (saying something) is a realm whose integrity is sometimes compromised by certain restrictions but that restriction, in the form of an underlying articulation of a world that necessarily (if silently) negates alternatively possible articulations, is constitutive of expression.[59]

---

[56]*Id.* at 394.
[57]*Id.* at 397.
[58]Fish, *supra* note 2, at 102.
[59]*Id.* at 103.

"Absolute" free speech is hence an impossibility. There will always come a point, relative to some "assumed conception of the good," at which a given community will refuse to allow certain speech, "not because an exception to a general freedom has suddenly and contradictorily been announced, but because the freedom has never been general and has always been understood against the background of an originary exclusion that gives it meaning."[60] In any community, in other words, there is no such thing as "free speech" because there is always some proscribed ground that gives unregulated speech its content and direction. Thus far, Fish's conclusions (if not his mode of reasoning) seem consistent with most interpretations of the First Amendment, except, perhaps (and even this is arguable), that of Justice Hugo Black.[61]

But First Amendment thought should not be absolved this easily. Not only is there no condition of "absolute" free speech, but the legal distinctions separating protected and unprotected expression are incoherent, Fish contends. He attacks in particular the speech/action distinction, which he labels the "preferred strategy" of avoiding the absoluteness of the First Amendment.[62] The speech/action distinction performs the function of separating speech from its consequences. As Fish puts it: "The difficulty of managing this segregation is well known: speech always seems to be crossing the line into action, where it becomes, at least potentially, consequential."[63]

Fish illustrates the problem with the "fighting words" doctrine from the U.S. Supreme Court's 1942 decision in *Chaplinsky v. New Hampshire*.[64] The Court defined "fighting words" as those that would provoke an average person to retaliation. Fish argues that if one considers "non-average" people in their full variety, there is no speech that will not incite someone, and thus the attempt to segregate "fighting words" from protected expression breaks down. This breakdown is inherent in all attempts to separate speech from action. Speech always has consequences (or is imbued with action), and "insofar as the point of the First Amendment is

---

[60]*Id.* at 104.

[61]On Justice Black's absolutism, *see* Rodney Smolla, Free Speech in an Open Society 23–27 (1992).

[62]Fish, *supra* note 2, at 105.

[63]*Id.* at 105. A similar conclusion is reached in the work of English philosopher J. L. Austin in How to Do Things with Words (1962). Austin's speech act theory pointed out that all language has a "performative" dimension that aims at accomplishing some end rather than simply describing the world. *See* Eagleton, *supra* note 14, at 118–19. *See also* Pierre Schlag, Cannibal Moves: An Essay on the Metamorphoses of the Legal Distinction, 40 Stan. L. Rev. 929 (1988).

[64]315 U.S. 568 (1942).

to identify speech separable from conduct and from the consequences that come in conduct's wake, there is no such speech and therefore nothing for the First Amendment to protect," Fish writes.

> Despite what they say, courts are never in the business of protecting speech per se, "mere" speech (a nonexistent animal); rather, they are in the business of classifying speech (as protected or regulable) in relation to a value—the health of the republic, the vigor of the economy, the maintenance of the status quo, the undoing of the status quo—that is the true, if unacknowledged, object of their protection.[65]

As an example, Fish points out that universities (institutions that are, in some cases, trying to regulate hate speech) have particular values and purposes. For this reason, Fish suggests that perhaps they should be able to regulate speech that is inimical to those values and purposes. Fish seems to engage in a bit of rhetorical hyperbole when he poses the question, "Could it be the purpose of [universities and colleges] to encourage free expression?" and then answers: "If the answer were 'yes,' it would be hard to say why there would be any need for classes, or examinations, or departments, or disciplines, or libraries, since freedom of expression requires nothing but a soapbox or an open telephone line."[66] This *reductio ad absurdum* presumably makes the point that freedom of speech is not the only social good to be found in higher education.

Fish chides Benno Schmidt, former president of Yale University, for a public statement to the effect that campus speech codes should not be allowed to undermine free expression. "'When the goals of harmony collide with freedom of expression,' Fish quotes Schmidt as saying, "'freedom must be the paramount obligation of an academic community.'"[67] Fish finds Schmidt's logic flawed because the very use of the word "community" reinforces Fish's point that "limitations on speech in relation to a defining and deeply assumed purpose are inseparable from community membership."[68] Speech of any meaningful sort is the product of limitations that both constrain speech and make it possible. "Indeed," Fish writes, "the very act of thinking of something to say (whether or not subsequently regulated) is already constrained—rendered impure and

---

[65]Fish, *supra* note 2, at 106.
[66]*Id.* at 107.
[67]*Id.* at 108.
[68]*Id.* at 108.

because impure, communicable—by the background context within which the thought takes shape."[69]

The second sense in which Fish suggests that "there's no such thing as free speech" is the notion that pure speech is free of harm to third persons. With particular attention to hate speech, Fish argues that traditional free speech justifications are specious. For example, Fish ridicules market-place of ideas justifications for free speech, which argue that short-run harms inflicted by hate speech are justified by the long-run outcomes that emerge when speech is unregulated, such as truth or better public policy. Fish mocks such forward-looking free speech justifications as continuing "in a secular form the Puritan celebration of millenarian hopes." He also questions the notion that harms caused by hate speech are minimal, purely mental injuries that should be endured by their targets. "The two strategies," Fish writes,

> are denials from slightly different directions of the *present* effects of racist speech; one confines those effects to a closed and safe realm of pure mental activity; the other imagines the effects of speech spilling over into the world but only in an ever-receding future for whose sake we must forever defer taking action.[70]

Despite what he sees as the illogic of such accounts, Fish concedes that many people embrace them. He even has a psychological explanation for why such reasoning is persuasive. Fish contends that

> people cling to First Amendment pieties because they do not wish to face what they correctly take to be the alternative. That alternative is *politics*, the realization (at which I have already hinted) that decisions about what is and is not protected in the realm of expression will rest not on principle or firm doctrine but on the ability of some persons to interpret—recharacterize or rewrite—principle and doctrine in ways that lead to the protection of speech they want heard and the regulation of speech they want silenced.[71]

Successful use of the First Amendment is never, Fish argues, the expansion of free speech, but rather the effective discursive maneuvering of some group that wishes to use free speech rhetoric for its own ends.

---

[69]*Id.* at 108.
[70]*Id.* at 110.
[71]*Id.* at 110.

Despite the apparent thrust of his argument, Fish hastens to point out that he is not counseling anyone to abandon First Amendment principles. Even though the First Amendment could never fulfill the purpose its advocates claim for it ("the elimination of political considerations in decisions about speech"),[72] First Amendment principles nonetheless may impede the hasty adoption of unwise restrictions on speech. The fact that First Amendment dogma requires would-be censors to "jump through hoops" may be worthwhile in itself. Nevertheless, Fish argues, the political nature of free speech is undeniable. Fish's Machiavellian counsel thus remains that

> so long as the so-called free speech principles have been fashioned by your enemy (so long as it is *his* hoops you have to jump through), contest their relevance to the issue at hand; but if you manage to refashion them in line with your purposes, urge them with a vengeance.[73]

Theory After Fish

Fish's work as examined here challenges classical notions of First Amendment theory in three fundamental ways. First, his claim that interpretive communities, rather than individuals, determine meaning undermines the role of the autonomous self, which is crucial to much First Amendment theory. Second, his claim that legal theory is irrelevant to practice eliminates any significant role for free speech theory in the creation of First Amendment doctrine. Finally, his deconstructive reading of the concept of "free speech" seems to undermine the idea of the First Amendment as carving out a neutral zone, uninfected by politics, for free expression. This section will discuss and critique these claims.[74]

Fish's view of interpretive communities as the locus of meaning has ominous implications for the freely choosing, autonomous self.[75] The

---

[72]*Id.* at 113.

[73]*Id.* at 114.

[74]It should be noted that some of the scholars whose ideas are drawn upon and cited in this section would perhaps disagree more violently with each other than they do with Professor Fish. It might well be asserted that the range of critics Fish has drawn is a testament to the power and importance of his ideas.

[75]The next chapter will take up, from a slightly different angle, various critiques of the "liberal self."

individual reader or self is constituted by these interpretive communities and acts as an extension of them. Fish notes that

> if the self is conceived of not as an independent entity but as a social construct whose operations are delimited by the systems of intelligibility that inform it, then the meanings it confers on texts are not its own but have their source in the interpretive community (or communities) *of which it is a function.*[76]

In much First Amendment theory (as in liberal political theory generally), it is a concern for the dignity and autonomy of the individual human person that compels the recognition of rights.

One serious difficulty with Fish's interpretive community construct is that he offers no particularly solid reasons for believing that interpretive communities actually exist as he describes them. Interpretive communities are, for an antifoundationalist like Fish, suspiciously foundational. A number of Fish's critics have pointed out that interpretive communities are themselves subject to antifoundationalist claims. Pierre Schlag, for example, argued that Fish's interpretive communities (or "interpretive constructs") are

> "theoretical unmentionables" in the sense that Fish has to (and to a large extent does) keep them relatively empty and unstructured. The more Fish says about the structure, content, or scope of these theoretical unmentionables, the more he looks like he's offering a positive theory of the generation of meaning—something he denies is possible.[77]

Moreover, while many of Fish's readers might agree that the interpretive community construct has some plausibility, his version seems overly deterministic. In many ways, acknowledging something like the interpretive community construct is similar to the insight in many academic fields that the "self" is socially constituted. Feminist legal scholar Martha Minow called this insight the "relational turn."[78] Some variant of this view is common to a host of disciplines influenced by Hegel, Marx, Foucault, the Frankfurt School, and other significant figures in the Continental tradition in philosophy and social theory. Human beings

---

[76]Fish, *supra* note 21, at 335 (emphasis added).
[77]Schlag, *supra* note 29, at 42.
[78]Martha Minow, Making all the Difference 192 (1990).

are not the free, presocial, autonomous selves of Locke, Kant, and the liberal political tradition. In fact, some relational theory claims, the general modes of thought and the very outlines of human identity are constituted by culture—in particular, by language.

While many readers might accept some version of the view that the self is not radically free from the community by which it is constituted, Fish's interpretive communities thesis goes further than most in eliminating individual autonomy. Creativity and imagination appear absent; the individual does not act independently, but as an extension of the community. Individual perception seems entirely constrained by an inflexible structure of interpretation that is "unknowable" because it is the individual's very means of knowing. Such rigid epistemic determinism does not describe how most human beings perceive their own situations, even if they acknowledge the constitutive nature of language and community. Individuals' "existential" experience alone cannot be conclusive, but Fish's picture is sufficiently counterintuitive that at the least one must expect him to carry the burden of proof. Nor do Fish's claims ring true as one observes the remarkable pluralism and adaptability of one's own and other cultures. As Steven Winter pointed out, "Fish's one-dimensional account fails to capture the maverick adaptive quality of human imagination: It lacks any conception of situated human agents capable of transformative action from within a given context."[79]

To the extent that interpretive communities lose their all-constraining power, so, too, does the claim that theory is irrelevant to practice. For it is the notion of "absolute situatedness" within an interpretive community that makes judges (as well as baseball players, literary critics, and others) both unwilling and unable to benefit from theory. If, on the other hand, judges, although situated agents, have cognitive room for both reflection and creativity, theory might well prove influential. And First Amendment theory—grounded not, like natural law, in some "brooding omnipresence in the skies,"[80] but in insights about human beings and their societies—might well help judges make free speech decisions that are conducive to individual and cultural growth and development.

Does First Amendment theory matter to decisions in particular free speech cases? While Fish implicitly contends that it does not, and could not, counterexamples seem abundant. Consider, for example, the U.S.

---

[79]Steven L. Winter, Bull Durham and the Uses of Theory, 42 Stan. L. Rev. 639, 681 (1990).

[80]Lon L. Fuller, Reason and Fiat in Case Law, 59 Harv. L. Rev. 376 (1946).

Supreme Court's decision in the 1978 case of *First National Bank of Boston v. Bellotti.*[81] The *Bellotti* case involved the constitutionality of a Massachusetts law that prohibited corporations from spending funds to affect the outcome of any referendum before Massachusetts voters unless the ballot issue materially affected the business or property of the corporation. In other words, unless corporate assets were involved, corporations could not speak out on ballot issues. The statute arose out of a fear of wealthy corporations dominating the political marketplace of ideas—the same fear that has led to the imposition of numerous limitations on corporate participation in federal elections. First National Bank of Boston wanted to spend funds to publicize its views on an individual income tax question that was coming before Massachusetts voters in 1976. However, the statute forbade the bank's participation in the debate. The Massachusetts Supreme Judicial Court upheld the statute, but a divided U.S. Supreme Court reversed the state high court and declared the statute unconstitutional.

One interesting thing about the *Bellotti* case is that the Supreme Court's majority and dissenters not only reach different results, but also seem to be operating with opposing conceptions of First Amendment theory. The majority chose largely to disregard the identity of the speaker and focus on the nature of the speech. In this case, the majority reasoned, the speech was "political speech," the protection of which the majority viewed as a vital purpose of the First Amendment. The free discussion of governmental affairs in a democracy is the central First Amendment value, according to the majority—a view most commonly associated with First Amendment theorist Alexander Meiklejohn.[82] Thus, the corporate speech that Massachusetts sought to suppress should be protected unless the corporate form of the speaker somehow deprived the speech of protection. After subjecting the Massachusetts statute to the Court's most exacting level of scrutiny, the "compelling interest" test, the majority of justices concluded that the state had not met its burden and that the statute must fall.

Justice Byron White, joined by Justices William Brennan and Thurgood Marshall in dissent, approached the question from a distinctly different theoretical perspective than that of the majority. The Massachusetts statute was constitutional, the dissenters argued, because corporate communications do not further "what some have considered to be the principal

---

[81]435 U.S. 765 (1978).

[82]*See generally* Alexander Meiklejohn, Free Speech and Its Relation to Self-Government (1948).

function of the First Amendment, the use of communication as a means of self-expression, self-realization, and self-fulfillment."[83] Corporate speech does not, the White dissent urged, "represent a manifestation of individual freedom or choice."[84] As a result, corporate speech deserved less First Amendment protection than individual speech, and the state interest in regulating corporate speech could be given more leeway. The White dissent focused, not on the primacy of political speech, but on the autonomy or self-realization theory, developed most fully in recent years by C. Edwin Baker.[85] The result is a conclusion on the merits of the case that is the opposite of that endorsed by the majority.

The *Bellotti* Court's use of First Amendment theory could be multiplied endlessly from free speech case law, both at the Supreme Court and lower court levels. One need only think, for example, of the landmark 1964 Supreme Court decision in *New York Times v. Sullivan*,[86] which revolutionized libel law. The Court's opinion clearly seemed to draw upon Meiklejohnian theory, something *Sullivan*'s author, Justice William Brennan, acknowledged in a *Harvard Law Review* article the following year.[87] The point *Bellotti* and other cases seem to make is that First Amendment theory matters—but does it really? Fish might well suggest that the arguments of the two sides in *Bellotti* are simply rhetorical window dressing. The justices actually reached a decision in *Bellotti* "immediately" upon hearing the facts, Fish might say, based on their already-in-place interpretive constructs. They then cast about for (or sent their law clerks in search of) appropriate rhetorical materials to turn those unreflective judgments into the formal materials of law—reasoned judicial opinions with theoretical support. Theory operates only as an after-the-fact rationalization of the decision that the judge, as a fully situated member (or "extension") of an interpretive community, had no choice but to make.

But this account seems reductionistic. Even granting that some (or even most) judges may "fly by the seat of their pants" and make unreflective decisions, judging might better be described as a process rather than a discrete and intuitive moment of discovery. Judges, both conservative and liberal, may indeed have knee-jerk reactions to cases, but there remains a

---

[83]435 U.S. at 804.
[84]*Id.*
[85]*See generally* C. Edwin Baker, Human Liberty and Freedom of Speech (1989).
[86]376 U.S. 254 (1964).
[87]William J. Brennan, The Supreme Court and the Meiklejohn Interpretation of the First Amendment, 79 Harv. L. Rev. 1 (1965).

process of crafting an opinion, perhaps in collaboration with others, to adequately support one's intuition. As Michael S. Moore stated his opposition to Fish's view of theory:

> A good recipe for discovery of the solution to a difficult mathematical proof, for example, is sometimes to think about something other than the puzzle itself. When the solution comes to me, however, *I cannot justify my belief that it is the solution by pointing out that I thought about something else.* Rather, the justification lies elsewhere, namely, in the other truths of mathematics and logic and their implications for this problem.[88]

Moore's point is that justification (which for a judge generally means a written opinion) is a separate process from discovery.

Moreover, justification need not simply mean a post-hoc rationalization for an intuition; it can be a process of reflection and reconciliation that may potentially lead to amending, or even discarding, the original intuition. Moore pointed out that "judges sometimes change their tentative decisions precisely because they cannot find reasons that will produce a plausible opinion. As judges say at such times, 'The opinion just wouldn't write.'"[89] Even if theory cannot affect the discovery process, it can affect the justification process.

Theory also need not come into play at the end of the decision process. It may be difficult to imagine a puzzled member of the *Bellotti* majority reaching for a dog-eared copy of one of Meiklejohn's tomes in order to decide the case. This is, of course, Fish's picture of "theory" as "something a practitioner consults when he wishes to perform correctly, with the term 'correctly' here understood as meaning independently of his preconceptions, biases, or personal preferences."[90] But the justice may well have read Meiklejohn earlier in his or her career, or the lawyer for the bank may well have invoked Meiklejohn (or some earlier judicial instantiation of his views) in the briefs or oral arguments. Even unreflective judging may be immersed in theory. The very interpretive construct within which a justice makes the Fishian intuitive leap may be saturated with Meiklejohn's thought.

---

[88]Michael S. Moore, The Interpretive Turn in Modern Theory: A Turn for the Worse? 41 Stan. L. Rev. 871, 910 (1989) (emphasis added).

[89]*Id.* at 916.

[90]Fish, *supra* note 22, at 378.

Fish himself seems to embrace something close to the latter point. In an essay titled, "Play of Surfaces: Theory and Law,"[91] Fish appeared to modify somewhat the extreme division of theory and practice he had formerly endorsed. He noted that

> in the process of making a decision the judge will pass through and incorporate the forms of thought the culture makes available, and these will certainly include theoretical formulations. It is just that those formulations will be components of the decision-making process rather than its source.[92]

This seems at the least a change in emphasis from Fish's position in the "Dennis Martinez" essay, in which theory is primarily a mode of self-presentation by a canny judge who knows the ropes. Even if it is not, Fish's embrace of such a thoroughly theory-soaked practice appears to render his dichotomy between theory and practice a distinction without a difference. Indeed, if Fish is willing to go this far, his critique of Dworkin and other theory proponents seems oddly without bite.

Of course, Fish's objection to theory is not only that situated agents have no need to consult it. Fish also argues that theory cannot have consequences for practice because persons embedded in interpretive constructs cannot "step outside" those constructs and achieve an Archimedean viewpoint from which to survey and evaluate those constructs. The constraining power of human situatedness renders human beings unable to attain a neutral spot from which to evaluate their beliefs and thus employ theory. Fish chided CLS theorist Mark Kelman for advocating such critical self-consciousness.

> [Kelman] has never seen anyone self-consciously select his interpretative constructs; indeed, I would go further and say that no matter how long he lives it is a sight he will never see, because there has never been or ever will be anyone who could survey interpretive possibilities from a vantage point that was not itself already interpretive. . . . It may be, as Kelman laments, that the thinking that goes on within [interpretive constructs] is biased (which means no more than that it has direction), but without them (a pun seriously intended) there would be no thinking at all.[93]

But this claim, like the interpretive community construct, is a psychological or cognitive theory for which Fish offers no real evidence.

---

[91]Fish, *supra* note 2, at 180.
[92]*Id.* at 198.
[93]Fish, *supra* note 22, at 394.

A number of commentators have advanced powerful arguments against Fish's "impossibility of critical self-consciousness" claim. For example, Steven Winter maintains that the force of Fish's argument flows from his choice of metaphors, and not from any particular insight into human psychology. Fish's argument represents beliefs or practices as a "containers" within which human beings think. If readers accept that crucial move, Fish's argument seems irresistible. "If beliefs are the kind of thing we are 'within,'" Winter writes, "then it is hard to see how we can achieve any 'distance' from them or find another 'position' from which to evaluate them."[94] Beliefs are not really containers, Winter maintains, although it may sometimes be helpful to think of them in that way. Moreover, if interpretive constructs really are the "containers" within which all knowing takes place, how would someone like Fish get "outside" of them in order to make his claims? By claiming to have found some perspective from which to assert that critical self-consciousness is impossible, Fish comes perilously close to what Richard Rorty accused both Neitzche and Derrida of—self-referential inconsistency; that is, "claiming to know what they themselves claim cannot be known."[95]

Aside from the theory-practice disjunction, the *Bellotti* example also raises unanswered questions about the idea of interpretive communities. How, exactly, do we account for the problem of disagreement? Are the justices who joined the majority opinion members of one interpretive community, whereas the dissenters belong (to use the term loosely) to another? Does the fact that then-Justice (now Chief Justice) William Rehnquist wrote a separate dissent on different grounds from the other three dissenters place him in yet a third interpretive community? Or is he in the same community as the other dissenters because his already-in-place interpretive construct led him to the same result as the other dissenters and only his post-hoc rationalization differed? What if (as sometimes happens) a justice's decisions vary unpredictably, both within and among various areas of constitutional jurisprudence? Presumably a justice cannot constitute an idiosyncratic interpretive community of one because the very modes of thought that make up one's repertoire of interpretation come from outside the self. These kinds of questions are largely unanswered in Fish's work because he seems to assume that once the interpreter is safely embedded in an interpretive construct, all else inevitably follows—and perhaps, as Schlag suggested, because too much

---

[94]Winter, *supra* note 79, *at* 682.
[95]Richard Rorty, Contingency, Irony, and Solidarity 8 n. 2 (1989).

positive explication of how interpretive communities operate causes Fish to run afoul of his own antifoundationalism. The potentially alarming proliferation of interpretive communities nonetheless suggests problems for the idea's explanatory force.

A related problem is how one explains obviously bad judicial decisions. In First Amendment law, lower court judges regularly issue restraining orders that are, just as regularly, struck down by appellate courts based on well-settled constitutional law. Is the injunction-happy lower court judge a member of a different interpretive community than the appellate judges who reverse him or her? Or is the lower court judge simply an improperly socialized agent in a single, monolithic judicial interpretive community? And if so, how should the problem be addressed? Could it be said that the incompetent judge needs to be exposed to some abstract formulations that govern practice in First Amendment law—in short, a solid dose of theory? These kinds of questions do not seem to arise in Fish's work because all of his judges (not just the good ones of whom Dworkin approves) are self-sufficient simply by virtue of being judges. That simply does not seem to be a convincing picture of how law works.

Finally, what is to be made of Fish's explicit attack on free speech? In part, Fish's "There's No Such Thing . . ." essay may simply be a case of a provocatively titled paper that does not completely deliver on its promises. First, Fish claims that speech is never "absolutely" free because, as in Milton's *Areopagitica*, there is always some point at which a community will pull back from its commitment to tolerance and forbid speech "subversive of its core rationale." Limits are "always and already" inherent in the realm of expression. Fish does not simply mean that at some point everyone will become fed up and outlaw certain speech; his point is the more subtle one that the very idea of free speech can only have meaning against some implicit boundaries. "Without restriction, without an inbuilt sense of what it would be meaningless to say or wrong to say, there could be no assertion and no reason for asserting it," Fish wrote.[96] That is, language is constituted by limits in the same way that chess *is* chess by virtue of a variety of rules and limitations on moves. There can no more be intelligible "free" speech than there can be a coherent game of "free" chess.

This claim seems to be a direct analog of Fish's antifoundational denial of an Archimedean point outside of one's beliefs and mental constructs. Such a "God's eye" position is impossible for a situated agent to

---

[96]Fish, *supra* note 2, at 103.

achieve, Fish claimed, as is any radical notion of free speech as absolutely unconstrained utterance. Fish reinforced this connection when, arguing against Benno Schmidt, he pointed out that

> independently of a community context informed by interest (that is, purpose), expression would be at once inconceivable and unintelligible. Rather than being a value that is threatened by limitations and constraints, expression, in any form worth worrying about, is a *product* of limitations and constraints, of the already-in-place presuppositions that give assertions their very particular point. . . . [T]he very act of thinking of something to say (whether or not it is subsequently regulated) is already constrained—rendered impure, and because impure, communicable—by background context within which the thought takes its shape.[97]

While Fish's argument may be fine as philosophy of language, it does not seem particularly helpful in any discussion of the scope of First Amendment protection, the ostensible point of Fish's essay. Indeed, the prelinguistic level at which Fish's claim functions can have no conceivable relation to limits on speech under the First Amendment. First Amendment advocates, including Benno Schmidt, simply do not argue about this level of communication. They are concerned with government-imposed limitations on speech that is already constrained, and thus meaningful in the sense Fish claims. Such speech is, as Fish himself seems to acknowledge, the only kind that could possibly matter in a First Amendment sense—or in any practical sense. For the sake of argument, one can concede Fish his claim about "absolutely pure" free speech because it can make no conceivable difference in any First Amendment analysis. This claim, at least (true to his own assertions), is indeed one theory without consequences.

At a more practical level, Fish's argument about absolute free speech seems gratuitous. It is unclear who the target of his argument might be. Almost no First Amendment scholars or Supreme Court justices (again, with the arguable exception of Justice Black)[98] have ever accepted absolutism as a possible First Amendment approach. As one treatise has noted "absolutism is fundamentally too simplistic to be a viable method of analysis . . ."[99] Many governmental limitations on

---

[97]*Id.* at 108.
[98]Rodney Smolla, for example, argues that Justice Black was only a "qualified" absolutist. Smolla, *supra* note 61, at 24.
[99]Smolla and Nimmer on Freedom of Speech: A Treatise on the First Amendment 2–54 (1994).

speech are routinely allowed under the First Amendment, including, to name only a few, regulation of libel, perjury, false (and some truthful) advertising, solicitation of murder, and obscenity. Thus, at the level of practice, Fish's assault on absolutism is both accurate and trivial.

Much the same could be said of Fish's attack on the speech-action distinction. While the Supreme Court has sometimes used the argument that the First Amendment protects speech and not action, the distinction has largely been discredited by constitutional scholars. One First Amendment treatise called it "the spurious speech/conduct distinction."[100] Laurence Tribe called it "persistent but oversimplified" and noted that "all communication except perhaps that of the extrasensory variety involves conduct."[101] In a 1975 *Harvard Law Review* article, John Hart Ely argued that expressive behavior is "100% action and 100% expression."[102] Again, it is not entirely clear to whom Fish's argument is addressed.

Given nearly unanimous scholarly agreement that free speech could never be absolute and that the speech-action distinction is incoherent, why does Fish argue against these dusty chestnuts? Surely it is not simply for the joy of demolishing the "rube" or "Fourth of July speech" version of free speech. A possible answer can be found in the requirements of Fish's deconstructive technique. John M. Ellis has argued that in order for deconstruction to operate, the deconstructionist must begin with the "literal" or "referential" meaning of words, that is, the idea that words denote some necessary truth about the world. This view of language is sometimes called essentialism. It is by starting with this naive concept of the meaning of words as somehow hooking onto some underlying reality that deconstruction gains its power.[103] Deconstruction is in part the process of undermining that essentialism.

But without essentialism, deconstruction runs into problems. Deconstruction thrives on binary oppositions—mind versus body, male versus female, truth versus error, and so on—that are naively accepted as expressing some "essence." Without someone, somewhere, who accepts the essentialist position, deconstruction has no target. As Ellis put it:

---

[100]*Id.*
[101]Laurence H. Tribe, American Constitutional Law 827 (1988).
[102]John Hart Ely, Flag Desecration: A Case Study in the Roles of Categorization and Balancing in First Amendment Analysis, 88 Harv. L. Rev. 1482, 1495–96 (1975).
[103]*See generally* Ellis, *supra* note 17.

> If deconstruction really needs the literal reading to use as the basis for its rejection and subversion, it will have to work with something that will have no currency at all in critical circles—and what would be the point of attacking and subverting something so insignificant?[104]

Moreover, Ellis pointed out, deconstruction can be for this reason oddly conservative. "Old views are not to be allowed to die and be replaced; they are to retain center stage in order to be debunked for all time," he wrote. "It is as if they are to be left in eternal purgatory instead of being laid to rest to make way for the next generation of ideas."[105]

Ellis's description sounds strikingly similar to what Fish has done to free speech. By setting up binary oppositions such as unconstrained expression versus constrained expression and speech versus action, Fish is able to demonstrate their incoherence. They are not "hard" distinctions based in reality, but rather linguistic distinctions that collapse into each other because each side of the opposition depends on the other for its very existence. The only problem is that serious First Amendment scholars simply do not accept the oppositions Fish creates. Thus, Fish demonstrates the conservative bias to which Ellis refers by resurrecting views that few embrace in order to debunk them. Again, Ellis's words, while explicitly addressed to the practice of literary criticism, seem on target.

> By keeping attention fixed on the initial simple view that is to be displaced and making the denunciation of that view a central aspect of the whole performance (rather than merely a starting point that is to be left behind and forgotten), deconstruction creates a sense of the excitement of intellectual progress beyond the commonplace, of the drama of intellectual confrontation, and of the exhilaration of provocativeness.[106]

Fish also appropriates a weak version of the marketplace of ideas theory to critique. He mocks what he views as the implicit "millenarian hopes" contained in the idea that speech, even offensive speech, should not be cut off in the interest of future benefits: "The requirement is that we endure whatever pain racist and hate speech inflicts for the sake of a future whose emergence we can only take on faith." Such an idea, Fish charges, "could be seen as the second of two strategies designed to delegitimize the

---

[104]*Id.* at 77.
[105]*Id.* at 81–82.
[106]*Id.* at 141.

complaints of victimized groups."[107] As deplorable as hate speech unquestionably is, it is quite an intellectual stretch to see marketplace justifications as merely "strategies" to "delegitimize" anyone's complaints.

A much more plausible interpretation of marketplace theory (which itself may not be the strongest claim for free speech) is that avoiding closure in the realm of ideas is *not* designed to lead to some ever-deferred moment of "Truth" with a capital *T*.[108] Rather, a relatively free exchange of ideas promotes a process of continual reflection upon, and readjustment of, political, cultural, scientific, and other ideas. Even if the truths discovered are only of the provisional variety, as pragmatism contends, an unrestricted process is necessary to avoid premature closure. The process might best be thought of in terms similar to that of the scientific method. As Richard Posner put it:

> The scientist is the inquirer who, disdainful of enlisting the power of the state to enforce agreement with his views—to obtain, in Justice Robert Jackson's striking phrase, the unanimity of the graveyard—offers those views to a community of inquirers in a form that makes them refutable if they are false. The process of falsification results in a shifting of perspectives, each of which leaves a deposit in a growing repository of knowledge.[109]

Indeed, if something like Fish's picture of interpretation is correct, and human perceptions are severely constrained within constructs that are in some sense unknowable, openness to alternate paradigms would seem quite important for any sort of progress to take place. In the final analysis, such a "fallibilist" defense of the marketplace justification would be subject to challenge[110]—in fact, as noted earlier, First Amendment scholars have regularly subjected the marketplace theory to serious challenge.[111] But Fish would clearly need to offer a more sophisticated critique than he

---

[107]Fish, *supra* note 2, at 109–110.

[108]For other accounts of the search for truth in First Amendment theory, *see* William P. Marshal, In Defense of the Search For Truth as a First Amendment Justification, 30 Ga. L. Rev. 1 (1995); Christopher T. Wonnell, Truth and the Marketplace of Ideas, 19 U.C. Davis L. Rev. 669 (1986).

[109]Posner, *supra* note 9, at 450.

[110]Rodney Smolla has noted the irony that we could "never empirically test the proposition that truth will triumph over error, because that would itself require some objective measure of what ideas are true and what ideas are false—a measurement that the marketplace theory itself forbids. The leap of faith thus required by the marketplace image, however, is not its weakness, but its deepest strength, for it spurs us to accept the noblest challenge of the life of the mind: never to stop searching." Rodney S. Smolla, Free Speech in an Open Society 8 (1992).

[111]*See, e.g.*, Baker, *supra* note 85, at 25–46.

does here. With his version of the marketplace of ideas, as with "absolute" free expression and the speech-action distinction, Fish has chosen a simplistic target to refute.

A final free speech "piety" that Fish challenges is the notion that the First Amendment could ever mark off for discourse a neutral area unaffected by politics. There is, Fish pointed out, "no such thing as a public forum purged of ideological pressures or exclusions."[112] In fact (and this point is closely related to Fish's claim that there is no "absolute" freedom of speech), the very lines that mark off protected and unprotected speech are fatally contaminated with politics. "The structure that is supposed to permit ideological/political agendas to fight it out fairly—on a level playing field that has not been rigged—is itself always ideologically and politically constituted," Fish writes.[113] Moreover, even knowing this and making "a good faith try" will not help the problem. The contamination is total, even to the point of "trying" to avoid political considerations.

Such totalizing claims create problems. Martha Nussbaum characterized this recurrent phenomenon in both Derrida's and Fish's thought as "if not the heavens, then the abyss."[114] Nussbaum claimed that Fish and other skeptical thinkers are deeply attached to the impossible goal of absolute foundations. "The failure of these thinkers to commit themselves to sorting out our human and historical practices of choice and selection, the insistence that we could have good normative arguments only if they came from heaven—all this betrays a shame before the human," Nussbaum wrote. "On the other hand, if we really think of the hope of a transcendent ground for value as uninteresting or irrelevant to human ethics, as we should, then the news of its collapse will not change the way we think and act."[115] All of this may simply be another way of making the point that Fish has produced another naive binary opposition—"absolute neutrality" versus "politics"—that he then proceeds to deconstruct.

There are two important problems with Fish's view of neutrality. Even conceding that transcendent neutrality is unavailable to human beings, courts nevertheless do a reasonable job of maintaining neutrality within limited domains of First Amendment law. Consider, for example, the virtual ban on prior restraints the U.S. Supreme Court

---

[112]Fish, *supra* note 2, at 116.

[113]*Id.* at 116.

[114]Martha C. Nussbaum, Skepticism about Practical Reason in Literature and the Law, 107 Harv. L. Rev. 714 (1994).

[115]*Id.* at 740.

announced in *Near v. Minnesota* in 1931.[116] With a few notable exceptions,[117] the Court simply has not countenanced prior restraints in the ensuing years. One could argue that the very definition of what constitutes a "prior restraint" is subject to dispute, and that would be correct. But it is difficult to deny that most attempts by government officials to halt speech before its transmission have been struck down by the Court, even in cases in which the political stakes were quite high, such as the Pentagon Papers case.[118] Or consider the fact that since the Court announced a First Amendment right of access to criminal trials in 1980,[119] very few criminal trials have been closed to the press and public. Admittedly, the decision to protect certain speech and not other speech is not unbiased, but the actual execution of doctrine proceeds with a remarkable degree of neutrality.

Indeed, this should not be surprising because, as Richard Posner pointed out, those who become judges probably do so in part because they gain significant satisfaction from deciding cases in a manner as free from bias as possible. One's best attempt at "neutrality," in Fishian terms, to some extent constitutes the role of "judge." Posner argued that most judges—as always, with some exceptions—try not to let inappropriate factors enter their decisions in the same way that many people derive great satisfaction from playing golf without cheating, even if they have the opportunity. It is part of the "pleasure of judging" to play the game by the rules. "It is a source of satisfaction to a judge to vote *for* the irritating litigant, *for* the lawyer who fails to exhibit proper deference to the court, *for* the side that represents a different social class from that of the judges," Posner wrote. "It is by doing such things that you know you are playing the judge role, not some other role; and judges for the most part are people who want to be— judges."[120] In light of this insight, it is unsurprising that political scientist Lief Carter reported that empirical data suggest low correlations between factors like judges' social backgrounds and attitudes and the outcomes of the cases they decide.[121]

---

[116]283 U.S. 697 (1931).

[117]*See, e.g.*, Cable News Network v. Noriega, 111 S.Ct. 451 (1990) (denying *cert.* in case of restraining order against the Cable News Network).

[118]New York Times Co. v. U.S., 403 U.S. 713 (1971).

[119]Richmond Newspapers, Inc. v. Virginia, 448 U.S. 555 (1980).

[120]Posner, *supra* note 9, at 131.

[121]Lief H. Carter, How Trial Judges Talk: Speculations about Foundationalism and Pragmatism in Legal Culture 222 in Legal Hermeneutics: History, Theory and Practice (Gregory Leyh ed., 1992).

But, Fish might object, even this kind of decision making is not neutral. Rather, it proceeds from an interested perspective, simply that of someone playing the role "judge" rather than some other perspective. This is true, but (and this is the second problem with Fish's critique of neutrality) Fish's analysis seems to ignore any difference of *degree*. Since the heavens are unavailable, the abyss must be unavoidable. When he asserts that a "good faith try" at neutrality is just as fatally contaminated with politics as an unreflective attempt at absolute neutrality, he seems to deny the position that we can better approximate neutrality by attempting to achieve it than by scrapping the concept altogether. First Amendment jurisprudence, while not perfect, is considerably more content neutral than the kind of reasoning that led to a death sentence against Salman Rushdie *in absentia*. All claims of liberal neutrality, Don Herzog argued, must be evaluated against actual historical alternatives.[122] "It's easier to live under the common law than it is to live under Caligula," Herzog wrote.[123] First Amendment neutrality is unquestionably infected with politics, but the degree of protection for speech it provides is historically rather remarkable. Presumably Fish would not disagree with this, but, if so, the point of his claim about neutrality becomes obscure. Is he criticizing First Amendment theory for the very lack of foundations his own position regards as an impossibility? Fish has, in fact, reified free speech doctrine by assuming that it tries to embody some eternal, transcendent truths when those who study it closely know that it never has, although they may believe pragmatically that its benefits outweigh its costs.

In light of Herzog's point, and Fish's own continued emphasis on situatedness, Fish's analysis seems strangely ahistorical. His critique seems blind to reasons why a First Amendment that is as "neutral" as partisan, situated human beings can devise might in fact be a pragmatic hedge around the all-too-human tendency to censor everything with which we disagree. Even a cursory examination of periods of repression of political speech in the United States in the 20th century reveals that differences of degree are indeed differences of consequence.[124]

---

[122]Don Herzog, As Many as Six Impossible Things before Breakfast, 75 Calif. L. Rev. 609 (1987).
[123]*Id.* at 626.
[124]*See, e.g.*, Vincent Blasi, The Pathological Perspective and the First Amendment, 85 Colum. L. Rev. 449 (1985). *See also* Michael Kent Curtis, Critics of "Free Speech" and the Uses of the Past, 12 Const. Comment. 29 (1995) (discussing the extent to which current free speech critics, including Fish, ignore history).

Of course, Fish's point is not exactly a celebration of First Amendment values—quite the contrary. His primary purpose seems to be to undermine First Amendment "pieties" in favor of a more pragmatic jurisprudence that presumably will not wince at upholding hate speech codes. Indeed, this is perhaps the oddest aspect of the entire exercise. While Fish claims he is "not making a recommendation,"[125] he also claims that the essay "is an attempt to pry [members of the liberal left] loose from a vocabulary that may now be a disservice to them."[126] In spite of his disclaimers to the contrary, Fish appears to be asserting that an understanding of the foundational emptiness of First Amendment theory may help clear the way for a more desirable jurisprudence. "Antifoundationalist theory hope," it seems, springs eternal. By making others aware that speech cannot be absolutely free—that "speech" and "action" collapse into each other—Fish appears to believe that he can loosen the grip of such foundational thinking and produce a corresponding change in practice. And although he nowhere claims it explicitly, he seems to hover perilously close to what he, in another essay, described as "the characteristically left error of assuming that an insight into our convictions (they come from culture, not from God) will render them less compelling."[127]

At the end of the day, it may be, as Fish himself pointed out, that his free speech thesis is "not, after all, a thesis as startling or corrosive as may first have seemed."[128] Few First Amendment scholars would be startled to learn that freedom of speech is not absolute, that the speech-action distinction is spurious, that the marketplace theory has flaws, or that unavoidable human bias enters into the process of drawing lines between protected and unprotected speech. Even fewer would likely think it corrosive to suggest that judges and legal scholars must contemplate the risks that speech may cause harm. In fact, it is the contemplation of just those risks that has resulted in the Byzantine structure that is modern First

---

[125]Fish, *supra* note 2, at 115.

[126]*Id.* at 102.

[127]Fish, *supra* note 22, at 395. Fish's apparent inconsistency here may not be as surprising as it appears. In an interview, he stated that although theory has no unique capacity to bring about change in an interpretive community, it can do so in the right circumstances. "However, theory—or as I sometimes say tendentiously in these essays, 'theory talk'—can like anything else be the catalyst of change, but it's a contingent and historical matter; it depends on the history of the particular community, the kinds of talk or vocabularies that have prestige or cachet or are likely to trump other kinds of talk. And if in a certain community the sense of what is at stake is highly intermixed with a history of theoretical discourse, then in *that* community at *that* time a change in practices may be produced by a change in theory." Fish, *supra* note 2, at 289.

[128]*Id.* at 114.

Amendment doctrine, with it varying levels of scrutiny and multiple three- and four-part tests for balancing the need for unregulated speech against other social needs. Whether that structure should be razed or remodeled is not the topic of this chapter, but Fish's argument seems to ignore its existence altogether.[129] By avoiding the hard questions, Professor Fish has left himself without a strong voice in this vital debate.

---

[129]Fish does, however, discuss the virtues of Learned Hand's "ad hoc" balancing formulation in *United States v. Dennis* in another essay. *Id.* at 126–30.

CHAPTER
4

First Amendment Theory and Conceptions of the Self

As the previous chapter's discussion of Professor Fish's views revealed, to explore the value and scope of constitutionally protected self-expression, it is necessary to have some understanding of the "self" that is engaging in expression. In fact, much First Amendment theory seems to derive from the liberal notion of a self that is detached from others and requires the freedom to pick and choose among ideas and conceptions of the good life. Liberal theorists from John Locke and John Stuart Mill to John Rawls have posited such a self as the basis for extensive individual rights that have precedence over the demands of the larger community. The "liberal self" is thus an atomistic individual with certain claims of autonomy from the state, including free speech.

The writings of a number of recent theorists have called this picture of the self into question. These theorists, including feminists, critical legal studies scholars, literary theorists and communitarians, have challenged the idea of the liberal self, both as a distorted picture of the human person and as an assumption that encourages excessive individualism at the expense of community. While few critics of the liberal self have spelled out precisely what their critique would mean for free expression theory, there seems little question that alternative conceptions of the self would lead to some significantly revised conclusions concerning individual rights.

This chapter will attempt to sketch, in a tentative fashion, the foundations of the conflict over the self and some possible implications for First Amendment theory. The chapter will first outline John Rawls's conception of the self as representative of liberalism generally. Next, it will explore the work of critics of Rawls's theory and other liberal conceptions of human personhood. Finally, it will consider how traditional First Amendment theory might be affected by the work of these critics.

The Liberal Self and the First Amendment

The liberal version of the self, which also underlies much First Amendment theory, has come under increasing attack from a variety of perspectives in recent years. The liberal self is said to be both an inaccurate representation of human personhood and a morally bankrupt conception that leads to disastrous social consequences in practice. Before discussing the critiques, however, it may be helpful to explore the nature of the liberal self as presented by one liberal theorist.

While notions of a liberal self may be traced to Kant,[1] Locke,[2] and Mill,[3] among others, perhaps the most discussed modern conceptualization came in John Rawls's enormously influential book, *A Theory of Justice*.[4] Rawls's theory was, in his own words, an attempt to "generalize and carry to a higher order of abstraction the traditional theory of the social contract as presented by Locke, Rousseau, and Kant."[5] It removes some of the difficulties posed by Kantian metaphysics, which

---

[1]*See generally* Patrick Riley, Kant's Political Philosophy (1983).
[2]*See generally* John Locke, Second Treatise of Government (C. B. Macpherson ed., Hackett Publishing Co. 1980) (1690).
[3]*E.g.*, John Stuart Mill, On Liberty 12 (A. Castell ed., 1947) (1859).
[4]John Rawls, A Theory of Justice (1971)
[5]*Id.* at viii.

involved [Kant] in claims about a noumenal realm beyond space and time in which all human beings participated insofar as they were rational; human beings were dual-aspect beings, a part of nature and yet simultaneously possessed of faculties that transcended nature.[6]

In addition to avoiding Kantian metaphysics, Rawls's theory provided a firm conceptual mooring for the liberal notion that individual rights should be conceived as both prior to and superior to any notion of the social good, in contrast to utilitarianism.[7] Thus, Rawls "sharply distinguished between 'the right' and 'the good,' identifying justice with the former and demanding 'neutrality' of the state on the latter."[8]

Rawls's method of providing a foundation for the priority of "the right" is to envision a hypothetical social contract.[9] That is, Rawls proposed reaching an agreement on principles of justice that rational persons, regardless of their particular social status or other characteristics, would freely choose. This agreement is made in Rawls's famous "original position."[10]

In the original position, according to Rawls,

no one knows his place in society, his class position or social status, nor does he know his fortune in the distribution of natural assets and abilities, his intelligence and strength, and the like. Nor, again, does anyone know his conception of the good, the particulars of his rational plan of life, or even the special features of his psychology such as his aversion to risk or liability to optimism or pessimism.[11]

The participants lack sufficient information about their own social position to bias the contract they must execute in their own favor.

What emerges from negotiations of the parties in the original position are two principles:

First Principle
Each person is to have an equal right to the most extensive total system of equal basic liberties compatible with a similar system of liberty for all.

---

[6]Stephen Mulhall & Adam Swift, Liberals and Communitarians 45 (1992).
[7]Rawls, *supra* note 4, at 29.
[8]Christopher Wolfe & John Hittinger, Introduction, in Liberalism at the Crossroads xii (1994).
[9]Rawls, *supra* note 4, at 12.
[10]*Id.*
[11]*Id.* at 137.

Second Principle

Social and economic inequalities are to be arranged so that they are both:

(a) to the greatest benefit of the least advantaged, consistent with the just savings principle, and

(b) attached to offices and positions open to all under conditions of fair equality of opportunity.[12]

Rawls's scheme further requires, among other things, that the provision of equal liberties cannot be overridden by the second principle, the so-called difference principle. Thus, basic liberties, whatever those may be, are prior to and cannot be abridged by the difference principle.[13] Rawls explicitly includes freedom of speech among the basic liberties the invasion of which cannot be justified by any social or economic considerations.[14]

Rawls's establishment of basic liberties as inviolable is hardly surprising. It is, of course, classic liberal thought, whether expressed as "natural rights" or by some other formulation. Rawls's scheme also closely mirrors constitutional law in the United States, in which certain basic liberties contained in the Bill of Rights can trump any other expression of positive law, except perhaps in the most extreme cases. In First Amendment law, for example, content-based restrictions on fully protected speech cannot be sustained without a "clear and present danger" or a "compelling government interest."[15]

First Amendment theory and doctrine also closely resemble Rawls's (and traditional liberalism's) notion of "the right" being prior to "the good." Liberal theorists frequently profess neutrality toward which ways of life should be promoted, but advocate protections against the state impeding citizens from choosing whatever version of the good life appeals to them.[16] Liberal neutrality, sometimes called antiperfectionism, arises from a vision of human autonomy. One commentator describing liberal theory noted that

---

[12]*Id.* at 302.

[13]*Id.*

[14]*Id.* at 222–223.

[15]*E.g.*, Simon & Schuster v. New York State Crime Victims Board, 502 U.S. 105 (1991); First National Bank of Boston v. Bellotti, 435 U.S. 765 (1978); Brandenburg v. Ohio, 395 U.S. 444 (1969). *See generally* Geoffrey R. Stone, Content Regulation and the First Amendment, 25 Wm. & Mary L. Rev. 189 (1983).

[16]*E.g.*, Mill, *supra* note 3, at 55–56. *See generally* Mulhall and Swift, *supra* note 6, at 25–33.

to show respect for individuals, the state must forego any authoritative vision of the good life. According to liberalism, in order to realize autonomy, individuals must be free to make those decisions most central to person identity—to pursue their own visions of the good—without collective interference.[17]

Similarly, much of First Amendment law and theory is concerned with government neutrality as to the value of speech.[18] This state neutrality is often expressed in the so-called content distinction. Professor Laurence Tribe has described the content distinction in his two-track model of the First Amendment. According to Tribe, when government attempts to regulate the "content" of speech—that is, its message—the regulation is presumptively violative of the First Amendment: "For if the constitutional guarantee means anything, it means that, ordinarily at least, 'government has no power to restrict expression because of its message, its ideas, its subject matter, or its content. . . .'"[19] Thus, First Amendment theory and doctrine echo liberalism's overall commitment to antiperfectionism. This coherence of free speech jurisprudence and liberal antiperfectionist theory is eloquently captured in the powerful rhetoric of Justice Jackson in the 1943 flag salute case, *West Virginia Board of Education v. Barnette:* "If there is any fixed star in our constitutional constellation, it is that no official, high or petty, can prescribe what shall be orthodox in politics, nationalism, religion, or other matters of opinion. . . ."[20]

Rawls's original position is also familiar, being a hypothetical restatement of social contract notions advanced by Locke and other liberal thinkers. As Locke described this contract in his Second Treatise of Government:

> Men being, as has been said, by nature, all free, equal, and independent, no one can be put out of this estate, and subjected to the political power of another, without his consent. The only way whereby any one divests himself of his natural liberty, and puts on the bonds of civil society, is by agreeing with other men to join and unite into a community . . .[21]

---

[17]Note, A Communitarian Defense of Group Libel Laws, 101 Harv. L. Rev. 682, 688 (1988).
[18]*E.g.*, Police Department of the City of Chicago v. Mosley, 408 U.S. 92 (1972); Cohen v. California, 403 U.S. 15 (1971).
[19]Laurence H. Tribe, American Constitutional Law 790 (1988) (quoting Police Department of the City of Chicago v. Mosley, 408 U.S. 92, 95–96 (1972)).
[20]319 U.S. 624, 642 (1943).
[21]Locke, *supra* note 2, at 52.

Locke may have actually believed that human societies formed in this unlikely way, while Rawls is clearly engaging in a hypothetical exercise to identify principles of justice. Nevertheless, in Rawls's theory, as in Locke's, individuals are conceived, in some sense, as existing prior to the political communities in which they find themselves and agreeing to the principles by which they are governed.[22]

Thus, one can see in notions of individual rights, antiperfectionism, and the social contract a privileging of the individual over the community. The liberal self is both the basis of, and in some sense the natural outgrowth of, this privileging. In recent years, however, the liberal self—as originated in classic liberalism, updated by Rawls, and mirrored in First Amendment theory and doctrine—has become subject to considerable criticism by diverse commentators. The next section will explore a sampling of those criticisms.

Challenges to the Liberal Self

The idea that true autonomous selfhood is problematic is hardly new. But recent criticisms of the liberal self go beyond the notion that autonomous selfhood is rare—often to claim that it is either ontologically impossible or based on morally flawed assumptions. Communitarians, for example, often view the notion that there is some core "self" prior to familial and community bonds as inherently flawed. Rather, it is through community that the self is created and realized. Community in this view is "constitutive" of the individual.

Communitarian theorist[23] Michael Sandel has taken liberalism to task for its "core thesis" that "society, being composed of a plurality of persons, each with his own aims, interests and conceptions of the good, is best arranged when it is governed by principles that do not *themselves* presuppose any particular conception of the good. . . ."[24] Sandel argues that the liberal self that can stand back from its own commitments and values and select its own conception of the good is a myth. Sandel views the self as emergent, while in Rawls's vision it is autonomous.[25] Further,

---

[22]Rawls, *supra* note 4, at 12.

[23]Some theorists labeled "communitarian" do not use the term to refer to themselves. For a helpful overview of modern communitarian thought, *see* Amitai Etzioni, New Communitarian Thinking: Persons, Virtues, Institutions, and Communities (1995) [hereinafter New Communitarian Thinking].

[24]Michael J. Sandel, Liberalism and the Limits of Justice 1 (1982).

[25]*See generally* C. Fred Alford, The Self in Social Theory 9–13 (1991).

the existence of an autonomous self, able to enter the veil of ignorance and choose principles of justice, is a requirement for Rawls's project to succeed.[26] Without the assumptions about selfhood that Rawls adopts, the priority of "the right" over "the good" that he seeks to vindicate is not assured.

For Sandel, Rawls's vision of the self is unrealistically "voluntarist."[27] The Rawlsian self does not look within its own nature to *discover* its proper ends and purposes, but instead stands back at a distance and *selects* those ends, as if selecting items in a cafeteria. The self could never, on Rawls's view, be regarded as constituted by its community in such a way that its values and ends are a necessary part of its identity.[28] This "thin" self precludes certain notions of community by its very ontology.[29] Moreover, Sandel argues, such a conception of the self, although unrealizable in the real world, requires a regime of "rights" superior to any broader notion of social good.[30] That is, the liberal view of the self requires certain political forms that belie the claimed neutrality of liberalism as to the content of "the good." Liberals thus smuggle in a conception of the good—an individualistic conception—while asserting that liberalism has no opinion on the matter:

> The assumptions of the original position thus stand opposed in advance to any conception of the good requiring a more or less expansive self-understanding, and in particular to the possibility of community in the constitutive sense. On Rawls' view, a sense of community describes a possible aim of antecedently individuated selves, not an ingredient or constituent of their identity as such. This guarantees its subordinate status. . . . As the self is prior to the aims it affirms, so a well-ordered society, defined by justice, is prior to the aims—communitarian or otherwise—its members may profess. This is the sense, both moral and epistemological, in which justice is the first virtue of social institutions.[31]

Communitarian theorist Alasdair MacIntyre, in his influential book *After Virtue*, points out that the "modern" self, stripped of its social context, is impoverished.[32] In earlier societies, MacIntyre maintains, the

---

[26]Sandel, *supra* note 24, at 19–23.
[27]*Id.* at 54–59.
[28]*Id.* at 62.
[29]*Id.*
[30]*Id.* at 64.
[31]*Id.* at 64.
[32]Alasdair MacIntyre, After Virtue 31–35 (1984).

human self was more closely linked to its social role and the overall social matrix in which it moved.[33] In "modern" (that is, liberal) societies, on the other hand, the self has been denuded of its social role. The modern self, unlike its classical counterpart, is

> able to stand back from any and every situation in which [it] is involved, from any and every characteristic that [it] may possess, and to pass judgment on it from a purely universal and abstract point of view that is totally detached from all social particularity. Anyone and everyone can thus be a moral agent, since it is in the self and not in social roles and practices that moral agency has to be located.[34]

MacIntyre attributes the advent of the modern self to the Enlightenment's failure to provide independent rational foundations for morality.[35] After efforts by thinkers such as Kant failed to ground morality in objective, rational principles, morality eventually became what MacIntyre calls "emotivist."[36] That is, political and moral debate is interpreted as simply being the arbitrary expression of personal preference. In arguments about important political issues, such as war or abortion, each side may advance rational arguments, but the starting points of such arguments have no rational foundation.[37]

MacIntyre notes, for example, that abortion opponents may begin their argumentation from the position that "murder is wrong," while pro-choice advocates often begin from the position that "women should have control over their bodies."[38] Although logical argumentation can proceed from either premise, the premises themselves are incommensurable. As MacIntyre puts it:

> But the rival premises are such that we possess no rational way of weighing the claims of one as against another. . . . It is precisely because there is in our society no established way of deciding between these claims that moral argument appears to be necessarily interminable.[39]

---

[33]*Id.* at 33.
[34]*Id.* at 32.
[35]*Id.* at 39.
[36]*Id.* at 35.
[37]*Id.* at 6–9.
[38]*Id.* at 6–7.
[39]*Id.* at 8.

Moreover, because individuals cannot convince each other on any rational grounds of the correct initial premise, it follows that their personal choice of positions is necessarily without any rational foundation.[40] One's position can only be an arbitrary choice of competing, but incommensurable, moral frameworks.

MacIntyre claims that this was not always the case, however. In making this claim, he invokes Aristotelian ethics, a system that was influential through the Middle Ages.[41] Aristotelian thought maintained that ethics was the system for human beings "as they were" to move toward realizing their true nature.[42] It was this notion of *telos*, or purpose, that gave morality its power. Within the Aristotelian scheme, according to MacIntyre,

> there is a fundamental contrast between man-as-he-happens-to-be and man-as-he-could-be-if-he-realized-his-essential-nature. Ethics is the science which is to enable men to understand how they make the transition from the former state to the latter. Ethics therefore in this view presupposes some account of potentiality and act, some account of the essence of man as rational animal and above all some account of the human *telos*.[43]

In this way of life, moral claims can be evaluated as either true or false, not without some disagreement, but without the incommensurability of "modern" moral claims.

The advent of modernity (and liberalism) removed the teleological element and thus detached the human self from its purposes or ends, which had in the past been embedded in one's society and one's role therein.[44] While the premodern self was defined by its roles and ends, the modern self, stripped of these constraints, finds itself adrift. MacIntyre, of course, does not view this shift as progress, although

> it is celebrated historically for the most part not as loss, but as self-congratulatory gain, as the emergence of the individual freed on the one hand from the social bonds of those constraining hierarchies which the modern world rejected at its birth and on the other hand from what modernity has taken to be the superstitions of teleology.[45]

---

[40]*Id.*
[41]*Id.* at 52.
[42]*Id.* at 52–53.
[43]*Id.* at 52.
[44]*Id.* at 33.
[45]*Id.* at 34.

For MacIntyre, the freedom of choice of the modern, emotivist self is the empty freedom of a ghost.

Although the preceding account cannot do justice to MacIntyre's complex project, the outlines of his argument sketched above make the point that, from his perspective, the liberal self is an insubstantial and somewhat pathetic creature. MacIntyre does not directly address Rawls to any great degree, but the implication of his work is that the notion of "the right" having priority over "the good" is a step backward from societies in which "the good" for human beings was embedded in cultural roles and practices. And it is exactly this shift that has produced the modern, unconnected self.

Another communitarian theorist, Charles Taylor, emphasizes similar themes in a number of his writings.[46] Taylor contends that primacy-of-right theories, which he connects to Hobbes and Locke, demand that individual rights be unconditional, while making principles of belonging or obligation purely voluntary.[47] Taylor suggests that earlier civilizations would have found the focus on individual rights to be "wildly eccentric and implausible. The very idea of starting an argument whose foundation was the rights of the individual would have been strange and puzzling— about as puzzling as if I were to start with the premiss that the Queen rules by divine right."[48] Taylor argues that the emphasis on individual rights in traditional liberal theories is incoherent because individuals need a certain kind of society in which to exercise their rights—a society that cooperatively supports and sustains freedom.[49] Taylor maintains that the excessive individualism of rights-based theories may contain the seeds of destruction of that very kind of society. Moreover, theories that assert the primacy of rights embody a particular, and to Taylor an unconvincing, conception of the self.[50] That is, they "derive support in those philosophical traditions which come to us from the seventeenth century and which started with the postulation of an extensionless subject, epistemologically a *tabula rasa* and politically a presuppositionless bearer of rights."[51] Such assumptions require, Taylor suggests, a serious debate about the nature of human subjectivity and its relationship to political theory.

---

[46]*See, e.g.*, Charles Taylor, Atomism, in Communitarianism and Individualism 29 (Shlomo Avineri and Avner De-Shalit eds., 1992).
[47]*Id.* at 30–31.
[48]*Id.* at 31.
[49]*Id.* at 43–45.
[50]*Id.* at 49.
[51]*Id.* at 50.

Communitarians are not the only ones who have opposed the liberal vision of the self and liberalism's concomitant fixation on individual rights. Some feminist jurisprudence identifies this "atomistic" view with male modes of thought.[52] Linda C. McClain writes that a

> central theme of [feminist] critique has been that the law embodies a masculine perspective in emphasizing autonomy and the individual over interdependency and the community. Liberalism has been viewed as inextricably masculine in its model of separate, atomistic, competing individuals establishing a legal system to pursue their own interests and to protect them from others' interference with their rights to do so.[53]

This atomistic self, as conceived by some feminist scholars, is a travesty of human personhood: an unconnected self whose identity is formed independently of others and whose only interests are selfish ones.[54]

Feminist legal scholar Martha Minow points out that feminism is one of many scholarly approaches that have taken, as noted in the previous chapter, the "relational turn," a reconsideration of the self and how it is constituted by the social world: "In field after field of scholarship, twentieth-century theorists have explored the significance of relationships and challenged modes of thought that rest upon autonomous and discrete items or persons."[55] Minow points to Carol Gilligan's "different voice" work in moral development as influential on a wide spectrum of feminist legal scholars.[56] Gilligan posited that a "different voice" emerges from feminine moral reasoning—not all of which necessarily comes from female subjects.[57] Minow notes that "Gilligan found that instead of viewing moral conflicts as the result of clashes between autonomous persons, who exist prior to their relationships, some people respond to statements of moral dilemma with concern for the failure of connection, or failure of care."[58] Gilligan's work also points out that this relational perspective tends to focus on situations in context rather than on rigid or absolute rules abstracted from their circumstances.[59]

---

[52]On feminist jurisprudence generally, *see* Gary Minda, Postmodern Legal Movements (1995).
[53]Linda C. McClain, "Atomistic" Man Revisited: Liberalism, Connection, and Feminist Jurisprudence, 65 S. Cal. L. Rev. 1171, 1171 (1992).
[54]*Id.* at 1177–78.
[55]Martha Minow, Making All the Difference 192 (1990).
[56]Carol Gilligan, In a Different Voice: Psychological Theory and Women's Development (1982).
[57]*Id.* at 7–11.
[58]Minow, *supra* note 55, at 196.
[59]*Id.* at 197.

Some feminist legal theory has even portrayed the liberal vision of the self and of individual rights in psychoanalytic terms. Linda C. McClain points out that

> "male jurisprudence," with its emphasis on individual autonomy and rights, has been interpreted by [feminist] critiques as the institutionalization of the male infant's psychoanalytic drama of development, whereby connection with and dependency upon the mother are rejected, often painfully, for autonomy, which is understood as separation and independence.[60]

The relationship between liberalism and fundamental psychological conflicts about "self" and "other" has also been a theme of critical legal studies scholarship. Critical legal studies (CLS) is an academic movement begun in U.S. law schools in the mid-1970s that critiques the dominant, liberal conception of law by incorporating elements of, among other things, "legal realist" thought of the 1920s and 1930s, Marxian thought, poststructuralist literary theory, and the Frankfurt School of critical theory.[61] Thomas Streeter made the point that CLS scholarship challenges the liberal separation of "the individual" and "society," in which the individual is the locus of freedom and change, while society is the locus of control and constraint.[62] "From this individual/society dichotomy thus come the familiar tenets of Liberalism, such as the belief that freedom of speech and individualism act as key mechanisms of resistance to social domination," Streeter wrote.[63] CLS writers, including Duncan Kennedy,[64] have challenged this dichotomy as paradoxical by noting that relationships with others are both a requirement of and a constraint on our freedom. As one commentator has explained Kennedy's "Fundamental Contradiction":

> [W]e desire to be free and autonomous individuals, to be let alone. Paradoxically, this requires interaction with others for two reasons: first, we must have the protection of others to ensure that we are not bullied by someone; and second, to become a person requires interaction with others in order to mature psychologically.[65]

---

[60]McClain, *supra* note 53, at 1180.

[61]For an overview of critical legal studies, *see* Andrew Altman, Critical Legal Studies: A Liberal Critique (1990); Minda, *supra* note 52.

[62]Thomas Streeter, Beyond Freedom of Speech and the Public Interest: The Relevance of Critical Legal Studies to Communications Policy, 40 J. Comm. 43, 48 (1990)

[63]*Id.*

[64]Duncan Kennedy, The Structure of Blackstone's Commentaries, 28 Buffalo L. Rev. 205 (1979).

[65]Donald F. Brosnan, Serious But Not Critical, 60 So. Cal. L. Rev. 262, 288 (1987).

The autonomy the liberal self seeks can only be gained in community with others, to the inevitable detriment of autonomy.

As discussed in the previous chapter, Stanley Fish's literary theory is another perspective from which the liberal self has been under attack. In particular, Fish emphasizes the role of interpretive communities in deriving meaning from texts, thus reducing the place of the individual reader (or self). The individual thus, in some sense, becomes a "branch office" of the larger interpretive community, although the exact outlines of that community remain somewhat shadowy. Pierre Schlag pointed out that Fish's advocacy of interpretive communities as the source of meaning has disturbing implications:[66]

> It seems to eclipse the 'self' entirely, leaving it at best an empty vehicle for the reiteration of meanings generated by interpretive communities. And not surprisingly, Fish has been criticized for annihilating the self as subject. Indeed, it would be easy to go further and suggest that Fish's concept of interpretive communities has totalitarian implications in that it overwhelms both reason and the self by appearing to locate meaning in the collectivity.[67]

All of these theorists, as well as numerous others not discussed, find something unconvincing, if not pernicious, in the idea of the liberal self. The next section will explore how these critiques might affect some of the First Amendment theories discussed in chapter 1.

Implications for First Amendment Theory

What implications do the various critiques of the liberal self have for First Amendment theory? Many of the assumptions deriving from the liberal self, including the priority of "the right" over "the good" and state neutrality, seem to be direct underpinnings of much First Amendment thought. What effect might these critics have on traditional First Amendment theory?

---

[66]Pierre Schlag, Fish v. Zapp: The Case of the Relatively Autonomous Self, 76 Geo. L.J. 37, 43 (1987)

[67]*Id.* Professor Schlag argues, somewhat whimsically, that in fact Fish's theory (or "antitheory") leaves the self quite a bit of room to maneuver. "The self cannot choose its interpretive constructs. It is always already within them. But at the same time (and quite conveniently) very little can be known about these interpretive constructs so the self need not feel closeted by an overly determined objectivity. The concept of interpretive communities offers the self a formal closure against the claims of theory, reason, and history. But at the same time, the concept is substantively empty, so that the self can project into 'interpretive communities' just about anything it wants." *Id.* at 45.

Before attempting to answer that question, it must be noted that the alternative theoretical stances discussed above do not constitute a unity. Among these diverse approaches are many serious differences, as there are within each camp. Theorists labeled "communitarian," for example, disagree with each other in significant ways, as they do with representatives of the other approaches mentioned. An exhaustive analysis of all of the implications of these theorists for free expression theory would be beyond the scope of this work. Nonetheless, one point of some convergence seems to be the critique of the liberal self, which is often contrasted with a vision of a "socially constituted" self. Perhaps this convergence provides an opportunity to offer at least a sketch of the free speech implications of these theorists.

Nonetheless, there are, in fact, key differences among the critics as to the nature of the self. At the risk of some oversimplification, it might be suggested that the critics of the liberal self can be divided for purposes of analysis into two groups: "descriptive" critics and "normative" critics. Some critiques of liberalism and its theory of the person seem to be primarily descriptive: that is, they hold that the liberal self is a mistake in apprehending the true nature of the human subject. The descriptive critique maintains that human beings are, in fact, not the atomistic, presocial selves of Rawls and Locke, and that this error in description leads to erroneous theories of politics and law. Normative critics, on the other hand, may grant that the atomistic liberal self is in fact a reality of our present era, particularly in the United States but argue that our social arrangements would be much improved if this were not the case. The normative critique focuses less on what sort of selves human beings are and concentrates more on the ideal human self, which finds its full expression through the political community.

Fish's critique, for example, seems to be primarily descriptive. He maintains that human beings are, always and already, embedded in their interpretive communities and that radical subjectivism is impossible.[68] Kennedy likewise suggests that his conception of the "Fundamental Contradiction" is descriptive.[69] MacIntyre's critique, on the other hand, seems largely normative. The modern individual is, in fact, an unconnected, ghostly subject.[70] But, MacIntyre argues, older traditions point the way toward a reclaiming of our connections with each other and with

---

[68]Stanley Fish, Is There A Text in This Class? The Authority of Interpretive Communities (1980).
[69]Kennedy, *supra* note 64, at 213.
[70]MacIntyre, *supra* note 32, at 31–34.

our communities, leading toward a higher good for human beings than liberal modernity can offer.[71] Some of the critiques, including Sandel's and those of some strands of feminism, seem to have both descriptive and normative elements. In fact, at least one critic of "antiliberal" thinkers has argued that some of these thinkers conflate both descriptive and normative claims in contradictory ways. Legal scholar Stephen Holmes accuses both MacIntyre and Sandel of this logical misstep. "It is obviously contradictory to say that liberal individuals do not exist and that the ones who exist are excruciatingly unhappy," Holmes writes. "Yet this beguiling contradiction is something like the official handshake of the communitarian movement in America."[72]

The descriptive and normative critiques of the liberal self would seem to lead to somewhat different views of First Amendment theory. For purposes of analysis, this section will examine each position separately in relation to three major theories of free expression discussed in chapter 1. Because these three theories are among the most widely adopted, in one variation or another, by courts and scholars, the hope is that pondering the effects of the critiques of the liberal self on these three theories will illuminate the broad implications of the critiques. The three theories are: (1) the self-government theory, which views free speech as primarily a means to an effective democracy; (2) marketplace theory, which emphasizes the role of free speech in the search for truth; and (3) the autonomy theory, which values free expression as an end in itself for human beings seeking to achieve self-realization.

Descriptive Critics and Free Speech

The descriptive critique, which argues that the liberal self is inaccurate as a matter of individual psychology, would probably embrace the self-government theory, at least to a limited extent. From the descriptive point of view, the fact that human beings are socially constituted rather than atomistic selves does not undercut the value of free speech for purposes of self-government. The socially constituted self is, for most theorists, perfectly capable of engaging in political discussion. This is true even if the "self," as in some strong descriptive claims, is in some sense an extension of the community in which it finds itself. In fact, descriptive critics generally, although not universally, seem to share with normative critics a strong

---

[71]*Id.*
[72]Stephen Holmes, The Anatomy of Antiliberalism 182 (1993).

desire that the political community be strengthened through exactly the sort of participation Meiklejohn's theory envisaged.[73]

While many descriptive critics presumably would have no quarrel with the self-government theory, a strong version of the socially constituted thesis leaves one wondering how productive political speech could be. In the strong descriptive account, individuals' views and ideas— indeed, the very categories by which they perceive the world—come from the community. That being the case, political speech would largely consist of ritualized repetition of conventional ideas rather than creating a forum for original thought for the benefit of all. The strong descriptive account suggests a kind of deterministic intellectual strait-jacket within which individual speech is unlikely to advance democratic goals. If the individual is simply a reflection of society—"community writ small"[74]—there is no particular reason to assume that anything other than platitudes and clichés would emerge from political debate. To the extent that the individual mirrors the community, there would seem to be no mechanism for productive and imaginative new ideas to emerge.

The marketplace theory poses similar difficulties. For the descriptive critic, the marketplace theory cannot be accurate. Human beings lack the capacity to stand aside from their values and commitments and freely choose among the fare offered in the "marketplace of ideas." The very idea of a self that can put aside its community connections, goals and values (which, after all, are what "constitute" the self) and find some Archimedian point from which to judge the truth and falsity of ideas is an impossibility. Moreover, this impossibility calls into question the notion that an unregulated marketplace of ideas will necessarily lead to a less partial truth or to better social policy. Lacking an objective or rational foundation for choice among competing ideas, there is no particular reason to suppose the socially constituted self will choose better—or truer— ideas to believe.

Fish, for example, mocks the truth-finding view of the marketplace of ideas.[75] He argues that the notion that uninhibited expression will, at some point in the future, yield indeterminate benefits "has a great appeal, in part because it continues in a secular form the Puritan celebration of millenarian hopes . . ."[76] While awaiting the forever-deferred arrival of truth, Fish

---

[73]*See generally* Sandel, *supra* note 24.

[74]Alford, *supra* note 25, at 11.

[75]Stanley Fish, There's No Such Thing As Free Speech and It's a Good Thing Too, 109 (1994).

[76]*Id.*

argues, First Amendment advocates ignore or minimize the genuine present harm of certain forms of speech, particularly hate speech.[77]

But it is the autonomy rationale that perhaps generates the greatest difficulty for descriptive critics of the liberal self. For while the marketplace theory presumes liberal selfhood, its primary focus is on a communal search for a less partial truth. The autonomy theory, on the other hand, is primarily concerned with the individual—with each person's right to discover his or her own personal conception of the good. The descriptive critic can only see the self that seeks autonomy and self-realization in First Amendment theory as a close cousin of—if not identical to—the presocial self of Rawls's original position. Rawls's theory emphasizes a self that is able to choose its own ends rather than the relational self that is embedded in, and constituted by, a social matrix. As one analysis of Rawls noted:

> Rawls sometimes seems to claim that a human being's capacity autonomously to choose its ends is not just one amongst many equally valuable capacities or features but rather forms the essence of his or her identity. It therefore follows that respect for human autonomy is not just one value amongst many in human life, but an absolutely fundamental one which must always trump any other; for to fail to respect that capacity is to fail to respect a metaphysically fundamental feature of personhood.[78]

To the descriptive critic, such an account of the self is simply mistaken. As a result, a free speech theory based on such a concept is untenable.

The descriptive critique has a number of fundamental weaknesses that make its application to autonomy theory problematic. At the most basic level, critiques that pose strong descriptive challenges to the liberal self as an autonomous center of self-generating meaning and activity run straight into what Frank I. Michelman called the "performative contradiction." As Michelman put this objection:

> How could anyone utter the call for attention, how could anyone give or have reason to give attention to anything, if not apprehending himself subjectively, as a consciousness sponsoring its own thoughts and exertions? The critique of subjectivity performatively affirms the subjectivity in question.[79]

---

[77]*Id.* at 110.
[78]Mulhall and Swift, *supra* note 6, at 46–47.
[79]Frank I. Michelman, Review Essay: The Subject of Liberalism, 46 Stan. L. Rev. 1807, 1810 (1994).

The performative contradiction does not, of course, rule out a "self" that is, to some extent, socially constituted. On the other hand, it does point toward the limits of some variety of Durkheimian holism as a valid alternative to liberal selfhood.

Another difficulty with the descriptive critique is that it may misapprehend liberal claims. Descriptive critics view the liberal self as a failed attempt by liberal theorists to paint an accurate portrait of the human self. In fact, however, that is often not the case. It may be more useful to view the liberal self as a heuristic device through which to analyze political and legal issues. In this heuristic view, the liberal self is something like classical economics' conception of *homo economicus*: not a real entity, but a useful tool for generating theory.[80] No human being is fully autonomous and free to choose her way of life, just as no human being is a fully rational utility maximizer. As in economics, the validity of the construct may lie, not in its descriptive correctness, but in the social value found in the principles it generates.

Rawls's recent work has adopted something like the heuristic view. In his 1993 book *Political Liberalism*,[81] he argues that

> [t]he veil of ignorance, to mention one prominent feature of [the original] position, has no specific metaphysical implications concerning the nature of the self; it does not imply that the self is ontologically prior to the facts about persons that the parties are excluded from learning.[82]

On the contrary, Rawls suggests, the original position is more akin to a form of role playing that allows one to think about principles of justice. Rawls contends that when

> we simulate being in the original position, our reasoning no more commits us to a particular metaphysical doctrine about the nature of the self than our acting a part in a play, say of Macbeth or Lady Macbeth, commits us to thinking that we are really a king or a queen engaged in a desperate struggle for political power.[83]

---

[80]*See* David Crump and Larry A. Maxwell, Health Care, Cost Containment, and the Anti-trust Laws: A Legal and Economic Analysis of the Pireno Case, 56 S. Cal. L. Rev. 913, 925–26 (1983).
[81]John Rawls, Political Liberalism (1993).
[82]*Id.* at 27.
[83]*Id.* at 27.

Political theorist Don Herzog makes a similar point when he argues that traditional liberal claims about the self may be regarded as "political" claims, responsive to specific social contexts, rather than ontological claims.[84] Specifically, in the historical context in which liberalism arose, communities demanded extraordinary things of their members based on notions of deference to one's betters and the supposed divine sanction of the state. "Describing individuals as presocial, imagining counterfactually what they might gain or lose by contracting to enter a political society . . . dramatizes the claim that persons are more than cannon fodder, more than eggs to be broke in the pursuit of omelettes," Herzog writes. "In a historical context where ordinary people had long been exploited and taken for granted, this bold egalitarianism is worth applauding, not condemning."[85] Descriptive critics, among whom Herzog includes CLS scholars, thus miss the point when they argue about the accuracy of liberalism's picture of the self.[86] And the point, Herzog maintains, is not purely a question of historical context: "Liberals today have nothing against a plurality of communities—indeed they may rightly urge that liberal toleration is the best safeguard of that plurality—but they may well worry that having only one community would rest on militant coercion."[87] In the realm of free speech theory, following Herzog's lead, the liberal conception of the self could be regarded as a strategic bulwark against what Justice Jackson in *Barnette* described as the "compulsory unification of opinion," which, according to Jackson, produced "only the unanimity of the graveyard."[88]

To the extent one views the liberal self in First Amendment theory as a heuristic device, the argument shifts from the liberal self's descriptive accuracy to the utility of the principles derived from its use. That, of course, is an entirely separate debate that involves the usefulness of theories of the First Amendment and the attractiveness of the kind of society that results when those theories are adopted. Descriptive critics can certainly engage free speech advocates on those issues, but the descriptive critics' claimed insights into human personhood guarantee no particular result. It will be the benefits of free speech, both individually and collectively, that will be under consideration.

---

[84]Don Herzog, As Many as Six Impossible Things before Breakfast, 75 Calif. L. Rev. 609, 614 (1987)
[85]*Id.* at 616.
[86]*Id.* at 614.
[87]*Id.* at 619.
[88]West Virginia State Board of Education v. Barnette, 319 U.S. 624, 641 (1943).

An even more serious objection to many descriptive accounts is their failure to justify the claim that a certain descriptive account somehow compels certain legal or political arrangements. Matthew H. Kramer has argued convincingly that metaphysical questions (such as the nature of personhood) have no necessary relation to how human beings should organize themselves, even though theorists sometimes mistakenly con-flate these two realms of inquiry.[89] Thus, descriptive accounts of the self compel no particular regime of free speech.

Kramer chides the frequent error that "taking into account the socially constructed nature of human beings and their realities must entail the spurning of individualism in politics."[90] Kramer points out that this "hasty passage between mutual creation and mutual support, between the neces-sarily social and the conscientiously sociable" is frequently employed by both Marxian theorists and communitarians like Sandel.[91] Kramer argues that the social and linguistic forces that constitute individuals may as eas-ily create individuals who are atomistic, rather than necessarily creating individuals who are bound to each other in fundamental ways that should be reflected in political and legal institutions.[92] Nietzschean philosophy, for example, combines a "self" that is created through culture with a supremely autonomous individual as the ideal.[93] Kramer notes that Marx himself recognized that "the *metaphysical* state of human beings as mem-bers one of another does not often incline them to behave very much like members one of another in *political* life."[94]

For free speech theory, this point makes clear that, regardless of the extent to which individuals are indeed socially constituted, no particular free speech jurisprudence necessarily follows from this fact. For example, a socially constituted individual, no less than an "atomistic" self, might

---

[89]Matthew H. Kramer, Critical Legal Theory and the Challenge of Feminism: A Philosophical Recon-ception 6 (1995).

[90]*Id.* at 10.

[91]*Id.* at 11. For a similar view, *see* Stephen A. Gardbaum, Law, Politics, and the Claims of Commu-nity, 90 Mich. L. Rev. 685, 702 (1992) (noting that the "consequence that Sandel derives from the social thesis is neither logically nor practically required. First, it is a non sequitur to argue that to deny 'the picture of the freely-choosing individual' is to imply 'that we cannot conceive our personhood without reference to our role as citizens.' Some argument is needed to move from the concept of the self as encumbered, to the essential nature of a particular encumbrance—that of citizenship").

[92]Kramer, *supra* note 89, at 11–12.

[93]*Id. See also* Gardbaum, *supra* note 91, at 702 (arguing that "if we are all constituted in part by our communities, then the type of individuals we are depends upon the nature of these communities.").

[94]Kramer, *supra* note 89, at 12.

obtain significant benefits from wide autonomy in the realm of expression, as might the community. One might even argue that the truth of the descriptive thesis suggests a good case for expressive autonomy. Assuming that the *degree* of social constitution varies from individual to individual—perhaps, for example, being less evident in those who have read and experienced the "forms of life" of other cultures and times—the only way to gain some perspective outside of one's limited horizon would be through protection of expression that would be seen as oppositional to the dominant culture. Only through broad protection of autonomous expression could individuals gain some reflective space from their own culture by experiencing alternative cultural frameworks or paradigms. To the extent that the descriptive thesis portrays individuals as trapped in a kind of cultural prison—reflecting, but unable to transcend, the community's ways of thinking—expressive autonomy could well be considered an essential escape mechanism.[95]

Normative Critics and Free Speech

Normative critics, who hold that the liberal self is a real but unfortunate development of modernity, sometimes evince hostility toward the very idea of individual rights. MacIntyre, for example, writes that belief in natural or human rights "is one with belief in unicorns and witches."[96] Moreover, he argues, the very existence of a *concept* of individual rights—conceived as a way in which individuals protect themselves against others—signals a serious breakdown of the social fabric.[97]

Despite this generally hostile tone, it seems likely that many normative critics of the liberal self would have some sympathy for the self-government theory. Political discussion and involvement promotes exactly the kind of relational values and sense of community that the normative critics generally support. For example, Charles Taylor argued that people "deliberating together about what will be binding on all of them is an

---

[95]*Cf.* C. G. Prado, Starting with Foucault 113 (1995) (arguing that for poststructuralist philosopher Michel Foucault, whose work emphasized the social construction of subjectivity by official discourses and "disciplinary techniques," an important method of struggle against established truths is to offer alternative accounts of truth in order to "gain those measures of intellectual freedom and well-being that are achievable by altering dominant relations").

[96]MacIntyre, *supra* note 32, at 69.

[97]Alasdair MacIntyre, Three Rival Versions of Moral Enquiry: Encyclopedia, Genealogy, and Tradition 184–85 (1990).

essential part of the exercise of freedom."[98] Taylor suggested that the atomistic self discourages political deliberation, which is a good in itself.[99] MacIntyre also made approving reference to Aristotelian notions of human beings as finding their highest good as participants in the *polis*, the city-state. MacIntyre noted Aristotle's assertion "that the city-state is the unique political form in which alone the virtues of human life can be genuinely and fully exhibited."[100] Thus, the normative critics of the liberal self would likely agree, although perhaps differing on its exact contours, that the self-government rationale reflects a self thoroughly grounded and participating in its political community. Such participation enables the self to move from its selfish, individualistic agenda toward a broader vision of its place in the community.

It should be noted that Meiklejohnian theory is largely *instrumental*: free speech about government is desirable because it promotes an effectively functioning democracy. The normative critic, on the other hand, might well regard citizen participation in government decisions through expression as *intrinsically* worthwhile because such participation is the highest good for human beings, who are by nature political animals. Only through political participation can atomistic individuals move toward the kind of strong community the normative critic embraces.[101]

The normative critic of the liberal self would likely find both worthwhile and undesirable elements in the marketplace theory. Marketplace theory encourages the discovery of truth, or at least pragmatic "warranted belief,"[102] by examining a wide range of alternatives. This search is a communal rather than an individual one, which might lead to its commendation by the normative critic.

On the other hand, the marketplace theory would almost certainly be problematic to normative theorists because of its heterodox tendencies. Normative critics, such as MacIntyre, see the self as finding meaning within the narrative structure of tradition: "Tradition tells us what the human good is, how to seek it, as well as providing standards of success and failure. This is what gives a life narrative unity."[103] The marketplace theory tends to downplay the importance of that grounding in tradition,

---

[98]Taylor, *supra* note 46, at 48.

[99]*Id.* at 47–48.

[100]MacIntyre, *supra* note 32, at 148.

[101]Jeffrey Abramson and Elizabeth Bussiere, Free Speech and Free Press: A Communitarian Perspective 218, 228 in New Communitarian Thinking, *supra* note 23.

[102]*See* Richard A. Posner, The Problems of Jurisprudence 112–15 (1990).

[103]Alford, *supra* note 25, at 14 .

instead emphasizing a continually evolving consensus that undermines all certainties. First Amendment theorist Rodney Smolla noted that the marketplace theory subjects all dogmas to "the intellectual acid bath of adversarial contest."[104] Justice Holmes, often credited as one of the architects of marketplace theory, was also a notorious skeptic.[105] It is this skepticism and the concomitant sense that truth is constantly up for grabs that might well make marketplace theory untenable for the normative critic. Marketplace theory encourages individuals to question community norms. Moreover, many of the ideas that move through the marketplace undermine the sense of community, including pornography, racist speech, and other divisive ideas.

For the normative critic, as for the descriptive critic, it is the autonomy rationale that would almost certainly be the most questionable free speech theory. For the normative critic, the autonomy rationale promotes an unhealthy obsession with individual judgment cut off from communal wisdom. As one commentator formulated the normative objection:

> Liberals think that autonomy is promoted when judgments about the good are taken out of the political realm. But in reality individual judgments require the sharing of experiences and the give and take of collective deliberations. Individual judgments . . . become a matter of purely subjective and arbitrary whim if they are cut off from collective deliberations.[106]

Moreover, the normative critic can only deplore the unconnected nature of the individual quest for autonomy. Autonomy theory posits an individual whose identity is created (or voluntarily "chosen") independently of others, and whose primary interest is self-interest. This excessively individualistic theory of free expression tends to ignore the pursuit of goals in community with others—the highest good for human beings. The autonomy theory, a normative critic might argue, helps to encourage the creation of a self with no real attachments to others. Embarking on a narcissistic quest to find his or her "true self," such an individual may jettison the only identity that can produce a worthwhile life—identity as a member of the group, within that group's practices and traditions. Particular forms of speech, for example, may be harmful to community cohesion

---

[104]Rodney S. Smolla, Free Speech in an Open Society 8 (1992).

[105]*See, e.g.*, Posner, *supra* note 102, at 221–23.

[106]Will Kymlicka, Liberal Individualism and Liberal Neutrality 165, 173 in Communitarianism and Individualism, *supra* note 46.

even though they satisfy some "autonomy" need of particular persons. Sandel wrote that "[c]ommunitarians would be more likely than liberals to allow a town to ban pornographic bookstores, on the grounds that pornography offends its way of life and the values that sustain it."[107]

To the extent that the normative critique is at odds with at least some streams of First Amendment theory, the critique raises some intriguing questions. MacIntyre's work, for example, seems to suggest that the only way that human beings can realize their ultimate good is through participatory citizenship in the political community.[108] To rescue the ghostly and insubstantial self created by modernity, a return to a strong community is required. For First Amendment theory, this approach seems to replicate the search of the autonomous individual to define the good life for herself through free expression at the level of the community. It is at the level of community that the good is identified, not at the level of the individual self. Free speech principles such as the autonomy rationale appear to be the result of confusion about how the good community should operate.

For First Amendment theory—and particularly autonomy theory—a crucial issue is exactly what "community" is under consideration. Certainly autonomy theory is not, by its nature, opposed to community cohesion. Atomism is not a requirement of autonomy theory. Individuals may voluntarily subordinate their personal visions to group norms and goals— whether these groups are political parties, religious organizations, or other voluntary associations. To the extent these groups constitute the relevant "communities," autonomy theory not only encourages but actively protects these choices and the communicative freedom to convince others to participate. Autonomy theory does, however, conflict with compulsory subordination of individual expressive autonomy to some state-sanctioned orthodoxy. If "community" is defined as an entity capable of invoking the legal apparatus of the state to enforce a particular vision of the good, autonomy theory appears irreconcilable with the normative critique.

Rawls's recent work recognizes this distinction. Rawls maintains his conception of "the right" being prior to "the good" operates in the political realm; that is, the original position is a "political conception of the person."[109] This view does not deny that citizens, in their nonpublic life, may

---

[107]Michael Sandel, Liberalism and its Critics 6 (1984).

[108]MacIntyre, *supra* note 32, at 219. There are, of course, numerous connections between the normative critique and the recent resurgence of interest in "civic republicanism." *See, e.g.*, Frank I. Michelman, Law's Republic, 97 Yale L.J. 1493 (1988).

[109]Rawls, *supra* note 81, at 29.

be deeply grounded in some community or other. The political conception simply maintains that for purposes of their relations with the state, they must be regarded as free citizens.

> It can happen that in their personal affairs, or in the internal life of associations, citizens may regard their final ends and attachments very differently from the way the political conception supposes. They may have, and often do have at any given time, affections, devotions, and loyalties that they believe they would not, indeed could and should not, stand apart from and evaluate objectively.[110]

While Rawls's political conception may itself create problems with its division between "public" and "private" selves, it does make clear that his liberalism is not completely opposed to the constitutive claims the normative critics advocate.

Moreover, Rawls's recent work supports the priority of the right over the good (and thus the inviolability of basic liberties such as free speech) on the practical ground that, in modern societies, there is simply no possible consensus as to what "the good" might be:

> A modern democratic society is characterized not simply by a pluralism of comprehensive religious, philosophical, and moral doctrines, but by a pluralism of incompatible yet reasonable comprehensive doctrines. No one of these doctrines is affirmed by citizens generally.[111]

Nor, Rawls adds, is one likely to be affirmed.[112] This intractable pluralism forms the basis for the requirement that no particular conception of the good be imposed by one group on others.

At the level of First Amendment theory, Rawls's response may insulate the liberal underpinnings of free speech from critics to some extent. If the concept of the liberal self is concerned solely with the individual's relations with the state, a free speech jurisprudence based on such a self need not be as morally dangerous as some normative critics claim. Moreover, in light of the pluralism of modern societies, the question of who should decide which communities are allowed to maintain their integrity by restraining others' speech becomes problematic. The seeming unavoidability of pluralism suggests that the normative ideal may be unavailable.

---

[110]*Id.* at 31.
[111]*Id.* at xvi.
[112]*Id.*

If so, it may be that the normative critique is a form of nostalgia for a social cohesion that, if it ever existed, may never exist again. In the absence of such cohesion, broad free expression rights, based on state neutrality, may be the only protection on which less powerful communities and individuals can depend.

Conclusion

Descriptive and normative critics have made powerful arguments challenging the liberal self that underlies much of First Amendment theory and doctrine. The individuated, freely choosing self of Rawls and other liberals, which also seems to be the self behind the marketplace of ideas and the autonomy rationales in free speech theory, may be an exaggeration of certain aspects of human personhood to the detriment of others, in particular, to our sense of community. Even if the liberal self is reasonably accurate as a picture of the modern individual, critics have maintained that such a self is the result of a liberal culture that cuts individuals adrift from the *telos* that they need to live satisfying lives in common with others.

For First Amendment theory, the challenge is to examine largely unexplored premises about the value of speech and its relationship to what human persons are, or should be. This chapter has attempted to take a first step in that direction by highlighting the nature of these critiques and suggesting some implications for free expression theory that seem to flow from the critiques.

For those concerned with maintaining strong protections for free expression, the critiques examined here may appear threatening. It may well be, however, that these critiques can provide worthwhile insights with which to improve a free speech tradition in which the picture of the human self is somewhat one-dimensional. Critiques of the liberal self— and the regime of rights tied to such a self—might productively be viewed as correctives to certain excesses of liberal political and legal theory.[113] Clearly, for example, a certain degree of social cohesion is a necessary

---

[113]For a similar view that communitarian thought, in particular, is limited to a largely corrective function, *see* Michael Walzer, The Communitarian Critique of Liberalism 52, in New Communitarian Thinking, *supra* note 23. Walzer notes that it is improbable that liberalism "can be replaced by some preliberal or antiliberal community waiting somehow just beneath the surface or just beyond the horizon. Nothing is waiting; American communitarians have to recognize that there is no one out there but separated, rights-bearing, voluntarily associating, freely speaking, liberal selves. It would be a good thing, though, if we could teach those selves to know themselves as social beings, the historical products of, and in part the embodiments of, liberal values." *Id.* at 62.

foundation for maintaining the efficacy of free expression. An open theoretical dialogue may yield rich insights that can enhance our understanding of First Amendment theory. Such an open dialogue is, of course, in the best traditions of the First Amendment.

5

The Public-Private
Distinction
and the New Realism

It is a truism of First Amendment doctrine that the constitutional free speech and press clauses are triggered only by state action. That is, unless state or federal governments take some affirmative steps to limit free expression, the protections of the First Amendment simply do not apply to the case. A corollary is that private actors' attempts to curtail speech generally are not subject to constitutional challenge. Thus, for example, the First Amendment applies to laws passed by the New York state legislature that limit free speech, but not to the *New York Times*'s refusal to print the views of a particular political commentator. As one commentator noted, the state action doctrine essentially asks:

> Under the Constitution, in what situations should government be held in some way
> responsible for harm inflicted by one person or entity (the wrongdoer) upon another

person or entity (the victim)? For purposes of this question, the terms "responsible" and "harm" should receive a broad construction.[1]

Since the time of the *Civil Rights Cases* in 1883,[2] the state action doctrine has largely been interpreted as limiting the reach of constitutional protections to affirmative acts of legislators or other governmental actors.[3]

The state action doctrine as presently articulated is not without its critics.[4] Recently, a number of commentators have challenged the state action doctrine, contending that, both in the First Amendment arena and in other domains of constitutional law, the doctrine is either confused or simply incoherent. Renewing a challenge that has been made since the high tide of legal realism,[5] these commentators contend that private action, no less than state action, can give rise to constitutional violations.[6] These "new realists" do not necessarily claim that private actors are universally converted into state actors. Instead, the claim is often made that the legal background against which private actors suppress speech—including the largely common-law domains of property, contract, and tort law—should be the subject of constitutional analysis in the same way as the affirmative acts of legislatures or other state functionaries. State inaction, no less than state action, should trigger constitutional scrutiny in the proper circum-

---

[1]G. Sidney Buchanan, A Conceptual History of the State Action Doctrine: The Search for Governmental Responsibility, 34 Hous. L. Rev. 333, 336 (1997).

[2]109 U.S. 3 (1883) (holding that the Fourteenth Amendment applied only to state, rather than private, violations of rights).

[3]The reality is slightly more complex, including as it does, in various iterations in the Supreme Court's state action jurisprudence, situations where "because of government involvement, assistance, encouragement, authorization, or delegation, the 'action' of nominally private parties can be fairly attributable to the state." Julian N. Eule and Jonathan D. Varat, Transporting First Amendment Norms to the Private Sector: With Every Wish There Comes a Curse, 45 UCLA L. Rev. 1537, 1544 (1998).

[4]Serious critiques of the state action doctrine have been advanced for many years. *See, e.g.*, Harold W. Horowitz, The Misleading Search for "State Action" under the Fourteenth Amendment, 30 S. Cal. L. Rev. 208 (1957); Charles L. Black, Foreword: "State Action," Equal Protection, and California's Proposition 14, 81 Harv. L. Rev. 69 (1967); Erwin Chemerinsky, Rethinking State Action, 80 Nw. U. L. Rev. 503 (1985).

[5]One might quibble about whether the new realist view is sufficiently "interdisciplinary" to warrant inclusion in this volume. In that regard, it is worth noting that the original legal realist attack on the public-private distinction originated, not in legal theory itself, but from the field of "institutionalist" economics. Neil Duxbury, Patterns of American Jurisprudence 98–106 (1995). In any case, because this view has been appropriated by recent interdisciplinarians and is central to many attacks on classical First Amendment theory, it seems worthy of discussion here.

[6]The "new realist" critique of state action explored here is but one mode of attack on the public-private distinction that is presently being explored by scholars. For example, for a study of the state action doctrine in the context of privatization, *see* Daphne Barak-Erez, A State Action Doctrine for an Age of Privatization, 45 Syracuse L. Rev. 1169 (1995).

stances. As a result, the new realists claim, many innovations that look like First Amendment *violations*, including hate speech regulation, laws mandating public access to mass media, and limitations on pornography, are, in fact, constitutionally required adjustments to the legal status quo.

A brief word about the term *new realist* might be in order. Theorists identified here as new realists do not claim this designation for themselves; it is a category created for purposes of this chapter to describe a variety of scholars of varying viewpoints who subscribe to some version of the views discussed in the previous paragraph. New realists include feminist scholars, critical race theorists, critical legal studies scholars, civic republican theorists and others.[7] While these scholars may differ with each other on a variety of theoretical and doctrinal legal issues, their views seem to converge and create a coherent, if not completely uniform, critique of the failure of contemporary First Amendment jurisprudence to incorporate the realist insight that state action comes in many forms, not the least of which is private actors using state-created property, tort, and contract claims to inhibit the speech of others.

This chapter will first examine the claims of the new realists that the state action doctrine and the constitutional baselines it assumes are incoherent. Next, it will offer a critique that will challenge some of those claims and their assumed implications. Finally, the chapter will offer suggestions for incorporating some of the important insights of the new realists without fundamentally imperiling free speech. It is hoped that the discussion here will clarify an ongoing debate in First Amendment theory and doctrine and demonstrate that while new realist claims certainly have some merit, it may not be wise to extend them as far as their proponents might wish.

The New Realist Critique

The state action doctrine, in essence, means that most commands of the Constitution apply to actions of government, not to actions of private

---

[7]Other legal scholars have recognized similarities in approach among the group this chapter refers to broadly as "new realists." Although, as noted in the text, no claim is made that the position of the new realists is absolutely uniform, sufficient similarities exist that a unified critique such as that presented in this chapter is warranted. *See, e.g.*, Steven G. Gey, The Case against Postmodern Censorship Theory, 145 U. Pa. L. Rev. 193 (1996) (describing the attack of "postmodern censors" on the public-private distinction); Kathleen M Sullivan, Resurrecting Free Speech, 63 Fordham L. Rev. 971, 977–78 (1995) (similar to Gey, but using the term "new speech regulators").

citizens. In the *Civil Rights Cases* in 1883, the Supreme Court considered the meaning of the Fourteenth Amendment and concluded that "it is state action of a particular character that is prohibited. Individual invasion of individual rights is not the subject-matter of the amendment."[8] This continues to be the dominant view of both courts and scholars, although various exceptions exist, including cases where private actors assume public functions or where a private actor's conduct is in some other way attributable to government.[9]

The new realist narrative, which contests the traditional view of state action, often begins with either the legal realist movement of the 1920s and 1930s or with Franklin D. Roosevelt's New Deal. Although the relationship between the realists and the New Deal is a complex question of intellectual history,[10] the assumption is that realist thinking had at least some impact both on New Deal policies and on constitutional law after the famous "switch in time that saved nine," when the Supreme Court in 1937 repudiated substantive due process and the view that the Constitution somehow required laissez-faire economics.[11]

Whatever its provenance, the key insight of this era, according to the new realists, was that law is everywhere, operating even in the "private" realm that is supposedly free of governmental coercion.[12] When legislatures choose not to act, the resulting state of affairs is not some prepolitical, "natural" state, whatever that might mean. Instead, even in leaving existing arrangements and distributions intact—in upholding the status quo—the state is always and already operating, if only through the preexisting common-law regime. Thus, one cannot say, for example, that the state is acting when it redistributes wealth through taxation, but not acting when it declines to do so. Both wealth and the markets that so often create wealth are creatures of the law. Moreover, one cannot assume that the status quo is "neutral," while disturbing the status quo somehow violates

---

[8]109 U.S. 3, 11 (1883).

[9]*See generally*, Buchanan, *supra* note 1.

[10]*See, e.g.*, Laura Kalman, Legal Realism at Yale, 1927–1960 (1986). *See also* Kermit L. Hall, The Magic Mirror (1989) (noting that "The New Deal, while not directly connected to the realist movement, nonetheless displayed in action the kind of pragmatic and instrumental approach to law with which the realists were identified." *Id.* at 271.).

[11]*See* West Coast Hotel Co. v. Parrish, 300 U.S. 379 (1937) (upholding a Washington state minimum wage statute).

[12]Important contributions to this debate from Legal Realists include: Morris Cohen, The Basis of Contract, 46 Harv. L. Rev. 553 (1933); Morris Cohen, Property and Sovereignty, 13 Cornell L.Q. 8 (1927); Robert Hale, Force and the State: A Comparison of "Political" and "Economic" Compulsion, 35 Colum. L. Rev. 149 (1935); Robert Hale, Value and Vested Rights, 27 Colum. L. Rev. 523 (1927).

neutrality. Existing common-law baselines provide no guarantee of neutrality.

Constitutional scholars Louis Michael Seidman and Mark V. Tushnet, in their book *Remnants of Belief*,[13] traced the erosion of the traditional baseline for determining state action to the 1928 Supreme Court case of *Miller v. Schoene*.[14] In *Schoene*, cedar tree growers challenged a Virginia statute that protected the growing Virginia apple industry by permitting the destruction of cedar trees that carried "cedar rust," a threat to apple orchards. The cedar tree growers claimed that statute was a constitutional "taking," which required compensation. The Court, in an opinion by Justice Harlan Fiske Stone, pointed out that the state was acting regardless of whether it passed the statute and allowed the destruction of cedar trees or failed to pass the statute and allowed the destruction of apple trees. "It would have been none the less a choice if, instead of enacting the present statute, the state, by doing nothing, had permitted serious injury to the apple orchards . . . to go unchecked," Stone wrote.[15] Seidman and Tushnet see this brief opinion, with its logic of "none the less a choice," as a conceptual revolution in constitutional law triggered by legal realist thought:

> The cedar tree owners' constitutional objections rested on the view that the Constitution took property law rules as the settled background: They argued that the Constitution bars the government from changing the rules (without paying for the change). The Supreme Court's decision brings the background rules of property law into the foreground and makes them completely subject to redetermination at any point . . .[16]

Legal scholar Cass R. Sunstein makes similar claims when arguing for a "New Deal" for speech.[17] Prior to the New Deal, Sunstein points out, the Constitution was read as prohibiting government from interfering with the "private" and "voluntary" realm of employment contracts, hourly wages, and the like. This era is often symbolized by the Supreme Court's infamous 1905 decision in *Lochner v. New York*,[18] which struck down a New York maximum-hours law aimed at limiting the working hours of bakery

---

[13]Louis Michael Seidman and Mark V. Tushnet, Remnants of Belief: Contemporary Constitutional Issues (1996).
[14]276 U.S. 272 (1928).
[15]*Id.* at 279.
[16]Seidman and Tushnet, *supra* note 13, at 28.
[17]Cass R. Sunstein, Democracy and the Problem of Free Speech (1993). *See also* Cass R. Sunstein, The Partial Constitution (1993).
[18]198 U.S. 45 (1905).

employees. *Lochner*, long viewed as the apotheosis of substantive due process, is equally famous for Justice Holmes' dissenting opinion, which argued that "the fourteenth amendment does not enact Mr. Herbert Spencer's Social Statics."[19] Holmes notwithstanding, the Court used its substantive due process jurisprudence to strike down a number of attempts to regulate economic matters over the ensuing decades, leading to a near-constitutional crisis in 1937 when Roosevelt introduced his "Court-packing plan" in order to alter the ideological composition of the Court. Shortly thereafter, several members of the Court changed sides, and a new majority began voting to uphold New Deal reforms and repudiate the legacy of *Lochner*.[20] Emphasizing the parallels, one critic of current free speech law has referred to "the Lochnerization of the First Amendment."[21]

As Sunstein notes, the New Deal reformers were adamant that private arrangements and economic markets were not immune from regulation. Treating employment relations, for example, as a naturally occurring, pre-political state of affairs into which government could not intrude was absurd because the existing system of legal rules, including property, tort, and contract law, made those relations what they were. As Sunstein put it:

> When the law of trespass enabled an employer to exclude an employee from "his" property unless the employee met certain conditions, the law was crucially involved. Without the law of trespass, and accompanying legal rules of contract and tort, the relationship between employers and employees would not be what it now is; indeed, it would be extremely difficult to figure out what that relationship might be, if it would exist in recognizable form at all.[22]

Moreover, it was equally absurd to treat the status quo as "neutral," while declaring regulation to be "partisan," or to claim that government intervention to change the law was "action" while governmental acquiescence in an existing state of affairs was "inaction." Government was, always and already, acting in a partisan way, even when it seemingly sat on the sidelines. Thus, Sunstein argues, the notion of "status quo neutrality," which holds that neutrality consists largely in leaving existing arrangements untouched, is inadequate.

---

[19]*Id.* at 75.

[20]*See generally* Hall, *supra* note 10, at 271–84.

[21]Morton J. Horwitz, Foreword: The Constitution of Change: Legal Fundamentality without Fundamentalism, 107 Harv. L. Rev. 32, 109 (1993).

[22]Sunstein, Democracy, *supra* note 17, at 30.

All of this clearly has dramatic consequences for the notion of a stable constitutional baseline against which to measure state action. It suggests something in the nature of a gestalt switch from the traditional view of state action, at least in First Amendment law. Sunstein maintains that while the New Deal understanding has infiltrated some aspects of constitutional law, it has yet to be felt to any significant degree in free speech law: "For purposes of constitutional understandings of the free speech principle, contemporary understandings of neutrality and partisanship, or action and inaction, are identical to those that predate the New Deal. The whole category of government 'intervention' is defined accordingly."[23]

Sunstein's "New Deal for speech" thus calls for explicit recognition of these conceptual shortcomings in free speech law. In certain cases, he maintains, government regulation might well promote free speech rather than hinder it. For example, requiring broadcasters to provide free air time for political candidates might promote First Amendment goals rather than impede free speech. Various content controls over broadcasters are not revolutionary, of course. The Supreme Court has upheld public interest obligations imposed on broadcasting stations based upon the scarcity of the electromagnetic spectrum and the governmental licensing of broadcasters.[24] Sunstein, however, raises the possibility of various regulations on newspapers, including access rights, that seem of dubious constitutionality under current law.[25] Given the fact that newspapers, for example, can exclude prospective "speakers" because of property law, Sunstein argues that newspapers are in a sense no less "licensed" by government than broadcasters. Thus a free-speech baseline derived from property law is neither natural and prepolitical nor necessarily neutral.

---

[23]*Id*. at 34. Interestingly, it was, in fact, New Deal era caselaw, in particular U.S. v. Carolene Products, 304 U.S. 144 (1938), that provided firm doctrinal grounding for special protection for individual rights, including free speech, from direct action by the state. Just as the Court was abandoning its laissez-faire economic theory, it was enshrining individual rights as especially protected. *Carolene Products*, with its famous footnote 4, seems to have been self-consciously crafted by the same forces on the Court, most notably Justice Stone, who represent the post–New Deal view for the new realists. Thus, it seems odd to argue that free speech law is somehow infected with a benighted, pre–New Deal conceptual scheme. Another irony, of course, is that the angry dissenter from *Lochner*, Justice Holmes, is also one of the founders of modern, laissez-faire free speech jurisprudence.

[24]*See, e.g.*, Red Lion Broadcasting v. FCC, 395 U.S. 376 (1969). As Lee Bollinger put it, "*Red Lion* . . . reads like a tract that treats the press as the most serious threat to the ultimate First Amendment goal, the creation of an intelligent and informed democratic electorate." Lee C. Bollinger, Images of a Free Press 72 (1991).

[25]*See* Miami Herald v. Tornillo, 418 U.S. 241 (1974).

New realists make versions of this argument in a variety of other speech contexts.[26] Laissez-faire First Amendment jurisprudence is not neutral, but instead grants power to certain speakers or viewpoints while withholding it from others. For example, J. M. Balkin notes that those who favor regulation of racist speech point out that the absence of tort remedies for racist speech is an implicit statement by the legal system of its values. "If the government is unwilling to allow common law causes of action for racial insult," Balkin writes,

> that reluctance is itself an admission that the state is responsible for the balance it strikes between speech rights and the perpetuation of racism—the state has chosen to value the expressive liberty of racists over the feelings of their victims. Put another way, this argument is really the familiar legal realist argument that the public/private distinction between direct state abridgment of rights and private abridgment collapses in particular contexts.[27]

Similarly, government's failure to regulate pornography is "none the less a choice" of a legal regime that eroticizes hierarchy and creates sig-

---

[26]David M. Rabban points out, "In attacking the invocation of First Amendment rights to protect actual inequality against legislation in the public interest and in viewing state regulation as a force for social good, current critics of First Amendment law employ the same arguments that progressives used against the liberal individualism that supported constitutional interpretation during the *Lochner* era." David M. Rabban, Free Speech in Its Forgotten Years 388 (1997). In addition to critics noted in the text, *see* Matthew H. Kramer, In the Realm of Legal and Moral Philosophy: Critical Encounters 112–134 (1999) (defending critiques of the public-private distinction); J. M. Balkin, Some Realism about Pluralism: Legal Realist Approaches to the First Amendment, 1990 Duke L.J. 375 (critiquing both state action doctrine and the public-private distinction); Richard Delgado, First Amendment Formalism Is Giving Way to First Amendment Legal Realism, 29 Harv. C.R.-C.L. L. Rev. 169 (1994). ("If, as a starting point, we posit a perfect marketplace of ideas, then, according to the old paradigm, the current distribution of social power and resources must be roughly what fairness and justice would require." *Id.* at 171.); Owen M. Fiss, The Irony of Free Speech (1996) (discussing the need for affirmative regulation by government to ensure freedom of speech); Charles R. Lawrence III, If He Hollers Let Him Go: Regulating Racist Speech on Campus, in Mari J. Matsuda et al., Words That Wound: Critical Race Theory, Assaultive Speech, and the First Amendment 53, 62–66 (1993) (critiquing both state action doctrine and the public-private distinction); Frances Olsen, Constitutional Law: Feminist Critiques of the Public/Private Distinction, 10 Const. Comment. 319 (1993) (similar to Lawrence); Tona Trollinger, Reconceptualizing the Free Speech Clause: From a Refuse of Dualism to the Reason of Holism, 3 Geo. Mason Ind. L. Rev. 137 (1994) (similar to Lawrence). A significant number of other First Amendment commentators have at least touched on the issue of affirmative government regulation (such as access regulation) to assure freedom of speech, although often with little or no explicit consideration of the state action issue. The *locus classicus* is, of course, Jerome A. Barron, Access to the Press—A New First Amendment Right, 80 Harv. L. Rev. 1641 (1967) (primarily considering statutory grants of access that could be created *consistently* with the First Amendment rather than access *compelled* by the First Amendment, as the new realists suggest). *See also*, Jerome A. Barron, Freedom of the Press for Whom? The Right of Access to Mass Media (1973). One work from the same era that devotes considerable attention to state action issues is Benno C. Schmidt, Jr., Freedom of the Press Vs. Public Access (1976).

[27]Balkin, *supra* note 26, at 381 (citations omitted).

nificant discrimination against women in all corners of the social world—discrimination that "silences" women by making their speech both less likely and less credible.[28] By not regulating pornography, government is allowing the silencing of one group (women), while regulation is simply the silencing of another group (pornographers). Seidman and Tushnet point out that every speech regime is a "subsidy" for some speakers and not for others: "We might, for example, imagine a world in which men and women have equal social power. According to this view, the Constitution might actually *mandate* antipornography regulation as an obligatory means of subsidizing the speech of women."[29] Much the same argument is made in the context of hate speech regulation: hate speech codes shift the subsidy from the racists to their victims.[30]

New realists sometimes reject another baseline in First Amendment thought: the baseline of private preferences. If viewers prefer *South Park* to C-SPAN, if citizens prefer professional wrestling or game shows to reasoned discussion of public issues, why should government disregard those choices? Sunstein's answer is that private preferences, much like newspapers' freedom from regulation, are simply an artifact of the existing system of legal rules. People's preferences are no more natural and pre-existing than is the present distribution of resources in the society: both are shaped by law. Sunstein's claim here seems little different from the familiar notion that human beliefs and desires are "socially constructed" and hence malleable. He places particular emphasis on the notion of "endogenous preferences," a term he uses "to indicate that preferences frequently are not fixed and stable, but instead adapt to a wide range of factors—including the context in which the preference is expressed, the existing legal rules, current information, past consumption choices, and culture in general."[31] Thus, the notion of endogenous preferences casts doubt on status quo neutrality in First Amendment law in a second sense. Moreover, the state action paradox rears its head again: not only does state action in the form of the current legal landscape necessarily shape preferences, but it would be no more and no less a form of state action if government enacted new regulatory regimes to produce "better" preferences.

---

[28]*See, e.g.*, Catharine A. MacKinnon, Pornography, Civil Rights, and Speech, 20 Harv. C.R.-C.L. L. Rev. 1 (1985).

[29]Seidman and Tushnet, *supra* note 13, at 130.

[30]*See generally* Mari J. Matsuda et al., Words That Wound: Critical Race Theory, Assaultive Speech, and the First Amendment (1993).

[31]Sunstein, Partial Constitution, *supra* note 17, at 164.

Doctrinal Vertigo

One immediate difficulty raised by the new realist approach is that it seems to obliterate the public-private distinction[32] and cast the constitutional interpreter into a doctrinal abyss. If everything the state forbids, requires, or permits through its legal regime is public, then everything is public. That being the case, all actions are potentially subject to constitutional scrutiny, not necessarily directed at the private actors themselves, but at the legal system that authorizes those actions. Moreover, the baseline for constitutional decision making is radically altered: the status quo no longer serves as a means to determine if government has infringed constitutional rights. It may be, for example, that government inaction is violative of the First Amendment in a given context, while an elaborate regulatory regime could be constitutionally required to ensure freedom of speech in another. It all depends on how one characterizes the situation. Thus, for those accustomed to a more familiar mode of First Amendment interpretation, a certain doctrinal vertigo may ensue.

It is not entirely clear that the simple insight that the private realm is interpenetrated with public power necessarily carries the theoretical weight new realists ascribe to it. It is true that the so-called private realm is both marked off and maintained by public power, particularly in the form of tort, contract, and property law doctrines. Nonetheless, this realization does not necessarily compel the conclusion that everything surrounding the public-private distinction is up for grabs. If the rationale for creating the private realm is normatively sound—that is, if there are solid political and legal reasons for creating a private sphere where individuals can have autonomy from the coercion of the state and their fellow citizens in certain ways—the simple fact that this sphere is created and maintained by the exercise of public power does not render the distinction either illegitimate or incoherent.[33]

---

[32]For a useful analysis of the distinction, see Alan Wolfe, Public and Private in Theory and Practice: Some Implications of an Uncertain Boundary, in Public and Private in Thought and Practice 182 (Jeff Weintraub and Krishan Kumar eds., 1997).

[33]Matthew H. Kramer points out: "Errors in reasoning, rather than political or moral shortcomings, are the direct targets of the critique of the public/private dichotomy. Of course, anybody who endorses such a critique may proceed to denounce the political or moral shortcomings that have been sustained in part by the errors of reasoning which the critique assails; but the additional step of moral or political chiding is not an integral element of the critique itself." Kramer, *supra* note 26, at 124. *See also* Brian Leiter, Legal Realism, in A Companion to Philosophy of Law and Legal Theory 261, 278–279 (Dennis Patterson ed., 1996).

In any event, even granting the problematic nature of the public-private distinction on which the state action doctrine rests, the new realist critique, by itself, does not compel any particular outcome. In the absence of common-law baselines, some other normative scheme is necessary to provide stability to constitutional doctrine. Sunstein, for example, holds a Meiklejohnian[34] view of the First Amendment as designed primarily to enhance democratic deliberation, and this is the master value he uses to determine what the First Amendment requires, distinct from existing baselines. Thus, even though common-law property rules keep me from forcing my op-ed contribution on the *New York Times*, Meiklejohnian deliberative democracy may require government intervention to ensure that public discourse is enhanced and a diversity of voices heard. Seidman and Tushnet seem to take a similar view, pointing out that "the ultimate question is, Which system of regulation exposes the society to the widest range of views?"[35] Commentators concerned with hate speech and pornography generally seem to regard the eradication of those evils as the primary values driving their First Amendment jurisprudence.

One difficulty with such approaches is that they simply push the problem back to another level: rather than determining if government is abridging speech within the "given" common-law background, courts are now required to contemplate a vast range of possible regulatory schemes to determine which will better serve the requirements of the First Amendment and to make sweeping adjustments to existing social arrangements in order to produce the "best" result. Moreover, the recognition of the new realist insight solves no substantive First Amendment problems. Instead, the new realist attack on state action has no necessary consequences for free speech: deconstructing the public-private distinction does not yield any normative program for change. Thus, the collapse of common-law baselines in no way implies that the existing free-speech regime is constitutionally suspect. It simply suggests that one must look at any given case in a new light—one might still arrive at the same result as suggested by status quo neutrality. One still needs an (almost certainly controversial) grand theory to yield any reasonably determinate result in a given case. To recognize, for example, that the state "acts" through its common-law libel doctrine does not tell us what adjustments to that doctrine the First Amendment requires, if any. One still needs a full-blown First Amendment theory to derive any normative principles or doctrine.

---

[34]*See* Alexander Meiklejohn, Free Speech and Its Relation to Self-Government (1948).
[35]Seidman and Tushnet, *supra* note 13, at 130.

Further, granting the new realist view of state action does not necessarily mean that the state must act to bring private conduct in line with the
state's own constitutionally required neutrality.[36] As Larry Alexander
points out:

> The ubiquity of state action as a conceptual matter does not affect the content of
> constitutional rights and duties. To say, for example, that the realm of the private is
> defined and buttressed by law—state action—is not to say that private choices
> within it are held to the same standards as the Constitution imposes on, say, the state
> police or welfare department.[37]

Alexander goes on to note that the state often has good reasons—and, in
fact, may be constitutionally required—to permit private actors to make
choices the state itself could never make, and on grounds the state could
never employ. For instance, the state may be constitutionally required to
allow people to choose their spouses or their religious faiths on grounds
the state itself could not apply to governmental decisions.

The crucial point is that even though the private realm is, in some
sense, constituted by state action, that does not imply that all choices
made in the private realm must or even should be made on the same bases
on which the state must make its own choices. The fact, for example, that
the state cannot normally forbid speech on the basis of content does not
compel the conclusion that private actors, such as newspapers, should not
do so. This is particularly the case where those private actors are themselves speakers who are exercising First Amendment rights through the
content of their publications. Any such judgment cannot be derived from
the new realists' revised conception of state action: it must come from
some independent value that must be argued for.

The notion that the state must alter the private realm in order to bring
all speech and conduct in line with constitutional values also has some
repellent implications. The private realm has been considered "private"
precisely because many people, including political and legal theorists,
conceive it as a domain the state may not enter without potentially grave
consequences for liberty. The concept of limited government, which has at
least as strong a constitutional pedigree as the new realists' republican
perfectionism, suggests that there are certain zones of private affairs

---

[36]For a discussion and critique of various attempts to do this, including through the use of state constitutional provisions and legislation, *see* Eule and Varat, *supra* note 3.
[37]Larry Alexander, The Public/Private Distinction and Constitutional Limits on Private Power, 10
Const. Comment. 361, 365 (1993).

where both good and bad things may happen, but which nonetheless must be allowed to exist free from governmental oversight and control. While the "private" realm may permit evils such as sexism or racism,[38] it also protects a space in which human flourishing is possible. Without some zones of private action, the power of government seems limitless, because all private actions are ultimately ascribed to the state. As Eric J. Segall pointed out, "this logic could be extended to make the state responsible for every criminal act, because the state has made a 'choice' to allow those people to live outside prison, or perhaps even to live at all." [39] Indeed, another commentator argued that

the sweeping assertion that individuals engaged in ordinary activities on their own behalf, far removed from the business of government, are wielding the power of the state—as though those individuals wore uniforms and badges—merely because their conduct is not prohibited by state law or protected by the Constitution, is a notion disquietingly totalitarian . . . [40]

The new realist version of the state action doctrine suggests a world in which government is responsible for all things—and responsibility implies the power, indeed the obligation, to control. As one commentator put it, the "permission theory," which claims that state inaction is always state action,

reminds me of scholastic brain-teasers about the omnipotence of God. If God is omnipotent, how can we explain the presence of evil in the world? What makes the question hard is the implicit assumption that God is morally responsible for allowing things to happen that he has the power to prevent. According to the permission theory, the state is like God. It is practically omnipotent; there are very few things it can't forbid.[41]

Needless to say, such a view does not comport well with some understandings of the importance of limited government and individual autonomy. The liberal theory that undergirds these understandings assumes that

---

[38]This discussion is addressed primarily to the state action doctrine in the free speech context, and so expresses no opinion regarding notions of state action in cases of private discrimination of various types. It may well be that the evils of discrimination call for a different analysis there than in the speech arena.

[39]Eric J. Segall, The Skeptic's Constitution, 44 UCLA L. Rev. 1467, 1483 (1997).

[40]Frank I. Goodman, Professor Brest on State Action and Liberal Theory, and a Postscript to Professor Stone, 130 U. Pa. L. Rev. 1331, 1338 (1982).

[41]John H. Garvey, Private Power and the Constitution, 10 Const. Comment. 311 (1993).

there must be zones of privacy and autonomy within which individuals can pursue their own version of the good life free from the preferences of those in power. A limited governmental role has been a particular emphasis in modern First Amendment doctrine because of the assumption that government officials cannot regulate speech in anything approaching a neutral manner, in part because of universal human frailty and in part because government officials have a particularly strong incentive to regulate speech in ways that enhance their hold on power.

Of course, new realists generally have no objection to government taking a larger role in the regulation of speech. Their argument is that the government is always regulating speech, and any given legal regime helps some speakers and inhibits others. Thus, government is not assuming a "larger" role when it regulates than when it seemingly sits idly by. This is actually a questionable premise, as legal scholar Robert Justin Lipkin points out. Lipkin argues that affirmative government regulation forecloses options that government "permission" does not:

> When the government forbids an activity, that ends the question of whether the forbidden practice, for example, speech, will legally occur. Forbidding is direct and final intervention. When the government merely permits action, however, it does not require it. An additional act must occur for the action to take place. Consequently, when the private sector "regulates," it does so only after competing private interests vie with one another for the opportunity to regulate. Once the government permits an activity, it has nothing more to do with the causal occurrence of that activity or its common law regulation. In short, the government is then neutral with respect to the occurrence of that activity, and with respect to prospective private regulators.[42]

Lipkin's point makes clear that there is, in fact, an asymmetry between affirmative regulation and permission that might well justify treating those two modes of government activity distinctly for constitutional purposes. In the realm of speech, for example, government regulation might well simply shut down various communicative options, while private domination of the channels of mass communication does not foreclose new and diverse speakers or media from making significant inroads on current distributions of speech "power." The rise of the Internet as a competitor of traditional media is, of course, a classic case in point.[43]

---

[42]Robert Justin Lipkin, The Quest for the Common Good: Neutrality and Deliberative Democracy in Sunstein's Conception of American Constitutionalism, 25 Conn. L. Rev. 1039, 1067 (1994).

[43]Lipkin points to the success of "smaller actors" such as USA Today and CNN, although these examples probably give little comfort to those concerned with present media structures. Id. at 1067.

Ultimately, the new realist First Amendment is an ironic creature that requires extensive governmental regulation to produce "free" speech. New realist Owen Fiss argues that "the State must act as a high-minded parliamentarian, making certain that all viewpoints are fully and fairly heard."[44] Whether we could ever expect the state, through either elected officials or bureaucrats, to perform such a delicate function properly is, of course, highly controversial. The record of speech regulation in the 20th century seems to suggest the contrary.[45]

Finally, it may be worth considering that although the traditional notions of government "action" and "inaction" are characterizations that do not capture the complexities of our legal order, they may be worthwhile heuristics that help us identify problems that are appropriate for courts to attempt to resolve. Frederick Schauer suggests that rethinking "background" assumptions such as property law may be beyond the institutional competence of courts, in part because the complex ramifications of such alterations would be widespread and unpredictable. As Schauer points out:

> Yes, markets are creatures of government, and, yes, existing distributions owe their existence to government action. Yet perhaps neither courts nor constitutional argument in general are particularly well-suited to unscrambling eggs, to readjusting the consequences of large-scale structures whose readjustment is likely to be more difficult than was their creation at the outset. Perhaps, therefore, constitutional argument and judicial review are best suited to dealing with more incremental or peripheral flaws. It may be that courts, for example, are better able to desegregate the public schools than they are to eliminate the racism that pervades so much of so-called private life.[46]

---

[44]Owen Fiss, State Activism and State Censorship, 100 Yale L.J. 2087, 2101 (1991).

[45]*See, e.g.,* Michael Kent Curtis, Critics of "Free Speech" and the Uses of the Past, 12 Const. Comment. 29 (1995); Vincent Blasi, The Pathological Perspective and the First Amendment, 85 Colum. L. Rev. 449 (1985).

[46]Frederick Schauer, Acts, Omissions, and Constitutionalism, 105 Ethics 916, 925 (1995). Schauer's discussion here has echoes of philosopher Karl Popper's distinction between "Utopian social engineering" and "piecemeal" engineering. The latter, which Popper sees as being less sweeping, is also both more effective and safer for human liberty. *See* Karl R. Popper, The Open Society and Its Enemies 157–63 (1963). Among the new realists, Sunstein at least recognizes the dangers of large-scale reinterpretations of property rights, as well as their questionable constitutionality under the takings clause of the Fifth Amendment. Sunstein argues that "the notion that a constitutional provision should protect existing holdings of property from governmental disruption seems not merely plausible, but on the contrary fully justified. That notion protects an important form of stability for individuals and for the system at large. It also creates and safeguards expectations that in turn help promote economic planning, investment, and prosperity. . . . A system in which private property is open to freewheeling public readjustment may well subject all citizens to open-ended state power. This form of insecurity introduces a kind of serfdom that is debilitating to democracy itself." Sunstein, Partial Constitution, *supra* note 17, at 128–29.

Schauer's pragmatic view of the dangers of large-scale modifications of the status quo and the unsuitability of constitutional adjudication by courts as the instrument of such modifications thus suggests an attractive epistemic humility that is lacking in some new realist thought.

The Problem of Historical Understanding

Although "originalist" theories of constitutional law have great difficulties, it is uncontroversial that there is a sense in which fidelity to original understandings must at least inform our interpretation of constitutional provisions in some attenuated way. We may not, for example, wish to interpret the First Amendment as necessarily limited by the subjective intentions of its framers or ratifiers (assuming we could ascertain those intentions), and yet a First Amendment completely cut adrift from historical understandings strikes many as arbitrary and illegitimate. Even granting the protean nature of "public" and "private" under the new realist gaze, if this conception is totally foreign to constitutional tradition, it must at least be suspect for that reason.

It seems reasonably clear that the First Amendment speech and press clauses as originally conceived were limitations on speech-restrictive legislation rather than the common-law "background" that creates the private sphere. Both the historical record and the text of the amendment itself—"Congress shall make no law . . ."—strongly suggest this understanding.[47] The Fourteenth Amendment, now interpreted as applying the First Amendment to the states, has somewhat broader language. That amendment explicitly refers to "any State" as the entity forbidden to deprive persons of life, liberty, or property without due process. Nonetheless, this wording offers no strong support for the new realist interpretation, and, indeed, subsequent free speech doctrinal development is largely to the contrary. As Richard S. Kay puts it:

> Few would argue with the general proposition that, at least in promulgating those rules of the Constitution whose text or history do not evince a broader intent, [the

---

[47]*See, e.g.*, Akhil Reed Amar, The Bill of Rights as a Constitution in The Bill of Rights: Government Proscribed 274 297 (Ronald Hoffman and Peter J. Albert eds., 1997) (arguing that "the amendment's historical and structural core was to safeguard the rights of popular majorities (such as the Republicans of the late 1790s) against a possibly underrepresentative and self-interested Congress"). *See also* Leonard W. Levy, Emergence of a Free Press (1985) (suggesting that the First Amendment as enacted was not understood to alter the common law, but that instead, "[t]he Framers intended the First Amendment as an added assurance that Congress would be limited to the exercise of its enumerated powers and therefore phrased it as an express prohibition against the possibility that Congress might use those powers to abridge freedom of speech or press." *Id.* at 268).

enactors] were not concerned with every action prescribed or permitted by the state, but with the injuries that flowed from the positive employment of the unique power of the state.[48]

Kay further notes: "Persons, property, contracts, and other legal artifices comprised a pre-existing background against which the Constitution was written. They were not its target." [49]

As Kay points out, any other approach suggests that constitutional law is not a variety of "higher" law that applies only to certain affirmative governmental acts. Constitutional law would apply to virtually every situation, because private actions can be recharacterized as artifacts of the present legal regime and thus products of state action. The fact that this view is almost certainly inconsistent with historical understandings of the Constitution must, at a minimum, call the new realist view into question.

The Private Preferences Paradox

New realists sometimes argue that private "speech" preferences are another baseline that can properly be disregarded, depending on the circumstances. Sunstein, for example, points out that "[p]references are often a product of legal rules. They are endogenous to the initial legal allocation of rights."[50] He suggests that private preferences for current television fare, for instance, are artifacts of current broadcast regulation. Because broadcasters operate in a legal regime that largely, although not entirely, protects their chosen content from governmental control, we have the existing state of affairs, complete with *Jerry Springer* and *When Animals Attack*. Again, the new realist approach would caution that this is not an absence of regulation—this is simply a particular regulatory regime that accords broadcasters great autonomy and other potential speakers very little. Moreover, under a different regulatory regime, private preferences would be different as well. "What viewers want" is produced by what is currently available, which in turn is a creature of current regulation. Affirmative governmental steps to provide "better" fare will simply result in "better" preferences.

As if suspecting the objections this proposal may elicit, Sunstein quickly suggested that it is "tempting but inadequate to object that this

---

[48]Richard S. Kay, The State Action Doctrine, the Public-Private Distinction, and the Independence of Constitutional Law, 10 Const. Comment. 329, 342 (1993).
[49]*Id.* at 343.
[50]Sunstein, Partial Constitution, *supra* note 17, at 193.

view embodies a form of 'paternalism' unjustifiably overriding private choices. If private choice is a product of existing options, and in that sense a product of law, the inclusion of better options, through new law, does not displace a freely produced desire."[51] No desires, presumably, are "freely produced" in the same sense that no forms of social organization are "natural" or "prepolitical," and thus free of the taint of existing distributions upheld by law.

Although the actual regulatory modifications Sunstein proposes are relatively modest—better children's programming, free time for political candidates, and the like—the implications of his argument are striking. To the extent that individuals' "preferences" (hence their beliefs, desires, and goals) are a construct of the legal regime, all government must do to reorient those preferences in a better, more democratic direction is to alter that regime. Problems emerge, however, when one begins to think about the issues of who will make such choices and where the criteria for those choices will come from. The preferences argument is, as J. M. Balkin suggested, a "self-devouring" one. Once one accepts that our preferences are shaped by our socialization—are socially constructed by the "private sphere" that emerges from a particular legal regime—where can our elected representatives, themselves victims of the same preference-shaping regime, turn to find the evaluative criteria needed to make judgments about "better" preferences? The best one can expect from such a system would be a battle to impose one's own "better" preferences upon the rest of the citizenry.

Although new realists seem confident about their ability to identify superior preferences, their own argument undercuts their claims. Once one makes this sort of "false consciousness" claim, the theorist is left scrambling to justify his or her own preferences. The problem is reminiscent of reflexive objections to the so-called "strong programme" of the sociology of knowledge. Strong programmers, most notably Karl Mannheim, suggest that all knowledge, including scientific knowledge, is distorted by various social factors, such as class interests. The objection, of course, is that the theory refutes itself: the theory itself is subject to the criticism that its claims are distorted in the same way as the scientific knowledge it criticizes.[52] By emphasizing the arbitrary and legally con-

---

[51]*Id.* at 221.
[52]*See generally* Brian Z. Tamanaha, The Internal/External Distinction and the Notion of a "Practice" in Legal Theory and Sociolegal Studies, 30 Law & Soc. Rev. 163, 172–73 (1996).

structed nature of preferences, new realists, not unlike the strong programmers, are left without the normative means to justify their own preferred brand of speech regulation. The new realists thus saw off the very
branch on which they sit. The problems are both epistemological and
political. Even assuming, *arguendo*, that someone, somewhere—say, Sunstein—did possess the necessary Platonic wisdom, what is the likelihood
that such individuals would actually be in positions of power making such
decisions?

A serious empirical problem with the new realist approach to private
preferences is the emphasis that new realists place on law and the legal
regime as a prime shaper of social reality. The largely unargued assumption is that human nature and attitudes, social organization, and the like
are infinitely malleable and that law is a chief instrument for shaping
them. The objection here does not turn on any particular resolution of the
age-old issue of whether human desires and goals are innate or socially
constructed. Even if social forces are much more powerful than genet-
ics—or indeed are the only operative forces—unless these forces can be
effectively manipulated and controlled to reliably produce certain ends,
the new realist position is untenable. As legal theorist Randy E. Barnett
points out: "Even were the processes of social construction the source of
what is thought of as human nature, if these processes cannot freely be
altered in any desired manner, human nature would still affect the manner
by which we must accomplish our ends."[53] New realists approach the
"preferences baseline" issue as if socially constructed preferences were
relatively simple to adjust, and further, that such adjustments could be
accomplished predictably via law, although they rarely say so explicitly.
This position seems counterintuitive enough that the burden of proof must
fall on the new realists, who have yet to offer very convincing accounts of
why one should accept such a view.

Even aside from these difficulties, the notion of manipulating preferences in order to produce true democracy, as Robert C. Post argues, is
nothing short of a wholesale abandonment of anything approaching
"democracy."[54] Governmental control of speech in order to engineer
"truly" democratic citizens has a somewhat Orwellian ring to it, and it is
in extreme tension with the sort of Kantian respect for individual auton-

---

[53]Randy E. Barnett, A Law Professor's Guide to Natural Law and Natural Rights, 20 Harv. J. of L. &
Pub. Pol. 655, 661 (1997).
[54]Robert C. Post, Meiklejohn's Mistake: Individual Autonomy and the Reform of Public Discourse,
64 U. Colo. L. Rev. 1109 (1993).

omy that seems to underlie much First Amendment theory and doctrine. Political philosopher Isaiah Berlin noted:

> This is the argument used by every dictator, inquisitor, and bully who seeks some moral, or even aesthetic, justification for his conduct. I must do for men (or with them) what they cannot do for themselves, and I cannot ask their permission or consent, because they are in no condition to know what is best for them . . .[55]

The contention here is not that the new realists have such goals in mind—from their writings, they seem genuinely concerned with positive social change—but that accepting their principles opens the way for the less scrupulous to subvert the very notion of democracy.

Extending *Sullivan*

As the new realists have noted, the state action problem and the resulting baseline issues are not purely academic questions in First Amendment theory. The Warren Court touched on these issues in its landmark 1964 libel decision, *New York Times Co. v. Sullivan*,[56] which is often considered one of the most important First Amendment decisions of the 20th century. New realists sometimes cite *Sullivan* as providing a foundation for their criticisms of current constitutional baselines.[57] Although *Sullivan* does offer some support for the general idea of scrutinizing background common-law regimes, the analogy between it and the more sweeping prescriptions of the new realists is often strained. As this section will discuss, *Sullivan* simply does not support the kind of free-ranging governmental role that new realists often propose.

In *Sullivan*, the Supreme Court overturned Alabama trial and appellate courts that had upheld a libel judgment against the *New York Times* and others based on a civil rights advertisement that appeared in the *Times*. The plaintiff, L. B. Sullivan, was a Montgomery police commissioner who claimed that references in the ad to illegal actions by police and other "Southern violators of the Constitution" defamed him. The Court held that common-law libel rules in Alabama (and numerous other states) violated the First Amendment. Specifically, strict liability for

---

[55]Isaiah Berlin, Four Essays on Liberty 150–51 (1970).
[56]376 U.S. 254 (1964).
[57]*See, e.g.*, Sunstein, Democracy, *supra* note 17, at 38–41.

defamation was unconstitutional in a case involving a public official because the rule inhibited public discourse about government. Instead, First Amendment considerations required plaintiffs who were public officials to establish a significantly higher level of fault: actual malice. *Sullivan* is a clear example of at least part of the new realist view in practice: the baseline common-law tort rules for protecting reputation were found to violate the First Amendment despite the absence of any "affirmative" state action other than the state courts' application of those common-law rules in a civil suit between private parties.

Despite the seeming happy coincidence between *Sullivan* and the views of the new realists, the case does not offer as much support for new realist claims as it might appear to at first glance. Although no claim is made here that *Sullivan* is the ultimate repository of all First Amendment wisdom, it may be useful to compare the relatively modest view of the state action doctrine suggested in *Sullivan* with the more extreme innovations advanced by the new realists.

First, *Sullivan* clearly illustrates a core new realist insight: state action is found not only in affirmative legislative or regulatory action. The background common-law rules—here, strict liability in defamation cases—must meet First Amendment standards as well. In *Sullivan*, there is a direct relation between the legal rule (strict liability in defamation) and the inhibition of important political speech about government officials. The speaker still must provide his or her own forum for the speech, but the inhibition—the "chilling effect"—of the common-law regime is regarded as state action and thus subject to constitutional remediation.

Compare this situation with Sunstein's claims for a right of media access. Sunstein argues that those seeking access to various media to present their views are not seeking any "positive" liberty. On the contrary, access proponents claim that trespass law (a common-law form of state action) is restricting their negative liberty to speak. Sunstein argues that the access advocates do not seek government assistance—they wish to eliminate government *interference*, through the law of property, with their speech rights.

One can certainly characterize the situation this way, and at first glance there is a certain analogical connection with *Sullivan*, but the analogy seems strained. Under current First Amendment doctrine at least (which certainly does not limit Sunstein as normative theorist), trespass law is not a form of state action that First Amendment rights override. In *Amalgamated Food Employees Union Local 590 v. Logan Valley Plaza,*

Inc.,[58] the Supreme Court, on first impression, held in 1968 that a union had a right, under the First Amendment, to picket a store in a private shopping center. In 1976, however, the Court overruled *Logan Valley* in *Hudgens v. NLRB,*[59] in which the Court concluded that speech on privately owned property is not protected by the First Amendment. Whether or not one agrees with the holding in *Hudgens,* this line of cases[60] is certainly a much closer call in terms of state action than is the question of access to print media. In the shopping center cases, the argument is essentially that the shopping center or mall is closely analogous to traditional public fora such as parks, streets, and the like. In fact, the argument often goes, privately owned shopping centers and malls have effectively replaced these traditional, government-owned public fora as gathering places for citizens. As a result, private property of this sort should be treated *as if* it were government-owned property, in which case all of the protections for speakers in a public forum would apply.[61] This argument has its strengths, but even if one accepts it, it does not follow that privately held media companies should likewise be treated as public fora. The columns of the *New York Times* are much less obviously analogous to parks and streets than are the corridors of the Mall of America.[62]

Moreover, another key difference between shopping centers and newspapers is that the latter are, in the very creation of the forum, engaged in speech. While a shopping center might metaphorically be said to "speak" to its intended audience through its very existence, its architectural design, its layout, and the like, a newspaper is literally engaging in protected speech in the very creation of the space new realists wish to appropriate. Allowing speakers with diverse views at the mall might disrupt business in some fashion, but allowing "trespassers" in "editorial

---

[58] 391 U.S. 308 (1968).

[59] 424 U.S. 507 (1976). The Court has held, however, that the states may grant state constitutional rights for speakers to protest on private property. PruneYard Shopping Center v. Robins, 447 U.S. 74 (1980).

[60] Even *Hudgens* appeared to acknowledge there were cases in which a private property owner might step into the shoes of the state. In such cases, the First Amendment might well override trespass law. *See, e.g.,* Marsh v. Alabama, 326 U.S. 501 (1946) (a company town could not exclude Jehovah's Witness since the town, while private property, was performing a "public function" and fulfilling role of a municipality; thus state action was present).

[61] For a good discussion of these arguments, see Steven Helle, Essay on the Bill of Rights: Whither the Public's Right (Not) to Know? Milton, Malls, and Multicultural Speech, 1991 U. Ill. L. Rev. 1077, 1088–1093 (1991).

[62] For a discussion of early cases reaching the conclusion that private print media are not state actors, see Schmidt, *supra* note 26, at 107–112.

space" would result in a much more direct and immediate interference with speech that is already in progress: the speech of the publisher. As will be discussed more fully, a legal theory of this sort would lead courts into the questionable territory of balancing the importance of the speech of one speaker against that of another speaker. Thus, the trespass argument seems considerably weaker in the newspaper access case than in the shopping center cases.

Sullivan and newspaper access claims are different in important ways as well. In *Sullivan*, the plaintiff's claim encompassed, and would, theoretically, have sought to punish *all* libelous speech about him, in any medium. Thus, there is a "breadth" issue with libel claims that truly imperils certain varieties of speech. In the newspaper access context, on the other hand, the newspaper presumably has little desire to stop speakers from speaking altogether—the newspaper simply wants to prevent speakers from impinging on *its own* speech. Ample alternatives are clearly available for the spurned op-ed contributor, as new media developments such as the Internet make abundantly clear. The newspaper, unlike L. B. Sullivan, enlists the help of government to prevent speech only in one place—its own columns—rather than punish it in all places, as in a libel claim. The newspaper's objections are largely content-neutral,[63] while the libel plaintiff's goals are closely related to the content of the speech in question. This content-driven aspect makes the libel plaintiff a significantly greater danger to free speech than the newspaper.

Not only do L. B. Sullivan and similar libel plaintiffs seek to squelch libelous speech based on its content and in all fora, they do so in a way that steps into the shoes of government much more directly than any newspaper seeking editorial autonomy. The facts of *Sullivan* may be viewed as quite close to traditional notions of state action in that the plaintiff in *Sullivan* was a public official bringing the action in order to stifle criticism of the performance of his governmental duties. In *Sullivan*, a state official was attempting to use tort law to accomplish that which he could not through the application of some civil or criminal action on behalf of the state itself: the halting or punishment of the political speech of critics. Indeed, Justice Brennan's opinion commented on the case's close relation to the law of seditious libel. Seen in this light, *Sullivan* is quite close to "genuine" state action in the traditional sense, and the application of First Amendment

---

[63]Clearly, an editorial decision not to publish a particular contribution might well be content-based, but the larger First Amendment objection of newspapers to compelled access is based more generally on editorial autonomy than on content considerations.

principles to the common-law regime that allows such action is less revolutionary than it might appear. *Sullivan*'s later progeny have departed somewhat from this model, but the progenitor itself does not provide as much support as the new realists might like for their position.

An additional problem with the new realist view is that the entire notion of the First Amendment overriding "property" law in the media access context is really a rhetorical gesture that cannot be meaningfully operationalized at the level of common-law doctrine. Unlike the *Sullivan* scenario, it is difficult to imagine any court actually striking down or altering the law of trespass on First Amendment grounds in the media access context. In *Sullivan*, libel law itself was fundamentally reinterpreted, with a constitutional gloss put on common-law rules in order to meet the strictures of the First Amendment. The law of libel was a direct infringement of political speech when enforced through state courts. In the access context, Sunstein's argument is purely an "in principle" argument: he does not literally intend, presumably, for courts to alter existing trespass law. What would such an alteration look like? "No one shall be liable for trespass in the newsroom of the *New York Times* if the actor actually intends to engage in protected speech?" One envisions a brawl among trespass-immunized "speakers" at the newspaper editor's terminal as the final version of the editorial page is sent off to the composing room. This admittedly silly fantasy makes clear that Sunstein does not intend any actual revision of trespass law based on First Amendment standards: his invocation of "property law" as violating free speech is abstract and formal, and it is not really analogous to the legal posture of the *Sullivan* case. Sunstein presumably wants courts to create affirmative access rights; such doctrine would have no direct relation to trespass law other than in a purely theoretical sense. For the common law to actually violate the Constitution, as in *Sullivan*, specific doctrines of the common law must be judged on constitutional standards and modified appropriately. Only by looking at specific portions of legal doctrine can one appropriately determine if the First Amendment has been violated: the level of abstraction at which Sunstein operates does not comport with the kind of fact-specific constitutional review exemplified in *Sullivan*. Instead, Sunstein's approach allows great latitude for the courts to reach various results with "in principle" arguments about existing legal arrangements.

Trespass law is arguably not even an appropriate category with which to analyze the problem—it is aimed at the exclusive possession and control of physical spaces, not at the ability to inject one's own communications into a particular medium. The critical aspect of content control at the *New York Times*, for example, is not based on one's right to be physically present in the newsroom. If this were so, the janitorial crew at the *Times*, who are certainly not trespassers, could presumably insert copy into the paper with impunity.

All of this points to the fact that, even if one accepts a modified view of state action, there is no concrete common-law rule that prevents non-editors from placing their copy into the newspaper. In the Supreme Court's state action jurisprudence generally, government has only been held to authorize a private act if it enforces the legal right to perform that act in the courts in some concrete way.[64] Since a right to be on the premises is not the same thing as a right of access, and since some sort of immunity from trespass law seems problematic in any event, Sunstein's approach seems unpersuasive.

Sunstein's suggestion, and those of other new realists who advocate access rights, also differs from *Sullivan* in that it allows courts to balance the free speech rights of one speaker against those of other speakers. In *Sullivan*, the balance was between a speaker (the *Times*) and the reputational interests of public officials. This reputational interest, while unquestionably important, had no constitutional dimension and did not involve competing speech by the defamed individual. In the newspaper access scenario, on the other hand, the new realist view presumably requires courts to balance the newspaper's free speech rights against those of the speakers seeking access to news or editorial columns. This sort of balancing would raise difficult questions: what, precisely, does the First Amendment mean in the newspaper context? Has one been allowed to "speak" simply by having one's political views set in type and placed somewhere between the front page and the classifieds? Or is the entire newspaper a seamless kind of speech—from news judgment on inclusion or placement of stories, through editorial decisions within stories, and the content of the editorial page—that requires coherence and editorial oversight over the entire product to constitute effective "speech" at all? Is removing the editorial control from portions of the newspaper simply "opening up" the opportunity for diverse views, or is it something like requiring a public speaker to interrupt her own prepared text every sentence or two in order to allow someone else to make some (possibly related) point? In the latter case, is the speaker even being allowed to "speak" at all?

---

[64] *See generally* Buchanan, *supra* note 1, at 705–6.

Moreover, at what point, exactly, does one become a speaker who will be required to give up control of a portion of one's speech to another? Is it simply when one owns a large, prosperous newspaper? What about a struggling start-up paper that may depend on editorial coherence for its economic life or a private citizen's Internet Web page? Would the latter forum be unavailable for access because of a need to protect the integrity of the speaker's "speech" or because it presumably would not reach a large audience and is thereby trivial? These sorts of issues raise disturbing questions about the intrusiveness of some new realist prescriptions.

New realist claims about hate speech and pornography are even less analogous to *Sullivan*. Assuming *arguendo* the empirical claim that hate speech or pornography silence some potential speakers, the affirmative act that brings about that silencing is itself speech, albeit often deplorable speech. For instance, racist speakers, unlike L. B. Sullivan, are not actively employing the machinery of state courts to punish the speech of others. They are simply exercising their own First Amendment rights and, in the process, perhaps either creating hesitancy in other potential speakers or creating a climate in which certain speakers may be taken less seriously. One can deplore such speech and at the same time question whether dramatic alterations in First Amendment doctrine are appropriate. When the common law permits a civil cause of action to inhibit speech, as in *Sullivan*, the assumption is that potential legal liability will be a significant hindrance to protected speech, and that the legal regime created by the state must bear significant responsibility for that chilling effect. When the common law (or the Constitution itself) simply permits one speaker to engage in discourse that may discourage other speakers, it is less clear that a similar level of state responsibility is present. While it may be argued that the difference is one of degree rather than kind, it still seems clear that courts may rightfully resist ascribing to the state sufficient responsibility to require affirmative steps to adjust the legal playing field. Of course, if one accepts the new realist argument that state inaction is always equivalent to action, the issue may be a closer call, but that argument seems questionable. The added disincentive to that course is the fact that one would have to engage in some sort of balancing of the speech involved— the value of the "spoken" speech versus that of the "silenced" speech— which seems almost guaranteed to lead to content preferences of exactly the sort that most First Amendment doctrine counsels against.

First Amendment Baselines Reconsidered

The preceding sections have discussed some of the weaknesses of new realist approaches to the First Amendment. It seems apparent that there are difficulties with reconceiving First Amendment baselines as the new realists advocate. However, it is also clear from cases such as *Sullivan* that the issue of constitutional baselines is not one that can easily be resolved by an unquestioning acceptance of the common-law background that underlies the private realm of speech. For example, *Sullivan* makes clear that it simply will not do to limit the concept of state action to the affirmative acts of government while simply taking the common-law background as given. This section will attempt, in a tentative fashion, to set forth a number of suggestions for dealing with constitutional baseline issues, drawing on the critiques of the previous sections.

First, in order to find state action, it seems clear that government must "act," either through constitutional, statutory, or common-law authority. This requires government enforcement through courts of some *specific* provision of law that suppresses speech. Thus, the First Amendment should not be triggered by vague generalizations about "property" law in the abstract or by protean claims that the world would somehow be different if a different background regime were in place. This sort of open-ended theorizing lacks the specificity necessary to produce sound incremental changes in current law while preserving justifiable expectations and social stability through existing legal rules. It is also, at least arguably, beyond the competence of the judiciary. This requirement of specific, identifiable harms caused by precise portions of legal doctrine also entails recognition that government is properly responsible at some level for private acts it prohibits or compels, but not those it merely permits, unless it also enforces those "permitted" activities through specific court enforcement. Such a requirement recognizes some private zone of liberty and discourages reflexive government intervention into every realm of life. As one commentator pointed out, in current state action doctrine, the "litmus test" is whether "the legality of the private action is sustained when that action is challenged in specific court proceedings."[65] Thus, a finding of state action should not be arrived at without specific common-law rights enforceable in courts of law.

Of course, it should be clearly noted that a finding of state action is a necessary, but not sufficient, condition for a First Amendment claim to

---

[65]*Id.* at 765.

succeed. Even if state action is found when one private party is using common-law remedies that prevent another private party from speaking, that is not the end of the inquiry. The First Amendment claim may still fail because, for example, the common-law interest being vindicated is particularly strong and the effect on speech is only incidental.

Second, there should be an identifiable, willing speaker whose speech is suppressed in order to trigger a finding of state action in suppressing speech. This requirement eliminates broad "silencing" arguments that claim a kind of generalized harm to First Amendment values without pointing to a specific "speaker" who has been silenced. The suggestion here is a kind of First Amendment "methodological individualism" that takes the unit of constitutional analysis to be individual speakers rather than groups or aggregates of various types. One advantage of this approach is that problems of proof and evidence are minimized: courts can restrict their attention to flesh-and-blood "speakers" who are able to establish how state action, broadly defined, abridged their speech. It avoids the potential problem of courts attempting to base constitutional analysis on controversial sociological theories about how groups are affected by various alleged speech-abridging activities, such as pornography. Moreover, this approach involves a frank recognition that broad "silencing"claims are often advanced simply as a way to restate what are fundamentally concerns with equality, but to do so in a way that acquires the strategic advantage of free speech claims. As Frederick Schauer noted, silencing arguments are often designed to serve this sort of strategic function rather than reflecting genuine First Amendment concerns. Schauer pointed out that

> if speech itself can be characterized not only as denying equality but also as denying speech, the argument from silencing moves to the rhetorically higher ground of seeing the speaker as censor, the talker as silencer. The political and rhetorical cachet of appeals to free speech makes it important to characterize, if at all possible, one's claims as based on the right of free speech. . . . As a matter of rhetorical strategy, the silencing argument can be seen as an attempt to compete for the high ground of anti-censorship in the free speech versus equality debate.[66]

First Amendment methodological individualism is one way to distinguish genuine First Amendment claims from such dubious characterizations.

---

[66]Frederick Schauer, The Ontology of Censorship in Censorship and Silencing 147, 152 (Robert C. Post ed., 1998).

Third, and related to the second point, courts should avoid, to the extent possible, "balancing" the rights of speakers against each other. Free speech is not, and should not be, a zero-sum game. It may be better in such circumstances to avoid a finding of state action and let speakers' ideas simply compete in the marketplace of ideas, even if that marketplace is something less than a level playing field for speakers based on disparities of wealth. The Supreme Court rightly suggested that balancing speech rights is dangerous, noting that "the concept that government may restrict the speech of some elements of our society in order to enhance the relative voice of others is wholly foreign to the First Amendment."[67] This balancing of speech rights is problematic in a variety of ways. First, it almost inevitably involves government in content distinctions that are questionable. Rather than maintain some approximation of neutrality between speakers (even accepting the new realist argument that absolute neutrality is not possible), direct balancing of speech rights is a much more invasive and content-driven methodology than current First Amendment jurisprudence. This seems to offer a dangerous warrant with which courts and other governmental actors can police the expressive realm for "benevolent" purposes. Moreover, it can lead to a constitutional version of an infinite regress, in which everyone who is allowed to speak, in whatever mediated or unmediated manner, can be accused of silencing someone or not permitting others access to the particular medium, forum, or other locus of speech. A much preferable approach may be simply to accept, for instance, some property law baselines as given. Current baselines in general do enable some speakers more "reach" for their speech than others, but for the most part they do not actually stop anyone from speaking. Even if one does not own a printing press or hold a broadcast license, there are numerous alternate ways to get one's message out. Technological advances from desktop publishing to the Internet suggest the development of an increasing convergence between individual communication and "mass" communication that may eventually render those distinctions less meaningful.[68]

Finally, the same concerns about government involvement weigh even more heavily against empowering government to adjust "preference baselines." As already discussed, the problems here range from the possibility and precision of such adjustments to the motives of governmental actors who might seek to make them. The suggestion that government reg-

---

[67]Buckley v. Valeo, 424 U.S. 1, 48–49 (1976).

[68]See Matthew D. Bunker and Charles D. Tobin, Pervasive Public Figure Status and Local or Topical Fame in Light of Evolving Media Audiences, 75 Journ. Q. 112, 116–18 (1998).

ulation (or lack of regulation) has produced current preferences, and that government regulation thus ought to be employed to produce better preferences, seems to overstate the power of any legal regime to socially construct preferences. Even if somewhat descriptively accurate, the argument essentially requires an abandonment of notions of democracy and individual autonomy that are central to First Amendment history and doctrine.

Although the new realists typically make much of the death of *Lochner* and the New Deal recognition of the artificiality of the public-private distinction, one key distinction between economics and speech should not be forgotten. New Deal regulation of private employment relationships and economic matters more generally is quite different from government regulation of the marketplace of ideas. Government officials often have no particular stake in the regulation of economic markets, other than perhaps the usual interest of lawmakers in helping their supporters and campaign contributors. The incentives may be quite different in regulating speech: illiberal regimes from time immemorial have used control over expression to suppress dissent and silence opposing voices. As legal scholar Kathleen M. Sullivan pointed out in an article emphasizing the asymmetry of speech and markets, "incumbents unfettered by term limits might stand united on one principle: suppress information or controversy that might lead voters to drive them from office."[69] There may be sound reasons why the Supreme Court routinely examines most economic regulation with mere rationality review, while saving heightened forms of scrutiny for issues of civil liberties.

Even more fundamentally, the new realist view is a dramatic reorientation of First Amendment theory and doctrine because it shifts the emphasis from the individual rights of speakers to overall social policy goals. The First Amendment thus ceases to protect individual speakers, no matter how misguided, and becomes an instrument of redistributing channels of communication and reeducating a recalcitrant citizenry. New realists seem eager to destabilize baselines because that shift facilitates the move from the rights of speakers toward a broader utilitarian calculus that can enhance or limit speech in terms of its contribution to deliberative democracy, the eradication of sexism or racism, or the production of a diversity of nonmainstream political views. While such values may certainly be highly desirable in the abstract, the price the new realists ask us to pay may simply be too high.

---

[69]Kathleen M. Sullivan, Free Speech and Unfree Markets, 42 UCLA L. Rev. 949, 961 (1995).

CHAPTER

6

The Normative First Amendment

Should constitutional jurisprudence employ the vocabulary and method-ologies of moral philosophy? This question is central to an important and recently revived debate within legal theory. As legal theory has increas-ingly turned to the theories and methods of other disciplines, a number of important theorists have explored the role of moral philosophy in legal reasoning. Although law and morality have long been viewed as inter-twined in some manner (at least by some theorists), the recent debate presents a more nuanced view of that relationship. On one side, propo-nents assert that the apparatus of moral philosophy is inseparable from sound constitutional law. On the other, opponents claim that moral philosophy is both indeterminate as to results and illegitimate as a means to derive constitutional doctrine. These debates often go to the heart of the proper definition of "law" and the appropriate mode of interpreting our Constitution.

In one sense, it seems obvious that legal reasoning and moral philosophy are two quite different enterprises. Legal reasoning is generally applied to some existing body of law, be it a constitution, a statute, or the more ambiguous realm of the common law. In any event, there are significant constraints on interpretive license, despite the claims of some theorists who assert that law is indeterminate or based upon what the judge had for breakfast. There may, in fact, be zones of discretion or vagueness, but there are also built-in constraints based on history, text, precedent, and other limiting factors. Judges cannot, in fact, bend the materials to reach any result. As John Hart Ely put it: "One doesn't have to be much of a lawyer to recognize that even the clearest verbal formula can be manipulated. But it's a very bad lawyer who supposes that manipulability and infinite manipulability are the same thing."[1] Moral philosophy is generally much more open textured, more subject to the assumptions, premises, methods, and temperament of the philosopher. That is not to deny the existence of moral truths, but simply to note that moral epistemology is uncertain. Perhaps the best way to capture the difference between legal and moral reasoning is that both the premises and many of the legitimate interpretive "moves" are relatively settled in law—despite the fact that judges or scholars may come to different conclusions—while moral philosophers are much more free to innovate as to both premises and methodologies. There are certainly limits within moral philosophy as well: at some point, the philosopher's community may exile her if her work falls too far outside any recognized paradigm. Nonetheless, moral philosophers appear to have significantly greater freedom from interpretive shackles than legal thinkers.

This chapter will first briefly set forth the traditional dichotomy in legal thinking between natural law theory and positivism. Next, it will explore the work of a number of contemporary thinkers who are attempting to explain the nature of the relationship, if any, between law and morality. Finally, the chapter will critique the work of the thinkers discussed and suggest how some of the best features of their work might be integrated for a better understanding of this difficult issue.

---

[1]John Hart Ely, Democracy and Distrust 112 (1980).

Law and Morality

Historically, the relationship between law and morality has been a problematic one. Theorists have often reached dramatically different conclusions as to the links, if any, between these two vital areas of human concern. As one commentator put it:

> In the Western tradition, there are two main approaches to these questions: natural law theory and legal positivism. At first approximation, we can say that natural law theory affirms the existence of a necessary connection between law and morality, while legal positivism denies the existence of such a connection.[2]

Natural law theory, which can be traced to Aristotle and Aquinas, among others, suggests that any given legal code must conform to and be interpreted in light of natural law. The latter may spring from some transcendent source, such as God or, less theologically, from human nature and reason. Natural law, according to this tradition, allows human beings to live good lives in society with others. Further, it applies universally in all times and cultures, based as it is in the dictates of human nature. To the extent that positive enactments of law conflict with natural law, those enactments are not truly "law." Natural law proponents often use the phrase *lex iniusta non est law* ("an unjust law is not law") to make this point.[3] So, for example, the argument has been made that the legal system of Nazi Germany did not truly qualify as "law."

Legal positivism, on the other hand, suggests that legal reasoning is simply the factual and historical investigation of official legal enactments, such as constitutions, statutes, and regulations. This view, associated with thinkers such as Jeremy Bentham, John Austin, and, more recently, H. L. A. Hart, asserts that what the law is on any given issue is based on the authoritative command of the sovereign. Positive law is entirely distinct from what the law ought to be. As early positivist John Austin noted:

> The existence of law is one thing, its merit or demerit is another. Whether it be or be not is one enquiry; whether it be or be not conformable to an assumed standard, is a different enquiry. A law, which actually exists, is a law, though we happen to dislike

---

[2]Andrew Altman, Arguing About Law 33 (1996).
[3]*See* Brian Bix, Jurisprudence: Theory and Context 70 (1996).

it, or though it vary from the text, by which we regulate our own approbation or dis-approbation.[4]

Although positivism may seem a bloodless doctrine, in the hands of a progressive reformer such as Bentham it was a way to cut through the mystification of "common law theology," which tried to defend the social and economic status quo by asserting that the English common law tracked natural law and thus was both inevitable and somehow divinely sanctioned. Bentham also hoped to place the study of law on a more "objective" basis. There is, of course, much variation among the views of thinkers designated as positivists, but the separation of law from morality seems a widely accepted tenet.

A number of theorists have sought a third way, which reconciles the division between morality and law suggested by positivism with natural law doctrine. For example, Lon Fuller proposed that law was more than simply the authoritative command of a sovereign. Instead, it had an "inner morality" that prescribed certain features for something to be properly called law. This inner morality was primarily procedural, and required such features as law that was general, publicly proclaimed, not retroactive, understandable, and relatively constant over time.[5] Fuller's was a morality of form rather than a substantive commitment to a particular moral vision.

Another theorist who has sought to reconcile natural law theory and positivism is Ronald Dworkin. Dworkin, whose work will be discussed in more detail, recognizes the (relatively) objective nature of positivism's "rules" but also posits "principles," based at least in part on moral reasoning, that underlie those rules. These principles apply in hard cases when the rules run out or are less than clear. Moreover, Dworkin's view is premised on judges deciding cases based on *both* the degree of "fit" with past precedent and on a moral component. Together, these two factors produce law as interpreted in its best light.

While the foregoing can only touch on a few of the basic elements of the sophisticated and nuanced debate between positivism and natural law theory, it does give a broad sense of where the battle lines have been drawn. As the brief description of Dworkin's work suggests, some of the debate has moved away from the question of whether law and morality have some necessary connection and toward the question of whether

---

[4]John Austin, The Province of Jurisprudence Determined (H. L. A. Hart ed., 1955).
[5]Lon Fuller, The Morality of Law (1969).

moral philosophy can play a legitimate interpretive role in legal reasoning, even assuming that positive law is in some sense separate from morality. That is, assuming that law and morality are not inextricably intertwined, can the techniques of moral philosophy assist in the explication of such "denaturalized" positive law—in particular, constitutional law? It is to this question that we now turn, first by examining the views of a critic whose answer is a vehement "no."

Posner *contra* Academic Moralism

Legal scholar and federal judge Richard Posner has offered a powerful critique of the use of moral reasoning to answer legal questions. In his recent book, *The Problematics of Moral and Legal Theory*, Posner first attacks the very idea of academic moral philosophy. He then argues that even if the latter attack fails, moral philosophy has nothing to offer jurisprudence.

Posner's attack on moral philosophy *qua* philosophy is hardly novel. He maintains that morality is relative—that moral standards are socially constructed rather than somehow existing independently of human cultures. Thus, moral realism is not an option for Posner—morality is not some mind-independent part of the furniture of the universe. Posner argues that "there doesn't appear to be a universal moral law that is neither a tautology (such as 'don't murder') nor an abstraction (such as 'don't lie all the time') too lofty ever to touch ground and resolve a moral *issue*, that is, a moral question on which there is disagreement."[6]

Posner is particularly critical of what he calls "academic moralists," his label for university professors who peddle various brands of applied ethics in hopes of affecting people's behavior. These hopes are entirely vain, Posner claims, because putative knowledge of the "proper" moral course provides no motivation to follow that course. Unlike Plato's claim that immoral behavior is the result of ignorance, Posner argues that for most people socially constructed moral intuitions, acquired through moral and religious instruction in childhood—or simple self-interest—will almost always trump the abstruse reasoning of the academic moralists. Thus, whether the philosopher is a utilitarian, a Kantian, a Rawlsian, an Aristotelian, or what have you, the academic moralist can have little effect on moral practice. "A person's moral code is not a balloon that the philosopher's pinprick will burst; it is a self-sealing tire," Posner notes.[7]

---

[6]Richard A. Posner, The Problematics of Moral and Legal Theory 19 (1999).
[7]*Id.* at 41.

In any event, the academic moralists' narrow training is not a recipe for moral innovation. "And even if it were," Posner writes,

> there is so much disagreement among academic moralists that their readers (who are in any event few outside the universities) can easily find a persuasive rationalization for whatever their preferred course of conduct happens to be. Indeed, moral debate entrenches, rather than bridges, disagreement. Exposure to moral philosophy may in fact lead educated people to behave *less* morally than untutored persons by making them more adept at rationalization.[8]

Academic moralists do not bring about significant moral change. That role, Posner claims, is filled instead by what he calls "moral entrepreneurs." Moral entrepreneurs (Posner cites Jesus Christ, Jeremy Bentham, and Martin Luther King, Jr., among others) do not use moral theory to persuade others to follow their lead. Instead, they use emotional appeals, charisma, and other nonrational devices to bring their audiences around. Moreover, successful moral entrepreneurs often succeed when social conditions are changing sufficiently to render existing moral codes anachronistic or dysfunctional in some way. Thus, for example, Lincoln and King succeeded as moral entrepreneurs at times when slavery and segregation, respectively, were already becoming anachronistic. As Posner puts it: "Successful moral entrepreneurs are like arbitrageurs in the securities markets. . . . They spot the discrepancy between the existing code and the changing environment and persuade the society to adopt a new, more adaptive code."[9]

Even if one refuses to accept Posner's position on the indeterminacy and impotence of academic moral philosophy, he argues that moral philosophy should not be applied to legal decision making, either directly or indirectly. After briefly exploring the theoretical positions of Hart, Dworkin, and Jurgen Habermas, Posner examines the overlap between law and morality. The extent of this overlap is often wildly overstated, he claims. It is true, Posner acknowledges, that law and morality often share a common subject matter, such as the culpability of one who harms another, the obligation to keep promises, and the like. However, this common subject matter simply means that morality and law "are parallel methods, the first being the earlier, for bringing about the kind and degree

---

[8]*Id*.at 7
[9]*Id*. at 44.

of cooperation that a society needs in order to prosper."[10] The commonalities do *not* mean that the techniques of reasoning of one method of social control are appropriate for making decisions in the domain of the other method. Moreover, Posner points out, law often does not enforce moral obligations, and many legal obligations have no particular moral valence. Law may, for historical reasons, have borrowed some of the vocabulary of morality (such as "fair," "unjust," and the like), but these borrowings are simply fortuitous and reflect no deeper connection.

Posner also briefly considers whether the Framers of the U.S. Constitution, as good followers of the Enlightenment, may have intended that the Constitution be interpreted in light of moral philosophy, but he finds no evidence for this proposition. The Framers may well have been influenced by Locke and others, but Posner argues that there is no warrant for thinking they intended the document to be interpreted philosophically. "Notions such as toleration or equality can be given a philosophical or religious construal—or they can be treated as policies instrumental to various social goals such as peace, strength, prosperity, and the conciliation of the disaffected," Posner writes. "It is open to question whether Locke was the inspiration or the rationalization for the thought of the American revolutionaries."[11]

Moral theory, then, is not the answer. Posner instead advocates what he calls "pragmatic adjudication," which he defines somewhat vaguely, but which seems to consist, at least in part, of a good bit of social scientific investigation. Posner is of course well known as a ground-breaking advocate of the economic analysis of law, and thus his pragmatic judge would not neglect the economic or other social consequences of legal rulings. Posner actually prefers that judges delegate the hands-on empirical work to law professors, who would accomplish much more through this research agenda than by "continuing the 200-hundred-year-old game of political rhetoricizing that we call constitutional theory."[12] Pragmatic adjudication also eschews precedent for precedent's sake, preferring to identify case-by-case results that will improve social conditions rather than worship at the altar of *stare decisis*. Pragmatic judges would not ignore precedent, however, both because having a reasonably predictable legal system is one important aspect of sound social policy and because prior decisions are often valuable repositories of wisdom. The pragmatic

---

[10]*Id.* at 108.
[11]*Id.* at 111.
[12]Richard A. Posner, Against Constitutional Theory, 73 N.Y.U. L. Rev. 1, 12 (1998).

judge is decidedly not a system builder, however, and, by definition, not a consumer of academic moral philosophy.

Dworkin's Moral Reading

Ronald Dworkin, who is unquestionably among the preeminent Anglo-American legal theorists of the 20th century, rejects the Posnerian, pragmatist approach, which he labels the "Chicago School of anti-theoretical, no-nonsense, jurisprudence."[13] Although Dworkin's published work spans vast areas of jurisprudence, moral philosophy, and political philosophy, this discussion will focus on several of his most recent articulations of moral philosophy's place in law. One of Dworkin's central arguments is that moral theory is an inescapable part of law, particularly constitutional law. Even more precisely, Dworkin singles out those abstract clauses of the Constitution dealing with such concepts as "freedom of speech," "due process," and "equal protection of the laws," as particularly appropriate for his "moral reading" of the Constitution. (By contrast, very specific constitutional provisions, such as the requirement that the President be 35 years of age, are not appropriate candidates for the moral reading.)

Dworkin begins a recent discussion of these issues by asking what sort of a statement it is if one says, for example, that the First Amendment protects flag burning. Such a statement is not purely descriptive, a straightforward positivist report of an historical reality. Nor is the statement simply predictive—as in, for example, predicting that the Supreme Court would uphold such a right (although the Court in fact has done so by a narrow majority).[14] As Dworkin points out, even if a decision of the Court contradicted one's assertion—either in the past or at some point in the future—one might still assert that the right to burn a flag is protected speech under the First Amendment. This makes sense, Dworkin argues, if we understand legal reasoning to be a "theory-embedded" activity that calls upon the reasoner to engage with a variety of legal, political, and moral principles:

> In practice, you cannot think about the correct answer to questions of law unless you
> have thought through or are ready to think through a vast over-arching theoretical
> system of complex principles about the nature of tort law, for example, or about the

[13]Ronald Dworkin, In Praise of Theory, 29 Ariz. St. L.J. 353, 355 (1997).
[14]Texas v. Johnson, 491 U.S. 397 (1991).

character of free speech in a democracy, or about the best understanding of the right to freedom of conscience and of personal ethical decisions.[15]

It is this engagement with theory, and, in particular, with the moral dimensions of constitutional law, that makes legal statements like the one about flag burning more than simple descriptive or predictive claims.

Dworkin suggests that the search for higher-level principles in the flag-burning case might lead to two quite different principles, which could result in conflicting holdings. The first, which suggests that the First Amendment freedom of speech is based upon fostering a well-functioning democracy, might lead to the conclusion that flag burning is not protected speech because it has little substantive content, other than as a symbolic expression of dissent, and does little to advance reasoned political discussion. The second principle justifies freedom of speech based on a Kantian respect for the equal citizenship of each person and the corresponding duty to respect each citizen's expression, no matter how offensive to the majority. Adopting the latter principle might well result in protecting a right to burn the flag.

The choice of one of these two principles (or other potential candidates) is not arbitrary, nor is it free-standing moral philosophy, Dworkin assures us. The choice of the "better" principle is based upon criteria Dworkin has developed for many years in his work.[16] "Better in what way?" Dworkin asks. "Better interpretively—better, that is, because it fits the legal practice better, and puts it in a better light."[17] That "better light" can be stated as the most morally attractive articulation of principle available. The issue of "fit" requires that the interpreter take the legal background as a given and begin the reasoning process with that background firmly in mind. Putting the material in its best light requires judges to

find the best conception of constitutional moral principles—the best understanding of what equal moral status for men and women really requires, for example—that fits the broad story of America's historical record. It does not ask them to follow the whisperings of their own consciences or the traditions of their own class or sect if these cannot be seen as embedded in that record.[18]

---

[15]Dworkin, *supra* note 13, at 354.

[16]*See, e.g.*, Ronald Dworkin, Law's Empire (1986).

[17]Dworkin, *supra* note 13, at 356.

[18]Ronald Dworkin, Freedom's Law: The Moral Reading of the American Constitution 11 (1996).

In another work, Dworkin uses the analogy of a "chain novel," in which different authors write succeeding chapters, to suggest the judge's role.[19] As the novel progresses, the later chapter authors are increasingly bound by what went before. The analogy nicely suggests the sense in which constitutional interpreters are neither entirely free nor completely constrained by history, text, precedent, and the like. Of course, Dworkin acknowledges, judges or other interpreters can act in bad faith and thus abuse their authority by importing their own idiosyncratic moral theories into the law. Dworkin's "moral reading" of the Constitution, however, assumes the good faith of constitutional interpreters.

Dworkin's moral reading also emphasizes what he terms "integrity," which calls, not only for consistency with past decisions concerning particular constitutional rights, but also for an overarching coherence of the entire Constitution as interpreted. Much as we expect individuals to have "integrity" in their views and actions across a range of moral issues, the Dworkinian judge must achieve a coherent interpretation of the Constitution as a whole. "The adjudicative principle instructs judges to identify legal rights and duties, so far as possible, on the assumption that they were created by a single author—the community personified—expressing a coherent conception of justice and fairness," Dworkin writes.[20] The document must "speak" a coherent moral vision, and when it does not, interpreters may have to reconcile anomalies. This reconciliation may require moving to some higher level principle in order to preserve the integrity of the constitutional vision. Moral philosophy, then, is critical in the sense of deriving the principles necessary to properly interpret the Constitution, although such philosophizing is constrained by the requirement of fit with the text, prior decisions, and the like.

It is important to understand that Dworkin's view, at least on his terms, cannot be contrasted with a positivist exhortation for judges to simply state "what the law is" or "what the rules are." For Dworkin, as for some literary theorists, there is no brute "fact" of what the law is: there is only a preinterpretive "something" consisting of text, precedent, and other factors that an interpreter must actively shape into the object to be interpreted. For many literary theorists, the same holds true for *Hamlet* or *Pride and Prejudice*.[21] As one commentator explained this point:

---

[19] Dworkin, *supra* note 16, at 228–38.

[20] *Id.* at 225.

[21] *See* Stanley Fish, Doing What Comes Naturally: Change, Rhetoric, and the Practice of Theory in Literary and Legal Studies (1989).

Law "as it is," law as objective and non-controversial, is only the collection of past official decisions by judges and legislators (which Dworkin refers to as the "preinterpretive data," that which is subject to the process of constructive interpretation). However, even collectively, these individual decisions and actions cannot offer an answer to the current legal question until some order is imposed upon them, and that order is the choice, the moral and political choice, between tenable interpretations of those past decisions and actions.[22]

This, in turn, means that those jurists and scholars who claim to simply present the law "as it is" are, on Dworkin's terms, being either disingenuous or naive. Judges always and already engage in the moral reading of the Constitution; some simply do not recognize what they are doing or choose to mystify the process. Since some type of "moral reading" is inevitable, Dworkin would prefer to see it performed in the open. "Constitutional politics has been confused and corrupted by a pretense that judges (if only they were not so hungry for power) could use politically neutral strategies of constitutional interpretation," Dworkin writes.

Judges who join in that pretense try to hide the inevitable influence of their own convictions even from themselves, and the result is a costly mendacity. The actual grounds of decision are hidden from both legitimate public inspection and valuable public debate.[23]

Thus, the moral reading is "moral" in at least two senses: it incorporates suitably constrained moral reasoning into constitutional interpretation, and it gives an honest account of how judges actually operate.

Sunstein's Minimalism

This chapter has already noted Judge Posner's objections to the Dworkinian view of moral theorizing in law. Other scholars have also rejected Dworkin's approach, although often for different reasons. Cass R. Sunstein, for example, rejects broad constitutional theorizing by judges in his recent book, *One Case at a Time: Judicial Minimalism on the Supreme Court*,[24] for several reasons. Sunstein, whom Dworkin grouped with Posner among the Chicago School of "antitheorists," argues in favor of deci-

---

[22]Bix, *supra* note 3, at 92–93.
[23]Dworkin, *supra* note 18, at 37.
[24]Cass R. Sunstein, One Case at a Time: Judicial Minimalism on the Supreme Court (1999).

sional minimalism, which he defines as "saying no more than necessary to justify an outcome, and leaving as much as possible undecided . . ."[25] In a work that suggests comparisons with Alexander Bickel's notion of the "passive virtues" of judicial avoidance,[26] Sunstein instead proposes that it is the method of deciding cases rather than the refusal to hear cases that is crucial.[27] Sunstein advocates both "narrow" decisions, which decide no more than the case at hand, and "shallow" decisions, which avoid the discussion of deep theoretical foundations for the particular result.

The virtues of this approach are many, Sunstein suggests. Decisional minimalism facilitates agreement among people (Supreme Court justices, for instance) who have broad theoretical disagreements at the level of fundamental principle. By avoiding first principles altogether, minimalism can increase the chances of reaching some consensus as to the result in a specific case. Sunstein calls this sort of consensus an "incompletely theorized agreement." As Sunstein points out:

> Of course many philosophical debates, including those about law, operate at a high level of abstraction, but the combatants can often be brought into agreement when concrete questions are raised about appropriate law. Kantians and utilitarians might well agree, for example, that speed-limit laws of a certain kind make sense, or that the law of negligence points in proper directions, or that there is no right to kill infants.[28]

Incompletely theorized agreements pave the way to decide specifics without invoking high theory. This strategic avoidance of first principles make sense not only within courts, but in society as well, where citizens may be more accepting of decisions that do not unnecessarily challenge their fundamental moral commitments.

Minimalism also helps to prevent the damage that may attend broad, large-scale rulings. For example, Sunstein cites with approval the Supreme Court's reluctance to promulgate broad principles or decide any more than the case at hand in recent disputes involving the First Amendment and new technologies, including the Internet. By moving slowly, one step at a time, courts are able to see the effects of their rulings and adjust course accordingly. Minimalist courts are able to preserve flexibility when

---

[25]*Id.* At 3.
[26]Alexander M. Bickel, The Least Dangerous Branch (2d ed. 1986).
[27]*See* Neal Devins, The Courts: The Democracy-Forcing Constitution, 97 Mich. L. Rev. 1971 (1999).
[28]Sunstein, *supra* note 24, at 13.

technology or values are undergoing adjustments, or simply when the court is unsure of its conclusions. Broad constitutional or legal pronouncements, on the other hand, can set in stone principles that can, in the long run, cause great harm.

Minimalism has another salutary effect, Sunstein contends, which is related to the previous point. By erecting few jurisprudential monuments and leaving the way forward relatively open, courts give democracy more room to operate. Sunstein argues that

> minimalist rulings increase the space for further reflection and debate at the local, state, and national levels, simply because they do not foreclose subsequent decisions. . . . If, for example, the court says that any regulation of the Internet must be clear rather than vague, and that a ban on indecent speech is therefore unconstitutional simply because it is vague, the Court will, in a sense, promote democratic processes by requiring Congress to legislate with specificity.[29]

Thus, Sunstein claims, appropriate minimalism not only can create space in which democracy can flourish, but it can encourage legislators and other officials to provide careful reasons for their decisions and to be accountable for those decisions. Sunstein therefore argues not for minimalism *per se*, but for modes of minimalism that effectively promote democracy.

Sunstein admits that the decision to issue a minimalist decision must be contextual. In certain contexts, minimalism may lead to unfairness or inconsistent results in similar cases. Minimalism can even undermine the idea of the rule of law by not setting forth sufficiently broad grounds for decision.[30] Despite these drawbacks, an appropriately contextual minimalism will often serve better than more expansive interpretive philosophies.

Other Views

A constitutional scholar who emphasizes modes of argument over explicit moral reasoning is Philip Bobbitt, whose work was discussed briefly in an earlier chapter. Bobbitt's influential book *Constitutional Interpretation*[31]

---

[29]*Id.* at 4.

[30]*See* Antonin Scalia, The Rule of Law as the Law of Rules, 56 U. Chi. L. Rev. 1175 (1989).

[31]Philip Bobbitt, Constitutional Interpretation (1991). *See also* Philip Bobbitt, Constitutional Fate: Theory of the Constitution (1982).

stresses what Bobbitt calls "modalities" of constitutional argument that precede the moral dimension of constitutional adjudication. The modalities are, Bobbitt asserts, "the ways in which legal propositions are characterized as true from a constitutional point of view." He identifies six modalities that function in contemporary constitutional debate:

> the historical (relying on the intentions of the framer and ratifiers of the Constitution); textual (looking to the meaning of the words of the Constitution alone, as they would be interpreted by the average contemporary "man on the street"); structural (inferring rules from the relationships that the Constitution mandates among the structures it sets up); doctrinal (applying rules generated by precedent); ethical (deriving rules from those moral commitments of the American ethos that are reflected in the Constitution); and prudential (seeking to balance the costs and benefits of a particular rule).[32]

Although the "ethical" mode might seem to offer opportunities for moral reasoning, Bobbitt circumscribes its use rather severely. The ethical mode in constitutional reasoning is not the same thing as moral argument. He points out that the prime "ethos" behind the American constitutional system is that of limited government, the assumption that those powers not explicitly delegated to government by the people remain in the private sphere. Thus, in Bobbitt's system, the ethical mode consists largely of reserving certain zones of autonomy to citizens in the private sphere. Other moral arguments, whether they deal with equality, fairness, or other fundamental moral notions, are excluded. As Bobbitt puts it:

> There is no constitutional legal argument outside these modalities. Outside these forms, a proposition about the U.S. constitution can be a fact, or be elegant, or be amusing or even poetic, and although such assessments exist as legal statements in some possible legal world, they are not actualized on our legal world.[33]

The place for moral deliberation comes, in Bobbitt's view, in the individual resort to conscience by the constitutional interpreter. The modalities often suggest conflicting resolutions to constitutional dilemmas; there is no meta-rule for sorting out these conflicts. No constitutional algorithm is available. Ultimately, Bobbitt suggests, the modes of argument set the stage for "the cultivation of our consciences and the rejection of systems

---

[32]Bobbitt, Constitutional Interpretation, *supra* note 31, at 12–13.
[33]*Id.* at 22.

and systematic approaches that, for all their idealism, are finally con-scienceless."[34] Agnosticism about the "objectivity" of the values thus defended does not diminish the process, Bobbitt argues.

> Rather, this agnosticism imposes on us the responsibility to constantly engage in a self-conscious examination of the premises of our decisions. That is the method of American constitutional interpretation, arising no doubt from the agnosticism of the Constitution itself, which studiedly refrains from endorsing particular values other than the structures by which our values are brought into being and preserved.[35]

Thus, for Bobbitt, moral reasoning makes its appearance in the final act, but it does so in a sort of "black box" appeal to individual conscience.

Moral deliberation in constitutional law is appropriate if properly lim-ited, according to renowned constitutional scholar Laurence H. Tribe. In *On Reading the Constitution*[36] Tribe and coauthor Michael C. Dorf emphasize that the constitutional interpreter must avoid both the Scylla of originalism—the view that the meaning of the Constitution must be lim-ited to the subjective intentions of its framers and ratifiers—and the Charyddis of broad interpretive strategies that allow the interpreter to cre-ate his or her own preferred Constitution, free of the actual Constitution as enacted. While agreeing with Dworkin that the abstract clauses of the Constitution require interpretation and moral deliberation, Tribe and Dorf prefer an approach that is cabined both by the specific history of constitu-tional clauses and by the overall structure of the document itself. As Tribe and Dorf note of Dworkin's less constrained approach:

> The moment you adopt a perspective as open as Dworkin's, the line between what you think the Constitution *says* and what you wish it *would* say becomes so tenuous that it is extraordinarily difficult, try as you might, to maintain that line at all. How can one maintain the line—given the ambiguity of the Constitution's text, the plas-ticity of its terms, the indeterminacy of its history, and possibility of making noises in the Constitution's language that *sound* like an argument for just about anything?[37]

Tribe and Dorf caution against "dis-integration," in which the consti-tutional interpreter examines discrete portions of the Constitution without

---

[34]*Id.* at 184.
[35]*Id.* at 184–85.
[36]Laurence H. Tribe and Michael C. Dorf, On Reading the Constitution (1991).
[37]*Id.* at 17.

regard to the entire structure of the document. For example, they point out, Chief Justice Burger once argued that the death penalty was constitutional simply because the Fifth Amendment allowed the deprivation of life, liberty, or property provided that the accused had the benefit of due process of law. That solution ignores the Eighth Amendment's prohibition against "cruel and unusual punishments," and thus offers a "disintegrated" interpretation of the Constitution.

Tribe and Dorf also counsel against the opposite extreme of "hyper-integration," which treats "the Constitution as a kind of seamless web, a 'brooding omnipresence' that speaks to us with a single, simple sacred voice expressing a unitary vision of an ideal political society."[38] Hyper-integration ignores the obvious fact that constitutional clauses were put in place at different times, by different people, and for different purposes. Hyper-integration, which seeks to achieve a single preferred vision on the entire document, is a particular temptation of constitutional theorists, who frequently identify their preferred vision and then selectively ignore all constitutional materials that contradict it. This approach, as Tribe and Dorf note, is a danger for a variety of commentators, including those who recommend a strong dose of moral reasoning in constitutional law.

Tribe and Dorf illustrate hyper-integration by considering whether a constitutional amendment that explicitly empowered Congress to outlaw flag burning could *itself* be struck down as unconstitutional, since it would fundamentally challenge the liberty interest at the heart of the First Amendment. That is, if one sees the protection of liberties such as freedom of expression as a central value of the entire Constitution, perhaps even a validly enacted amendment that contravened such liberties should not be given force by the courts. Tribe and Dorf are sympathetic to the moral and political motivations of such a view, but deny that any such interpretation could be legitimate.

> To be sure, there may be no adequate political *theory* that can reconcile wide-ranging freedom of expression generally with an explicit exception for the United States flag; yet the need for doctrinal consistency does not empower the Supreme Court to ignore the text or the undeniable purpose of a duly enacted amendment. Difficult as the task might be, the Supreme Court would have to go about drawing lines between protected expression on the one hand, and unprotected flag-defilement on the other.[39]

---

[38]*Id.* at 24.
[39]Tribe and Dorf, *supra* note 36, at 26.

While it is not at all clear that Dworkin's approach would reach a different result—after all, Dworkin requires "fit" along with moral reasoning—there is at least a difference in emphasis between Dworkin's insistence on "integrity" and Tribe and Dorf's caveats against hyper-integration. Dworkin seems much more willing to promulgate (or "ascend" to) an overarching moral framework that produces results deductively, while Tribe and Dorf caution against too much of that style of broad theorizing.

Moral Theory in Constitutional Law

While the theorists discussed in the preceding sections certainly are not the only important voices in the debate, their views may provide a worthwhile starting point for assessing the persuasiveness of the case for moral reasoning in constitutional adjudication—and specifically in First Amendment law. The following section will briefly critique some key points and offer some suggestions for integrating moral reasoning in free speech law.

Judge Posner's views, while sophisticated and provocative, seem to elide some crucial points. First, Posner's conflation of the use of moral thinking in law with moral realism obscures rather than advances his argument. Second, Posner's call for pragmatism fails to acknowledge the place that moral considerations almost inevitably must occupy, if only implicitly, in the kind of adjudication he seems to be suggesting. However, Posner's enthusiasm for empirical research seems well founded and might be a useful corrective for some of the armchair theorizing in which many legal philosophers engage.

One difficulty with Posner's view is that his claims about moral realism—the view that questions of morality have "objective" answers—do not really advance his argument with regard to moral reasoning in law. As legal philosopher Jeremy Waldron argues, the fact that one agrees with moral realism does not imply that one should use moral reasoning in legal decisions. In fact, one's view on moral realism or antirealism (such as, for example, varieties of noncognitivism) is irrelevant to the use of moral philosophy in law. As Waldron points out, the existence of moral disagreement does not provide evidence for moral anti-realism: people can disagree about all kinds of things without that disagreement alone proving that there is no "fact of the matter" about which to disagree.

Moreover, the mere fact that one happens to be a moral realist does not significantly advance the case for the use of moral reasoning in law. Dworkin, for example, is an advocate of moral reasoning in law and yet apparently not a moral realist. Waldron notes that in many matters, such as facts about the physical world, when we disagree, there are more or less agreed-upon methods with which to settle those disagreements. While Kuhnians and some other academic critics of science might disagree, most scientists would assert that while there may be substantive disagreements about particular facts or physical processes, basic questions of epistemology and methodology are generally not disputed. This is simply not the case in ethics, as Waldron points out. "Among moralists, there is nothing remotely comparable [to the scientific consensus on method]," Waldron writes.

> Instead each view comes along trailing its own theory of what counts as a justification: utilitarians have one view, Kantians another, Christian fundamentalists yet another, and so on. . . . Yet unlike their counterparts in the scientific community, they share virtually nothing in the way of an epistemology or method with which these disagreements might in principle be approached.[40]

Waldron notes that most moral realists elide this point in their disputes with anti-realists. The realists often simply assert that the antirealists are incorrect, but without specifying how moral facts are to be acquired.

> For a proposition to be a possible object of knowledge, there must be some gesture in the direction of justification for the true belief in question, and in particular a nontrivial sense of justification that would have some connection and sensitivity to the distinction between the genesis of true belief and the genesis of false belief.[41]

Posner presumably would not disagree with this, yet, examined carefully, it suggests that much of his argument about realism is beside the point.

The upshot of this predicament is that moral reasoning in law is no more or less unpredictable or irrational for the committed moral realist than it is for the moral antirealist. Even assuming that moral facts exist in some mind-independent fashion, without some consensus on moral epistemology or method, realist judges will disagree about moral questions just as will antirealist judges. As Waldron noted, if antirealism is correct, moral reasoning in law will consist of the struggle between different judges' merely subjective feelings about morality. If realism is correct, moral reasoning in law will consist of the struggle between different

---

[40]Jeremy Waldron, Law and Disagreement 178 (1999).
[41]*Id.* at 179.

judges' contrasting "beliefs" about moral reality, none of which can be justified satisfactorily because of the absence of any consensus on moral epistemology. Neither realism nor antirealism would be less arbitrary than the other. Thus, the battle between realism and antirealism is, in Waldron's words, "irrelevant" to the issue of moral reasoning within legal thought. All of this suggests that Posner's arguments against moral realism miss a crucial point. In any event, even if there are no objective answers to moral questions, that conclusion alone provides no support for the notion that serious intellectual inquiry and discussion about such matters might not produce better answers—if not "true" answers—than would be engendered by a refusal to engage in such thinking at all.

A more fundamental difficulty with Posner's argument is that his "pragmatic adjudication," at least as he somewhat vaguely describes it, seems a wholly inadequate alternative to moral reasoning in law. In fact, pragmatic adjudication presupposes moral reasoning while explicitly claiming to replace it. Pragmatic adjudication, according to Posner, is future oriented; respectful toward, but not a blind follower of, precedent; anxious to avoid distinctions without differences; and consequentialist with a vengeance. Posner's pragmatist judge "wants to come up with the decision that will be best with regard to present and future needs."[42] The obvious problem with this thin definition is that it begs several questions. "Best" in what way? Using what criteria? Whose "needs," precisely? How are conflicting "needs" to be accommodated? Quite clearly, these value-laden terms call for what can only be called "moral" determinations, which is exactly the sort of inquiry that Posner wishes to eschew. The Posnerian judge must make determinations about both our ultimate values and the appropriate means to achieve them, but is forbidden to consult moral theory. Despite protestations to the contrary, Posner seems to be advocating a form of utilitarianism that he wishes to install at the center of the judicial enterprise without either moral justification for the system itself or moral reasoning about the how it should be operationalized.

Posner is quite sanguine about the vagueness of his formulation. After discussing several examples of pragmatic adjudication, he notes:

> I leave open the criteria for the "best results" for which the pragmatic judge is striving, except that, *pace* Dworkin, they are not simply what is best for the particular case without regard for the implications for other cases. Pragmatism will not tell us

---

[42] Posner, *supra* note 6, at 242.

what is best; but, provided there is a fair degree of value consensus among the
judges, as I think there is, it can help judges seek the best results unhampered by
philosophical doubts.[43]

"Value consensus" seems a rather disturbing and undeveloped substi-
tute for reasoned deliberation. Moreover, the eradication of "philosophical
doubts" might be regarded as an ominous rather than a welcome development. Posner in fact *wants* "doubt" in his system; he asserts that pragmatism *à la* Peirce and Dewey emphasizes doubt as the key force behind
intellectual inquiry. Strangely, however, when it comes to the fundamental
values that drive the entire system, Posner wishes to fall back upon an
unreflective conventionalism. Dworkin has written that Posner's pragmatism "is empty because it instructs lawyers to attend to facts and consequences, which they already know they should, but does not tell them
which facts are important or which consequences matter, which is what
they worry about."[44] Posner's answer here is in some ways similar to
Bobbitt's, and similarly unsatisfactory. Where Bobbitt inserts the black
box of "conscience," Posner inserts "value consensus." Neither chooses to
delve too deeply into what those vague solutions will mean in practice.

At times, Posner seems to flirt with the naturalistic fallacy, by assuming that once enough empirical facts are assembled, the way forward will
be clear. However, in the constitutional realm, as elsewhere, one cannot
derive "ought" from "is." The fact that a judge knows, for example, that
social scientific research suggests a causal link, for some individuals,
between consumption of violent motion pictures or video games and subsequent violent behavior cannot, and should not, answer the question of
whether such material can be suppressed by government consistent with
the First Amendment. One still needs some theory of why speech is protected under the First Amendment and what level of harm would justify
suppression. A judge would also, it appears, have to at least contemplate
whether the overall value of an "open society" outweighs—even if on a
purely consequentialist basis—the marginal improvements (say, in the
crime rate) created by official censorship. The latter determination may be
beyond any empirical methodology, except perhaps some rather loose
comparative, qualitative analysis. Many more questions would need to be
addressed (for instance, the slippery slope problem comes to mind), but

---

[43]*Id.* at 262. One wonders what Posner's reaction would be if the "value consensus" among his fel-
lows judges was that judges should use moral philosophy to decide legal issues.

[44]Ronald Dworkin, Order of the Coif Lecture: Reply, 29 Ariz. St. L.J. 431, 433 (1997).

the point is that facts and empirical data are only the beginning of such an inquiry; they certainly cannot dictate its outcome. Whatever the results of social scientific research, such answers alone cannot obviate the need for value choices.

The naturalistic fallacy recurs in Posner's apparent claim that because "academic moralists" cannot influence most (or many) people, they should not do so. The latter simply does not follow from the former. Perhaps, one could argue, the solution is not to eliminate moral philosophy but to educate citizens more completely so that rational deliberation enters more fully into their moral lives. Posner's largely unstated premise appears to be that human beings are "hard-wired" to defend their acculturated moral paradigms at all costs, no matter how convincing moral reasoning may be, but this undefended claim may say more about its author than about human nature.

Posner's reasoning also seems oddly self-refuting when he seeks to invoke the prestige of science for his enterprise in order to distinguish it from moral reasoning. Posner alludes to empiricism, replicability, claims that are subject to refutation via observation, and the like as the antidote to grandiose and ungrounded moral philosophizing. The Vienna Circle, it seems, lives.[45] The problem is that Posner's own claims about the separation of law and moral reasoning cannot meet these epistemic criteria. Posner offers us a nonrefutable "theory" that cannot meet his own standards. Posner appears to recognize this objection,[46] but fails to answer it.

Nevertheless, Posner's advocacy of empirical investigation in legal interpretation seems promising. This theme, which extends back to the "Brandeis brief" and the legal realist movement, is at least underemphasized in the rationalist jurisprudence of someone like Dworkin. Answers to constitutional questions cannot be derived exclusively from first principles, and although it is a caricature, there is nonetheless a strain of this sort in the thought of Dworkin and others to which Posner seems to be reacting. Posner opposes a certain style of *a priori* moral theorizing in law. In that way, Posner's view is a valuable corrective. The problem, however, seems to be that Posner throws the baby out with the bathwater. He wishes to dispense not only with *a priori* moral reasoning, but with any moral

---

[45]Classic logical positivism asserted that truth claims consist solely of synthetic statements (empirically testable) or analytic statements (true by definition). It soon became apparent, however, that such a general rule does not qualify as a truth claim by its own standards, and thus is self-refuting. *See, e.g.*, Harry J. Gensler, Ethics: A Contemporary Introduction 64 (1998).

[46]Posner, *supra* note 6, at 29–30.

reasoning at all. The point of Dworkin's that Posner seems to miss is that this is not only a bad idea, it is an impossible one as well.

Moral reasoning, properly applied, might in fact facilitate rather than inhibit the empirical approach Posner champions. As one commentator pointed out, Posner's view of moral philosophy is misguided in that he assumes moral philosophers always seek to deliver definitive answers to moral questions and change people's minds about morality. In fact, moral philosophers more frequently seek to clarify the debate and offer deeper understandings of positions people already hold rather than effect dramatic conversions in their readers.[47] This clarification of the terms of moral debate may well help judges and others identify what empirical information is needed to answer constitutional questions. As philosopher Martha C. Nussbaum notes:

> Probably argument rarely persuades people to depart altogether from their most settled views. What it more commonly does, however, is to bring to the surface part of one's moral view that has been obscured or inconsistently applied. Frequently the systematic power of ethical theory is a great help in this sort of argument, ordering what is until then disordered, rendering explicit what is nameless and thus easily denied or effaced.[48]

It is the power of moral reasoning to illuminate, rather than convert, that can aid in determining precisely what empirical data may be useful and how that data should be evaluated and applied to the problem at hand.

Of course, not every case requires grand theory. Sunstein's minimalism seems a workable strategy for a certain class of cases: those cases in which agreement on results can be obtained without resort to higher level principles. It seems a sound tactic for collegial courts, such as the Supreme Court, where deep ideological divisions can make even simple cases extremely difficult. Nonetheless, Sunstein's approach seems almost purely "strategic"—it certainly does not contradict Dworkin's assertion that high-flying justificatory ascent is only necessary in relatively rare cases. In that class of cases, avoidance of fundamental premises seems perverse or obfuscatory. As Jeffrey Rosen put it, "for the Justices to extend Bickel's notion of 'passive virtues' to a judicial opinion itself, refusing to say what they think about a constitutional issue after they have promised to do so, is a peculiarly coy vision of the judicial role. It seems

---

[47]Laura Carrier, Note: Making Moral Theory Work for Law, 99 Colum. L. Rev. 1018 (1999).
[48]Martha C. Nussbaum, Still Worthy of Praise, 111 Harv. L. Rev. 1776, 1793 (1998).

not so much passive as passive-aggressive."[49] Minimalism certainly has its place, but it is precisely in the most difficult and divisive moral and legal issues that it will not prove helpful. If one believes that the Constitution protects certain vital rights and values, and that judges have a duty to struggle to operationalize those rights and values, Sunstein's emphasis on minimalism at times seems like a sophisticated defense of judicial irresponsibility. Minimalism in the support of greater "democracy" is not without its potential problems as well. Whatever its merits, democracy is not an unqualified good—particularly in the context of a Bill of Rights that was enacted in part so that democratic majorities could not run roughshod over individuals with different ideas. Sunstein nowhere suggests the contrary, but his enthusiasm to encourage democracy seems at times to overlook this key point.

In cases where minimalism is not appropriate, Dworkin's approach seems the most persuasive, although some modifications may be in order. Dworkin captures the sense in which many judicial decisions are routine and require no "justificatory ascent." Hemmed in by text, precedent, and other factors, judges frequently reach straightforward, determinate decisions in such routine cases. Here, Sunstein's minimalism seems an appropriate but not a particularly revolutionary innovation. However, in the cases where this is not so—and particularly in many constitutional cases that reach the Supreme Court—justificatory ascent of some sort seems both inevitable and undeniable. Simply reading such decisions seems convincing proof that judges—whether explicitly or implicitly, consciously or unconsciously—engage in the kind of moral reasoning (or at least moral "positing") that Dworkin describes. Dworkin's project, in part, is to bring that process into the open.

To illustrate both the descriptive accuracy and the normative bite of Dworkin's account, consider a 1991 U. S. Supreme Court First Amendment decision, *Cohen v. Cowles Media Co.*[50] In this case, moral reasoning lies at the heart of the decision, although it is not always presented as explicitly as Dworkin might advocate. In *Cohen*, the Supreme Court considered the enforceability of a promise by two newspapers to preserve the anonymity of a confidential source for a political story. Both newspapers elected to "burn" the source: that is, reveal his name despite the promised confidentiality. He subsequently sued for breach of contract. The case

---

[49]Jeffrey Rosen, Foreword: 1999 Survey of Books Relating to the Law, 97 Mich. L. Rev. 1323, 1328 (1999).
[50] 501 U.S. 663 (1991).

came to the U. S. Supreme Court after the Minnesota Supreme Court had decided that there was no binding contract, but that the source would have had a valid claim of promissory estoppel—an equitable doctrine that protects promisees in the absence of a binding contract—but for the First Amendment. First Amendment doctrine, of course, is particularly concerned with the protection of truthful political speech, which was precisely the speech in question in *Cohen*. The Court was thus faced with a Dworkinian "hard case": there were lines of precedent that seemed to support either outcome, as the majority acknowledged.

The source won, but only by a slim 5–4 majority. The majority noted that two lines of precedent might apply. On one side, there were cases in which the First Amendment overrode civil causes of action, particularly those that sought to penalize truthful political speech. On the other side, there were cases in which the press was held to be subject to laws of general application, such as tax laws, labor laws, and the like. The majority endeavored to show that the latter cases were controlling, making much along the way of the newspapers' voluntary assumption of promises of confidentiality. Despite the doctrinal window dressing, it seems unavoidable that the majority was in fact reaching what was at bottom a moral determination: newspapers, like everyone else, should keep their promises. This was a clear case of the majority learning everything it needed to know to decide this particular case in kindergarten. The problem is not so much with the precise outcome the majority reached—although broad *dicta* in the opinion may, in fact, be doing some harm—but with the disingenuousness of the opinion. By its unconvincing attempt to demonstrate that the result was compelled by precedent—that the process was an almost algorithmic application of "legal" reasoning—the majority missed the opportunity to honestly confront the moral dilemma before it. Justificatory ascent was mandatory in *Cohen*, but the majority sought to pretend it was staying close to the (doctrinal) ground.

The dissenters, on the other hand, were much more straightforward about the competing moral currents in the case. Justice David Souter's dissent admitted that a fundamental principle of law is that people should keep their promises. The difficulty was that also operating was a political imperative, embodied in First Amendment law, that speakers not be punished for truthful political speech—not only for the speaker's benefit, but for the benefit of the hearers. The political theory that the First Amendment operates primarily to ensure an informed, self-governing citizenry thus was fully in play in the case. Justice Souter's dissent acknowledged the competing principles, noted that either might prevail depending on the precise facts of a given case, and at least implied the existence of a balancing mechanism to make the determination. Thus Justice Souter, by confronting the moral dimension more or less head-on, delivered an opinion that was intellectually honest and subject to further debate and development. Even if one disagreed with Souter's preferred result, the moral premises were laid bare and thus available for further intellectual inquiry. The majority's disingenuousness, on the other hand, concealed the moral reasoning at the heart of the decision, thus both frustrating reasoned doctrinal development and bringing the entire process into question. One could even argue that to the extent judges avoid acknowledging even to themselves what they are truly doing, they are depriving themselves of the ability to bring their full intellectual abilities to bear on the resolution of the case.

Obviously, *Cohen* is not a typical First Amendment case, but based on Dworkin's theory, one would expect justificatory ascent only in rare cases. *Cohen* does seem to illustrate the validity of Dworkin's claim that at least some hard constitutional cases inevitably require recourse to fundamental moral principles—constrained, of course, by the requirement of fit with existing legal doctrine. It also at least suggests the normative soundness of Dworkin's call for judges to acknowledge the moral dimension and bring moral reasoning into the open in judicial opinions.

Nonetheless, Dworkin's picture of adjudication can be usefully supplemented by the thought both of Bobbitt and of Tribe and Dorf. Bobbitt's modalities add a more precise picture of the constraining forces operating in modern constitutional practice. Dworkin's notion of fit seems somewhat underdeveloped in comparison with Bobbitt's perceptive account of the modalities of constitutional argument. Tribe and Dorf, on the other hand, bring a sense of balance to the process, particularly through their caveats against hyper-integration, a monistic search for the single overriding vision of the Constitution that Dworkin's approach can tend to encourage. While the quest for the "best" moral principles that fit with text and doctrine seems sound, Tribe and Dorf remind us that there is no one unifying, moral vision contained in the Constitution and that each constitutional clause must, in some sense, stand on its own.

At the end of the day, it appears that constitutional jurisprudence simply cannot be divorced from moral reasoning. The Constitution is not a warrant for free-ranging moral philosophy but at the same time, its proper interpretation cannot ignore the moral dimension. Clearly, in a pluralistic society, the answers are not easy to ascertain. Nonetheless, judges and legal scholars must seriously and openly grapple with the questions with all the skill they can muster.

Shall We Commit First Amendment Theory?

Above all, those who practice self-ratifying discourse are attracted to what they regard as interdisciplinarity, conceived not as the actual practice of a second discipline but as the duty-free importing of terms and concepts from some source of broad wisdom about history or epistemology or the structure of the mind. This is of course not inter-disciplinarity at all but antidisciplinarity, a holiday from the method-ological constraints that prevail in any given field.

—*Frederick Crews*[1]

Although the authors and schools of thought explored in this book have been many and varied, there are some common themes worthy of discussion. This chapter will touch on some key issues of interdisciplinarity in First Amendment theory and make some schematic suggestions for doing First Amendment theory in a more satisfactory way. At the risk of some repetition, I want to revisit briefly some particularly important points made in earlier chapters and sketch a few ideas for how those points might shape future theorizing. In particular, I wish to provide at least a general outline for a method of First Amendment theorizing that can draw upon interdisciplinary insights without losing claim to the rubric *law*. No rea-

---

[1]Frederick Crews, The End of the Poststructuralist Era, in The Emperor Redressed: Critiquing Critical Theory 52 (Dwight Eddins ed., 1995).

sonable conception of the scope of this work would allow me to work out all of the details here, but I hope the following remarks will at least stake out the territory.

Is First Amendment Interdisciplinarity a Good Thing?

As the earlier chapters demonstrated, interdisciplinarity in First Amendment theory has become a powerful force. The interdisciplinarians have, of course, always been with us, but in recent decades their presence has been more strongly felt and their theoretical structures have increasingly begun to diverge from the classical theoretical views that both sprang from, and were internalized within, First Amendment history, text, and doctrine.

The new interdisciplinarians have contributed much. Communitarians and their allies, for example, have shown that a purely individualistic conception of rights is untenable. Rights, for their very existence, depend upon a certain type of community and the institutional structures that derive therefrom. Without such a community, our picture of individual rights—and, perhaps particularly, free speech rights—would look dramatically different. Feminist and critical race theorists, among others, have identified, often with dazzling narrative power, the harms that our free speech regime can inflict. Likewise, feminist theorists and proponents of literary theory, particularly Stanley Fish, have pointed toward the situatedness of human thought and action in ways that tend to undermine the "Enlightenment extremism" that sometimes undergirds our free speech rhetoric. Judge Posner's economic analysis of free speech opens up new ways of thinking about the value of speech and provides the kind of gestalt switch that enables us to think more clearly about the existing tradition. New realist critics of state action doctrine have demonstrated that a much more nuanced analysis of the state action question may be required. And debates on the desirability of moral philosophy in First Amendment and other legal doctrine force us to think hard about the nature of constitutional law and the always slippery legal balance between the positivistic need for legal certainty and authoritative provenance and the aspiration for justice. An ardent Millean might even suggest that the interdisciplinarians, even if their claims are untrue, have performed the valuable function of shaking First Amendment thought from its dogmatic slumber. That claim, of course, presupposes a view of truth and the marketplace of ideas that a good number of free speech critics might well find uncongenial.

Of course, the picture is not all rosy. As I have endeavored to show in the preceding chapters, a number of recent interdisciplinary approaches have serious problems. Some operate at a level of abstraction that does not allow any meaningful contribution at the level of legal doctrine. Others commit one to a reductionism that runs roughshod over the existing tradition by simply ignoring key aspects of the First Amendment ethos. Still others begin from premises that are wholly foreign to the origins and development of First Amendment theory and doctrine. And, finally, some do all three. Moreover, a few partake in the freedom, and attendant difficulties, identified by Frederick Crews in the epigraph of this chapter: abjuring the constraints of disciplinary boundaries, they occupy the academic equivalent of a no man's (or woman's) land, where anything goes. This kind of intellectual freebooting, while often exciting to watch, is rarely very satisfying or helpful to the onlookers.

At a more concrete level, many of the specific proposals of the interdisciplinarians seem problematic. Certainly the private exercise of power poses some dangers to free speech, but empowering government to intercede could weaken or destroy the great good that has come from the concept of a private realm as espoused in our constitutional tradition. Certain types of speech do have costs, in particular hate speech and certain types of (nonobscene) pornography, but the doctrinal remedies for these costs threaten to undermine the entire edifice (and, to some extent, the tremendous individual and social benefits) of free speech doctrine.

Top-Down and Bottom-Up Reasoning

Given all this, in what direction should First Amendment theory go? I certainly do not claim to have all of the answers, but I have a few suggestions. One answer, the essentially conservative one, would be simply to resume the dialogue from the comfortable point before the new interdisciplinarians came onto the scene. In other words, we should simply pick up the mantle of Mill, Holmes, and others and move forward on those well-beaten paths. (This is, in fact, what some First Amendment scholars have already chosen to do by simply ignoring the new interdisciplinarians' intellectual assaults.) This can be a fruitful option, and it should not be dismissed out of hand.

Another, more ecumenical, approach might be to refashion First Amendment theorizing to take heed of the methodological innovations and useful theoretical perspectives of the interdisciplinarians while avoiding their weaknesses. A useful way to think about this might be through the concept of top-down versus bottom-up theory. Top-down legal theory generally begins with some indubitable (to the theorist) premise, value, or insight, the implications of which are then explored and ultimately brought down to earth to be operationalized in legal doctrine. The key here is deductive reasoning. Many of the interdisciplinarians discussed in the preceding chapters are top-down theorists. They identify a grand theoretical insight, epistemology, or method and then relentlessly work out the implications, even though their premises may be far afield from the First Amendment tradition. Stanley Fish, notably, is not a top-down *legal* theorist (hardly surprising given his views on theory), but operates in a much more ad hoc manner when it comes to legal doctrine—exactly as he suggests that judges do. However, his analyses of others' theoretical shortcomings are driven from the top down by his a priori assumptions about interpretive communities, the impossibility of theory, the impotence of principles, and the like. Once one is familiar with Fish's rhetorical toolkit, all else follows fairly predictably (something Fish himself freely admits in his writings). Judge Posner, a self-professed pragmatist, seems relentlessly top-down in his First Amendment analysis (discussed in Chapter 2), as is much law and economics scholarship, although some of Posner's later work would suggest a change of heart. Top-down theory is, of course, not the exclusive province of the interdisciplinarians; a good number of the classical First Amendment theorists discussed in the first chapter applied a similar methodology.

Another alternative is bottom-up theory, which often simply goes by the name of doctrinal scholarship. The pejorative term is *legal formalism*, although the vast majority of doctrinalists are almost certainly not full-on Landellians. Induction is the *modus operandi* here, with all of the shortcomings that style of reasoning is known for. The bottom-up approach is to aggregate case law, perhaps along with relevant textual evidence, and provide a theory for what courts are doing in practice. For the most part, such theories are explicit or inchoate in the decisions themselves; rarely, they are surprising or even counterintuitive, given the legal materials.

The problems with each of these approaches are obvious. Top-down theory is often disconnected from the concrete reality of constitutional law, and thus not only unconvincing to practitioners and judges, but so far removed from First Amendment history, text, and doctrine as to be of questionable legitimacy even if it *were* convincing. Thus, it is impotent, and often rightfully so. Top-down approaches, to the extent their premises are radically divorced from the constitutional tradition, founder on Tribe and Dorf's distinction between "reading the Constitution and writing one."[2] This, of course, is a difficulty commented on numerous times in the previous chapters. Bottom-up theory, on the other hand, can be little more than descriptive of existing practice, even if it reconceptualizes that practice in some way. As such, it has no normative bite, although it may be empirically sound. Thus, with top-down reasoning one is often cut off from constitutional reality, while bottom-up reasoning allows faithful description (perhaps with some minor policy arguments) but gives one little normative purchase.

An Agenda for First Amendment Theory

What seems to be called for is some other brand of First Amendment theorizing that can transcend the limitations of the top-down and bottom-up approaches. The approach must avoid the Scylla and Charybdis of a utopian constitutional transubstantiation, on the one hand, and a narrow constitutional positivism, on the other. It must be grounded in constitutional realities, and yet be capable of an immanent critique of the sort that doctrinal scholarship lacks the resources to achieve. Such an alternative already exists, and it often goes by the name of *reflective equilibrium*. This insight is hardly novel and I disclaim any originality in suggesting it, although it does appear that the utility of reflective equilibrium is often underappreciated. First Amendment theorists and other constitutional scholars have used theoretical schemes not unlike reflective equilibrium for a very long time, although not always with that terminology. Despite this, it seems that closer attention to some of the best thinking about reflective equilibrium could improve First Amendment theory for the better. My aim in the following remarks is not to provide a complete account of reflective equilibrium in First Amendment theory, but simply to offer some suggestions for further thought about its application.

Reflective equilibrium is often associated with political theorist John Rawls[3] The concept is also associated with philosopher Nelson Goodman.[4] Reflective equilibrium is a method employed in moral philosophy, political theory, and a number of other philosophical disciplines. "Narrow" reflective equilibrium, according to philosopher Norman Daniels, is the familiar "process of working back and forth between our moral judgments about particular situations and our effort to provide general reasons

---

[2]Laurence H. Tribe and Michael C. Dorf, On Reading the Constitution 13 (1991).
[3]*E.g.*, John Rawls, A Theory of Justice (1971).
[4]Nelson Goodman, Fact, Fiction and Forecast (2d ed. 1965).

and principles that link those judgments to ones that are relevantly similar."[5] Already this coherentist method of justification has similarities to what judges and constitutional scholars do as they go about their work, provided one substitutes broad constitutional principles and individual cases in place of general moral principles and individual moral judgments.[6]

However, narrow reflective equilibrium needs to be expanded to avoid an arid conventionalism, and it is particularly in this expansion that the method can both accommodate interdisciplinary learning and avoid the top-down propensities of its advocates. In "wide" reflective equilibrium, as philosopher Kai Nielsen describes it, the theorist seeks

> an equilibrium that takes into account our best corroborated social scientific theories and theories of human nature, firmly established social and psychological facts and political realities, such as the extent and intractability of pluralism (reasonable or otherwise) in the society or cluster of societies where the reflective equilibrium is sought. . . . The thing is, considering all these matters, to achieve a consistent cluster of moral, factual, and theoretical beliefs that would yield the best available account of what the social situation is, what possibilities obtain in the society or societies, and what it is reasonable and desirable to do. Such an account is both descriptive and normative, and it is through and through coherentist and holistic, justifying our beliefs and practices by showing the consistency and coherency of their fit with each other, if they can be seen to have it, or, what is more likely, by forging one if they do not.[7]

Thus, in wide equilibrium, the theorist consults considered judgments and broad principles, as in narrow reflective equilibrium, but then broadens the enterprise by considering what Norman Daniels calls relevant "background theories." These might include, in the First Amendment context, theories and empirical work dealing with the nature of persons, the effects of various types of speech, the unintended consequences of certain communications, the distribution of resources in the society, the nature of the public-private distinction, and the like. Many other forms of background knowledge of various types might be relevant. The theorist moves back and forth among the three elements (considered judgments; broad, general principles; and background theories), revising where necessary

---

[5]Norman Daniels, Justice and Justification 1 (1996).

[6]Sometimes, of course, constitutional adjudication, like common-law adjudication, operates in a more casuistic or analogical mode.

[7]Kai Nielsen, Naturalism Without Foundations 15–16 (1996).

until a reasonable coherence (or equilibrium point) among the elements is achieved. Such a method, when applied to the First Amendment by starting with broad constitutional principles (the precise content of which can never be entirely uncontroversial, of course), on the one hand, and First Amendment text, history, and doctrine, on the other, can be inclusive of a wide variety of both critical and empirical interdisciplinary work without simply abandoning core First Amendment principles and doctrine, as many interdisciplinarians would have us do. Those core principles and doctrines may, of course, be subject to some modification or, conceivably, rejection in light of powerful background theories or empirical findings, but the coherentist[8] nature of wide reflective equilibrium keeps us firmly grounded in constitutional reality and constrains the urge to hurl the baby out with the bathwater. Norman Daniels notes that

> marshaling of the broadest evidence and critical scrutiny is the attraction of *wide* as opposed to *narrow* reflective equilibrium. We must not only work back and forth between principles and judgments about particular cases . . . but we must bring to bear all theoretical considerations that have relevance to the acceptability of the principles as well as the particular judgments.[9]

The method is conservative in that a complete abandonment of fundamental constitutional principles, derived from text, history, and doctrine, is unlikely, but it does not advocate a quiet acceptance of the status quo. Instead, it critically examines the entire edifice of our constitutional tradition and forces us to reconsider those judgments that cannot be squared with wider clusters of knowledge. It facilitates the incorporation of knowledge and theoretical perspectives from other disciplines into constitutional theory while curbing the interdisciplinary impulse toward colonization and reductionism. It allows us to claim plausibly to be dealing with "law" as a set of authoritative norms without lapsing into a shallow and unreflective legal formalism. As Nielsen puts it, starting with our considered judgments (or, in the case of constitutional theory, with text, history, and doctrine) "involves—indeed inescapably involves—seeing things by our own lights. Where else could we start? We can hardly jump out of our cultural and historical skins."[10] And, in the case of constitu-

---

[8]For a critique of global coherence theories in law, such as Dworkin's, see Joseph Raz, The Relevance of Coherence, 72 B.U. L. Rev. 273 (1992). Raz is less critical of "local" coherence theories that aim at specific fields of legal doctrine.

[9]Daniels, *supra* note 5, at 6.

[10]Nielson, *supra* note 7, at 17.

tional theory, it might be added that to the extent theorists do depart from the legal materials, the legitimacy of the enterprise becomes highly problematic. As Nielsen also noted, wide reflective equilibrium is thoroughly fallibilist, which makes both for a nice conceptual isomorphism with First Amendment doctrine itself and for a useful constraint upon the absolutist pretensions of some of the interdisciplinarians. It is also, in contrast to natural law theories, constructivist: the resulting theoretical structures are created rather than discovered. Moreover, wide reflective equilibrium is interpretive;[11] there are no deductive techniques available in this realm. Nor, if we think carefully about it, could there be.

The theorist achieves equilibrium when the theory and the individual judgments are consistent, after adjustment by the various other clusters of knowledge that have been brought to bear. As a result, wide reflective equilibrium steers a dialectical path between top-down and bottom-up reasoning. It incorporates both descriptive and normative elements. As Robert Burns has pointed out:

> [Reflective equilibrium] is situated in that the policy results of the theory purport not to float in "from heaven knows where." The norms on which his theory relies, Rawls argues, are already incarnate in "our considered judgments" on policy matters. These norms are, then, not only grounded but concrete: they are defensible against the charge of empty formalism traditionally leveled against "Kantian" theories. On the other hand, the discipline of Rawls' theory allows these consensual or traditional norms to be refined (to reach reflective equilibrium) and extended to new issues of justice or to the revision of old resolutions of those issues. Rawls' theory is situated but normative: it is rooted in our convictions but not bound by them. . . .[12]

Wide reflective equilibrium calls upon the theorist to test every part of the entire structure in relation to every other part. Any equilibrium is inevitably temporary and will, almost certainly, be superseded as additional information becomes available.

The process of achieving equilibrium is an exercise of judgment that, while a clear account of the process can be given, is not reducible to any algorithm. Based on the Quinean notion of the underdetermination of theory by evidence, it seems unavoidable that a number of inconsistent, yet

---

[11]As Richard H. Fallon noted, interpretive constitutional theories, while normatively significant, also reflect an understanding of actual constitutional practice "with all its peculiarities and deficiencies, in what I take to be the most favorable light." Richard H. Fallon, A Constructivist Coherence Theory of Constitutional Interpretation, 100 Harv. L. Rev. 1189, 1237 (1987).

[12]Robert P. Burns, Rawls and the Principles of Welfare Law, 83 Nw. U.L. Rev. 184, 186–87 (1988).

internally coherent, theoretical structures could "explain" the legal materials. Here one of the limits of wide reflective equilibrium becomes clear—it does not eliminate controversy and disagreement from constitutional theory. This limitation is, of course, neither surprising nor grounds for rejecting wide reflective equilibrium. No approach to constitutional theory can promise universal agreement. Nor does wide reflective equilibrium deny that the interpretation of the legal materials is itself somewhat theory dependent. There is no simple fact of the matter, no neutral observation language, when it comes to questions about history, text, and doctrine: one's interpretation is invariably affected by one's theoretical commitments (dare I say, interpretive community), and often vice versa. *Pace* Fish, however, such interpretation is limited by the brute legal materials themselves as least as much as by the interpreter's theoretical framework. The view here might usefully be compared with Karl Popper's philosophy of science, which, while acknowledging the theory-impregnated nature of experience, still contended that it was empirical reality that determined the fate of theories, rather than the reverse.[13] The primary materials are not infinitely manipulable, in any event, and disparities in interpretation are simply a condition of any human enterprise.

The fact that wide reflective equilibrium seems familiar is hardly surprising. It is often the (unarticulated and less than fully developed) way in which human beings seek to reason about many things in life.[14] Wide reflective equilibrium certainly has similarities to the way in which common law judges operate, although the common law is a rather more closed system and might be more fruitfully compared to narrow reflective equilibrium. As well, we have already encountered echoes of it in theorists discussed in this book. Bobbitt, for example, with his modalities of constitutional argument, has a coherentist orientation, although he rather sharply limited the permissible materials to the six modes. Perhaps most strikingly, Dworkin's project, particularly the activities of his fictional judge, Hercules, bears considerable similarity to wide reflective equilibrium.[15]

---

[13]See Geoffrey Stokes, Popper: Philosophy, Politics, and Scientific Method 15 (1998).

[14]Kai Nielsen makes a similar point about the commonsense nature of wide reflective equilibrium. Nielsen, *supra* note 7, at 13.

[15]See Ronald Dworkin, Taking Rights Seriously (1977); Ronald Dworkin, Law's Empire (1986). *See also, e.g.*, Fallon, *supra* note 11; Robert J. Lipkin, Beyond Skepticism, Foundationalism and the New Fuzziness: The Role of Wide Reflective Equilibrium in Legal Theory, 75 Cornell L. Rev. 811 (1990); Frank Michelman, In Pursuit of Constitutional Welfare Rights: One View of Rawls' theory of Justice, 121 U. Pa. L. Rev. 962 (1973).

The fact that wide reflective equilibrium began as a tool for moral and political philosophy suggests that it may require some adjustment if it is to be applied to constitutional theory. For one thing, the constitutional theorist has less freedom than the pure philosopher to ignore existing doctrine. As Cass Sunstein suggests:

> Some of the fixed points in law are precedents reached by others, not judgments genuinely accepted by oneself. These points may be fixed either because the legal culture genuinely renders them unrevisable (for the particular judge on, say, a lower court), or because the principle of stare decisis imposes a strong barrier to revision.[16]

Of course, we might assume there is at least a difference in *degree* between the constraint faced by a judge versus that faced by a legal scholar, but the difference ought not be a difference in *kind*, at least if we want to develop theory that is reasonably connected to the actual Constitution. Thus, wide reflective equilibrium in constitutional theory might have to give greater weight to existing precedent than a moral philosopher might give to considered moral judgments. As legal theorist Robin West pointed out, sometimes it makes more sense simply to acknowledge that *this* Constitution does not incorporate one's preferred principles than to torture the material in order to make it cohere with one's favored scheme. West cited the hate speech debate as a good exemplar of the almost universal tendency of scholars simply to assume that the Constitution must protect their preferred values:

> [O]ne group of scholars and litigators (generally liberal) argues that hate speech regulations are simply unconstitutional under the First Amendment, while a second, more or less minority (and generally progressive), position argues that they are constitutional either by virtue of the similarity between hate speech regulations and traditionally accepted limits on the First Amendment, or because of limits we should imply into that amendment through the "penumbral" and balancing, or counterbalancing, effect of the Fourteenth Amendment's equality clause. The position that seems to have no adherents is that hate speech regulations are desirable, for progressive reasons, but are nevertheless unconstitutional, but shouldn't be, and that this shows that, at least from a progressive perspective, the First Amendment is morally flawed. But again, this position seems to have no adherents. Instead, those

---

[16]Cass R. Sunstein, On Analogical Reasoning, 106 Harv. L. Rev. 741, 778 (1993).

who think hate speech regulations are a good idea generally think they are constitutional while those who think they are not a good idea generally find them unconstitutional.[17]

This seemingly obvious point goes unheeded in great swaths of contemporary constitutional discourse of both the theoretical and everyday varieties. The use of wide reflective equilibrium, properly executed, would bring this constitutional unmentionable to the fore.

It is also worth pointing out that general principles in constitutional law need not be monistic. In considering the First Amendment, for example, we might construct a set of general theoretical principles (or subprinciples) that encompasses many free speech justifications, rather than a simple, unitary one. General principles of First Amendment free speech might, for example, include appeals to democratic self-governance, the marketplace of ideas, autonomy, tolerance, or other justifications, as long as these multiple justifications adequately cohere with the considered judgments of the legal system in individual cases. Without demonstrating that point here, it appears that a basis in multiple justifications might be the only way to account for the sheer variety of Supreme Court First Amendment jurisprudence. Indeed, the Court itself has at various times alluded to a wide variety of the classical theories. Of course, to fully articulate First Amendment general principles, it might be necessary to establish contextual rules for the circumstances in which various justifications operate, but that sort of ordering seems entirely possible. One way to do this, for example, would be by limiting the scope of individual justifications to some specific doctrinal area or "zone" within First Amendment law rather than attempting to cover all First Amendment cases with a single unitary principle. This zoning approach would almost inevitably result in some border disputes, but nonetheless it seems promising. Another alternative would be the development of what legal theorist Ken Kress calls "meta-principles," which function in coherence theories by resolving conflicts among principles.[18]

The critical point to remember, however, is that whatever principles were constructed could not simply be *imposed* from the top down, as is often the new interdisciplinarians' wont. Furthermore, as the quest for reflective equilibrium moves wide, both the general principles and the

---

[17]Robin L. West, Constitutional Scepticism, 72 B.U.L. Rev. 765, 768 (1992).

[18]Ken Kress, Coherence, in A Companion to Philosophy of Law and Legal Theory, 533, 542 (Dennis Patterson ed., 1996).

individual judgments are subject to revision (at least on the pages of the law reviews, if not necessarily in legal effect), based upon other clusters of knowledge, be they theoretical or empirical, provided the force of those arguments is sufficiently compelling. However, the (constructed) principles and the individual judgments would exert a powerful grounding force that would tend to keep theoretical extravagances in check. That is as it should be in a legal system in which authoritative legal norms can only be overturned in the face of compelling evidence, based both on the legitimacy interests associated with fidelity to text, history, and doctrine and on the values of stability and predictability associated with *stare decisis.*

Wide reflective equilibrium allows the theorist to take account, not only of moral and political theories outside of law, but also of empirical evidence that bears on legal interpretation. Here is one area where most of the interdisciplinarians discussed herein have not ventured. Judge Posner gave a nod toward empiricism in his economic theory of the First Amendment but did not seem overly inclined to actually engage in empirical research to support his assumptions. It may be that some other theorists mentioned, especially those interdisciplinarians with a postmodernist bent, have philosophical disputes with all or some of empirical social science. Those issues are important but will be deferred for another day.[19] In any event, many debates about the meaning of the First Amendment could benefit from empirical evidence. Wide reflective equilibrium provides a useful perspective with which to bring such evidence to bear on a fully developed First Amendment theory. Do hate speech and pornography really silence members of certain groups? Is the media market really so concentrated that the marketplace of ideas is a sham? One could no doubt generate a host of such questions (which may or may not have adequate empirical answers in the literature), which could be useful in attaining equilibrium. To the critics who maintain that First Amendment law is the last bastion of formalist legal thought, this attention to empirical questions would be a significant advance.

Conclusion

Many details obviously remain to be worked out. My intent here is not to offer a full-blown methodology for First Amendment theory, but simply to suggest a direction that future research might follow. The method pro-

---

[19]See Alexander Rosenberg, Philosophy of Social Science (1988).

posed here is, clearly, no panacea. To those with serious doubts about the liberalism, individualism, and negative liberty conceptions that seem built into the First Amendment tradition, the coherentist approach suggested here is almost certainly insufficiently critical. On the other hand, to those with a legal positivist or originalist bent, the adoption of wide reflective equilibrium would offer judges (and scholars) far too much room for jurisprudential mischief and tend to undermine fidelity to law. Nonetheless, the approach seems to hold promise as a technique of remaining faithful to our First Amendment heritage and staying grounded in something that can reasonably be called "law," while continuing the task—so central to many conceptions of the First Amendment itself—of advancing toward a more complete and just vision of freedom of expression.

Author Index

Subject Index